D1562759

Geographies of Campus Inequality

Mapping the Diverse Experiences of First-Generation Students

JANEL E. BENSON
ELIZABETH M. LEE

OXFORD

UNIVERSITY PRESS

OXFORD
UNIVERSITY PRESS

Oxford University Press is a department of the University of Oxford. It furthers
the University's objective of excellence in research, scholarship, and education
by publishing worldwide. Oxford is a registered trade mark of Oxford University
Press in the UK and certain other countries.

Published in the United States of America by Oxford University Press
198 Madison Avenue, New York, NY 10016, United States of America.

© Oxford University Press 2020

Library of Congress Cataloging-in-Publication Data
Names: Benson, Janel E., author. | Lee, Elizabeth M., 1974– author.
Title: Geographies of campus inequality : mapping the diverse experiences
of first- generation students / Janel E. Benson and Elizabeth M. Lee.
Description: New York, NY : Oxford University Press, 2020. |
Includes bibliographical references and index.
Identifiers: LCCN 2020013330 (print) | LCCN 2020013331 (ebook) |
ISBN 9780190848156 (hardback) | ISBN 9780190848170 (epub) |
ISBN 9780190848187
Subjects: LCSH: First-generation college students—United States. | People
with social disabilities—Education (Higher)—United States. | Student
aspirations—United States. | College environment—United States.
Classification: LCC LC4069.6 .B46 2020 (print) | LCC LC4069.6 (ebook) |
DDC 378.1/98—dc23
LC record available at https://lccn.loc.gov/2020013330
LC ebook record available at https://lccn.loc.gov/2020013331

Contents

Acknowledgments

This project is the result of a five-year equal collaboration between the authors that was inspired by current and former students. We are indebted to the 64 first-generation students who shared their deeply personal narratives with us and to the amazing student researchers who worked on our research team over the years and helped collect these data. We would also like to thank Doug Massey and Camille Charles, the Principle Investigators of the National Longitudinal Survey of Freshmen, and their research team for collecting the survey data used in this book and generously making them available to scholars. The project would not have been possible without the generous financial support from the Spencer Foundation, Colgate University's Faculty Research Council, and Ohio University, which provided us with the resources to collect these data, share our ideas at conferences, and write this manuscript.

We are grateful to have received lots of encouragement and constructive feedback as our ideas evolved into a full manuscript. A number of colleagues were instrumental in helping us frame the ideas presented in the book, including Mary Simonson, Susan Thomson, Meg Worley, Alicia Simmons, Richard Shin, Donnell Butler, Katherine McClelland, Cyierra Roldan, Eddy Sihavong, Rory Kramer, Sarah Hayford, Rob Crosnoe, and Glen Elder. We are especially grateful to Jessi Streib, Katherine McClelland, Rory Kramer, Tim Englehart, and the anonymous reviewers for reading and providing constructive feedback on earlier drafts of this book. This project also benefited from rich conversations and support from our departmental colleagues at Colgate and Ohio University and from conference presentations. Finally, we also are grateful to Oxford University Press, especially Abby Gross, Katharine Pratt, Fabian Shalini and the OUP editorial staff, for supporting this project and believing in our work. We thank Tan Nguyen for contributions to the book cover design.

We also would like to thank our mentors, family, and friends. Janel especially thanks Edward Weisband, Kent Trachte, and Katherine McClelland for providing critical guidance as she navigated college as first-generation student. She also thanks her partner Tom Cambier, daughter Beverly, and her family and friends for their love and encouragement. Liz thanks her friends and family, especially Lauren Gutterman for sharing friendship and work stress, and her wife Tan Nguyen for making work–life balance happen. For generous ongoing support and encouragement, she also thanks Tim Haney, Debbie Warnock, HyunJoon Park, Ashley Rondini, writing group colleagues and friends Nicole Kaufman and Paula Miller, and Keith Brown and the Saint Joseph's University sociology department.

1

More Than One Way to Be First

Dan and Brianna are both low-income first-generation[1] students at Hilltop College (HC)—a selective, predominantly White institution at which nearly 90% of the students have at least one parent who graduated from college.[2] For Dan, a White student from a large southern city who joined HC as a recruited athlete, it took a little time to get used to campus: the preppiness, the small size of the place, the East Coast weather, and being in a more rural setting were all unfamiliar. Overall, however, Dan recalled his transition being pretty smooth. He made friends easily with teammates, and then with their friends. More broadly, he found the campus community to be friendly—as he put it, "the student body was welcoming, they made you feel a part of the school." By the time he was interviewed at the end of his sophomore year, Dan had a strong social life based largely around his teammates and fraternity brothers.

These two overlapping circles of sports and friends form the basis of Dan's time on campus. While he reported that he does his best in the classroom and gets his work done, descriptions of typical weekday and weekend activities highlight how athletic commitments and social activities shape Dan's life. On weekdays, "typically I have some sort of athletic activity planned in for me, whether that be a run or workout. . . . I usually have about two classes a day. You know, just a normal schedule: shower, go to class, go to work out, come home, eat, do my work, hang out with some friends, go to sleep." On weekends, Dan's schedule became more social, with friends and good times:

> The night probably starts around nine o'clock, start to get dressed, I'll put some music on, me and my roommate will probably have a few drinks, we'll meet up with other people in an apartment complex, go over to the fraternity house, then head downtown, hit a few places there.

Dan's campus life unfolds seamlessly out from his student-athlete peer ties into the mainstream social scenes on campus where he spends time interacting primarily with White, affluent male peers.

Geographies of Campus Inequality. Janel E. Benson and Elizabeth M. Lee, Oxford University Press (2020). © Oxford University Press. DOI: 10.1093/oso/9780190848156.001.0001.

Brianna's experience is very different. Like Dan, she was of the first generation in her family to go to college, and like Dan, she found the transition from the urban setting in which she grew up to HC's campus to be an adjustment. An African American[3] woman, Brianna came to HC through the Summer Bridge (SB) program, an orientation course designed to welcome underrepresented students to campus during the month before the fall semester begins. Her first encounters at HC were therefore with a large number of students who shared her background. However, once fall classes began, she quickly realized that this was not the norm—in fact, she was one of only a small number of Black students on campus. Brianna described feeling like "a fly in a bowl of milk" and it took her awhile to "find her niche" of friends. Despite this, she kept up with friends from SB and found spaces to call her own through several campus clubs focused on social justice. She also devoted lots of time to her academic work, pursuing a philosophy major. Unlike Dan, Brianna preferred more low-key social settings: "A typical weekend night is me with one of my best friends or groups of friends just watching movies, chilling out. . . . We have dinner together. We go to various events on campus together, like lectures, movie screenings." She found Greek Letter Organizations (GLOs) and the party scene on campus "very homogenous and very exclusive."

Brianna also described her weekday life very differently, with academics and studying taking up a much larger percentage of her time than Dan's account. Having been "your typical, like, straight-A valedictorian, model student," Brianna continued her focus on academic work at HC. A typical weekday for her centered on schoolwork and clubs: "My time is spent in the classroom, and when I'm not in the classroom, it's attending various lectures offered on campus or like group meetings. And doing homework." Clubs also provided the spaces in which Brianna felt the most comfortable on campus, what she called the "quote-unquote multicultural spaces on campus." While Dan's HC life is organized around sports, friends, and fraternity life, Brianna's is focused on academics; smaller gatherings of friends from similar race, class, and gender backgrounds; and extracurricular life in places that speak to her personal identity.

How is it that two students who share both a campus and first-generation status—typically associated with lower college satisfaction, participation in extracurricular activities, and likelihood of graduation[4]—have such different experiences from one another? And how do Dan and Briana's experiences fit in with scholarly assessments of first-generation experiences? In fact, neither are described by current sociological research—Dan as a White fraternity brother and frequent partier with a wide circle of friends and Briana as a Black woman deeply involved in campus activities and a close, supportive circle of friends. Scholars and campus policymakers alike tend to conceptualize first-generation students as a homogenous group, focusing on their collective differences from those students who have at least one parent who is a college graduate (i.e., continuing-generation students).[5] In these examinations, first-generation students at selective campuses are largely isolated and unable to locate a sense of belonging on campus. Compared to continuing-generation peers, they are less likely to participate in extracurricular activities or to form close relationships with faculty, students, and staff.

While this perspective on first-generation student life is deeply important in highlighting the struggles faced by many first-generation students, narratives like Dan's and Briana's suggest that it is not the whole picture. In this book, we problematize the notion that there is only way to be a first generation student, and we consider the implications that first-generation students' varied routes into and through college have for post-college mobility. We focus on three broad questions: First, what are the different ways that first-generation students organize their social, extracurricular, and academic lives at selective and highly selective colleges? Second, how do first generation students sort themselves and get sorted into these different types of campus lives? Third, how do these different patterns of campus engagement prepare first-generation students for their post-college lives?

Overview of the Argument

We address these questions by investigating how institutional practices and the peer cultures they support shape students' access to and experiences within "the experiential core"[6] of college life—friendships, social life, and extracurricular activities—as well as academic experiences. We found that, rather than developing a sense of belonging or isolation on campus at large, our respondents located smaller multidimensional niches—what we refer to as *campus geographies*.[7] Participating in these geographies shapes students' experiences on campus and also what they learn about college life, including what is important and how to obtain it.

We characterize these geographies with reference to how most respondents described the idealized HC campus life: work hard, play hard. At one end of this spectrum is a geography based around play, whether leisure and/or partying—our student Dan would fit into this grouping. At the other end is a geography based around work, including both academic and extracurricular involvement, as we saw for Briana. Between these two, we find a Multisphere geography, students who are able to navigate both the Play Hard and Work Hard ends of the spectrum. Finally, perhaps outside this spectrum entirely is a Disconnected geography: respondents who struggle to find connection and belonging anywhere on campus. This geography is the closest to what is typically described for first-generation students at selective campuses. Each geography involves trade-offs and limitations and, with the exception of the Disconnected geography, each brings benefits.

Campus geographies illuminate the social embeddedness of college relationships and the resources they provide. While first-generation students can gain social support, networks, and new social and cultural competencies through interaction with campus peers and faculty,[8] we argue that these potential benefits are context-specific and vary across campus geographies. We show that first-generation students are not only more likely to participate in some types of geographies than continuing-generation students (reflecting the role of socioeconomic factors) but also that students' race/ethnicity[9] and gender positions also shape their ability to participate in (i.e., meet the norms and expectations of) these geographies. We also highlight how college campuses play important, often unseen roles in creating geographies by sorting students through targeted orientation programs, support structures, campus activities, dorms, and other social spaces, much of which is shaped by underlying race, gender, and class considerations. While we acknowledge students' individual choices, we focus primarily on the social and structural contexts within which those choices are made.

Why is this approach important? An increasingly large number of selective campuses are developing support systems for first-generation students—these include orientation programs, student support offices, targeted advising and mentorship, and smaller-scale programming to increase first-generation enrollment, academic success, social satisfaction, and graduation rates. These systems need to be based on a full understanding of first-generation experiences, including both those students who are fully marginalized and those who are finding different ways to make community on campus. Limiting our focus means we don't understand the costs and benefits to students of participating in different campus scenes or activities. Moreover, when we assume all first-generation students have the same experiences on selective campuses, we miss how students' experiences are conjointly shaped by the ways college contexts reflect and reward different types of racialized, gendered, and classed positions.[10] Much current research leaves these analyses out to hone in on comparisons to continuing-generation students. Finally, those seeking to support first-generation students need to take into account the ways campuses themselves contribute to stratification among first-generation students, whether through programming or other structures.

In the rest of this chapter, we elaborate on how geographies work and how participants are distributed across them after explaining our analytical processes and the setting in which our qualitative data takes place. We close this chapter by contextualizing our findings within a larger, ongoing discussion of first-generation students at selective colleges and finally providing a chapter-by-chapter overview.

Methods and Setting

Data

We draw our findings from two sources of data: in-depth interviews and a national survey of undergraduate students at selective and highly-selective campuses.[11] We use survey data to identify larger patterns of selective college student engagement and the qualitative data to provide rich and personal descriptions of how students experience and perceive these different campus contexts.

Quantitative data came from the National Longitudinal Survey of Freshmen (NLSF), a probability sample of approximately 4,000 students who entered 28 selective U.S. colleges and universities in the fall of 1999.[12] The survey was designed to speak to race/ethnic differences in campus life and therefore oversampled students from racial/ethnic minority groups. We use these representative data to frame our analysis. The quantitative data provide a broad perspective on the ways students at selective colleges across the country organize their academic, extracurricular, and social lives, and they allow us to examine whether patterns of engagement differ by college generational status, race/ethnicity, and gender.

We combine these national survey data with 64 interviews with first-generation students conducted between 2014 and 2016 at a selective campus that we call "Hilltop College."[13] We conceptualize first-generation college students as those who grew up in households where no residential parent or caregiver graduated from a four-year college. These rich qualitative data provide an important window into the lived experiences of first-generation college students on selective campuses, allowing us to unpack patterns identified in survey data. The interview sample includes an approximately equal number of men and women from White, Black, and Latinx racial/ethnic positions. Our sampling strategy was purposive, intended to allow us to analyze race and gender variation within a group of first-generation students. In line with similar studies of inequality in higher education, we choose to focus on African American and Latinx students rather than other marginalized racial and ethnic groups because they share similar disadvantaged educational outcomes compared to White students,[14] and they make up a significant proportion of first-generation college students.[15] Most respondents' parents were gainfully employed in blue- or pink-collar jobs. Mothers and female caregivers tended to work in service-oriented jobs, including grocery clerks, home healthcare aids, waitresses, retail workers, house cleaners, custodians, and administrative assistants. Fathers and male caregivers worked as cab and truck drivers, contractors (electrical, lawn care, construction), mechanics, security officers, and government workers.

Hilltop College as a Campus

HC, located in a small northeastern city in the United States, is a selective liberal arts college enrolling about 3,000 students. Roughly two-thirds of the student body is White and slightly less than 1 in 10 students are from first-generation backgrounds. Although the overall graduation rate is 92% (within six years, the metric utilized in national ranking systems), the rate is only 85% for underrepresented racialized minority groups; no data are available on graduation rates by socioeconomic background. On par with other similar private colleges, the cost of attendance is approximately $72,000 annually in estimated costs in 2019–2020. The campus is selective, with most students graduating in the top 10% of their high school class and having obtained high SAT or other standardized test scores.

The 200-plus-year-old HC campus, known for its immaculate landscape and preserved stone buildings, stands out for its academic prestige but also for its social life. Current students and alumni often use the "work hard, play hard" motto to describe the HC student culture as intensely focused on academics, extracurricular activities, and socializing. With limited opportunities off-campus, HC's residential campus is the social hub of student life, offering over 200 extracurricular opportunities. Although students are involved in a range of activities, HC is well-known for its historic Greek system and well-regarded competitive athletic programs. It is nearly impossible to walk through this carefully manicured campus without seeing students sporting HC athletics or GLO gear. The significant impact of these two institutions on campus culture is reflected in high student participation rates, with over 20% and 30% of students participating in each, respectively.[16] When asked about campus life, respondents invariably mention Greek Life and athletics as prominent features, and with limited social opportunities off-campus, these status systems are difficult to step outside of or escape.

In examining campus life participation, we also investigate students' campus entry points—the first time they arrive on campus for enrollment. We distinguish between those who arrived on campus with all HC incoming students for regular orientation from those who participated in one of three different types of HC sponsored pre-college programs: SB, recruited athletic team training, and thematic pre-orientations. Here we'll describe each very briefly as a setting. We highlight the role of each space within the relevant geographies.

For the past several decades, HC's SB program has invited a highly selected group of 30 to 40 students who have overcome significant challenges to come live on campus during the summer while they take two academic courses. Like other college SB programs, a majority of participants come from lower-income backgrounds and are students of color, and invited students are required to attend.[17] SB students are supported by faculty and staff directors, teaching faculty, and upper-level student mentors both during the program and throughout their four years at HC.

In addition to SB, first-year HC students can also enter campus before the start of the fall semester for pre-season athletic training and thematic pre-college programs. Many recruited athletic teams at HC invite student athletes to campus two to four weeks before classes begin for pre-season training. During this time, teams prepare for their seasons, and first-year student-athletes have an opportunity to meet new friends and learn about campus life. HC also offers first-year students the opportunity to apply

for a number of short (up to two weeks) programs that bring students together around a shared interest (i.e., physical education, music, writing,
environmentalism) as a way to introduce new students to HC and develop
bonds with other students. Unlike the others, these programs require an
application and, for some programs, a small fee; financial aid is available.
Finally, all incoming students participate in a short orientation program
just before fall classes start in which they take care of logistical issues like
getting mail and dorm keys, meet new peers, and begin to get to know the
campus.

First-Generation Students on Selective Campuses: The Big Picture

The number of first-generation students attending college has increased over
time, yet this group continues to be grossly underrepresented at selective
colleges and universities.[18] Low-income, first-generation students are less
likely to apply to and attend selective colleges compared to their more affluent, continuing-generation peers.[19] Sociologists and policy thinkers often
focus on selective and highly selective campuses because they offer very
strong sources of socioeconomic mobility. They also provide first-generation
students with a stronger infrastructure of social and academic supports compared to less selective institutions, resulting in higher graduation rates even
after accounting for precollege academic qualifications.[20] Moreover, they are
often able to provide generous financial aid packages that make attendance
affordable.

At the same time, however, research suggests that first-generation
students do not necessarily reap the same benefits from attending selective colleges as their continuing generation counterparts. They have lower
rates of participation in campus social life and extracurricular activities,
work longer hours for pay, and have less time for academic pursuits than
continuing-generation peers.[21] In addition, first-generation students are,
on average, less satisfied with college and less likely to say they belong on
campus.[22] Finally, first-generation students are more likely to come from
low-income families (in this work we focus specifically on low-income
first-generation students)[23] and have fewer connections to sources of advice about college or post-college opportunities, especially within the white
collar world.[24]

Variation

The research above characterizes first-generation students in broad strokes, the average experience of a large group. However, we also know that there is variation within these patterns.

First, based on the large body of work on race and gender stratification in higher education, we would expect that first-generation students from different race/gender positions would have different experiences. Research consistently finds that students of color at predominantly White institutions perceive the campus climate and their social interactions are far more negative compared to White students[25] and often experience racial harassment and social isolation.[26] Students of color are often presumed to be less academically competent (or, in the case of Asian American students, to have advantages, masking academic effort) and to benefit from affirmative action.[27] These stereotypes and resulting micro- or macro-aggressions play out in myriad ways in daily life and often constrain social roles available to students of color on predominantly White institutions. For example, White students often perceive of African American men as unserious and athletic. On a majority-White campus, this avenue of participation therefore becomes the most direct source of recognition or social status for Black college men.[28]

Overall, selective, predominantly White colleges operate as a White space within which racialized stratification dynamics unfold not only among peers but also at institutional and classroom levels.[29] Examples of these may be seen in current news media, as students of color have the police called on them for napping or simply being on campus, and in scholarly research showing the ways that predominantly White college campuses commodify, devalue, and/or "other" students who are Black, Latina/o, Asian, Native American, and multiracial.[30] Students of color entering these spaces from educational and residential contexts in which they are not minoritized often face significant "culture shock"[31] and must adjust not only to college life broadly but also to these racialized dynamics. Importantly, these dynamics play out not only at the personal level but also at the institutional level.[32]

Similarly, gendered expectations within peer cultures lead to highly gendered (and racialized) performances, with men and women facing unique interactional pressures shaping all aspects of daily life, from personal appearance to the amount of effort put into academics. Women learn to perform perfection in both the academic and social realms, which includes an intense dedication to academics and pleasing others through both appearance and providing social support. Men, on the other hand, learn to perform hegemonic masculinity, prioritizing sports, leisure, and hetero-sexual relationships while strategically minimizing academic effort to con-form to masculine ideals of "coolness."[33] While both men and women are subject to these gender systems and their links to social status or belonging, the ways in which students access even individual sources of status are much more constrained for women. Women are judged more harshly for their physical appearance, clothing choices, and personality traits like nice-ness and friendliness. For example, sociologist Jenny M. Stuber and her colleagues described the ways that undergraduates perceived themselves as being looked down upon by privileged women peers while feeling much more comfortable with privileged men.[34] Notably, these expectations are maintained and policed by women as well as men, making gender expec-tations a much broader issue than heterosexual romantic or sexual popu-larity. These gender dynamics are also racialized, with appearance norms and gender scripts set to White ideals.

As in the case of race, gender stratification at the peer level is undergirded by institutional arrangements through single-sex dorms, athletic teams, GLOs, and, to some extent, clubs. On campuses that have fraternities and sororities, the regulation of GLOs plays an important role in shaping gen-dered social dynamics. For example, GLO regulations dictate that fraterni-ties may throw parties while sororities are unable to do so. Women therefore seek entry to men's spaces, spend social time in spaces physically and socially dominated by men, and the key venues for social life are typically those man-aged by men. This, in turn, has consequences for how gender is performed and enacted within these spaces. Women who seek status in the heterosexual dating marketplace face expectations for performances of femininity, both from male students who serve as gatekeepers to social events and also from female peers who wish to create peer groups of high-status friends, whether through sorority structures or friendship groups.

Second, institutional structures and programming shape the resources available to students and the types of peers with whom they come into con-tact.[35] We would therefore expect that students' varied location within the campus structure might shape their experiences. These variations may be the result of targeted programming for particular categories of student (e.g. first-generation, students of color, women, athletes), or they may be broad-based structures that relate to the full student body. For example, sociologists Daniel Chambliss and Christopher Takacs (2014) highlight the role of the institution in arranging pre-orientation programs that connect new students to peers and to campus faculty and staff. These provide important lead-time in making friends and getting to know the campus and its resources for those students who participate.

In other cases, campus policies privilege particular students or student lifestyles more than others. Sociologists Elizabeth Armstrong and Laura Hamilton (2013), for example, found that a "Party Pathway" through college was not only highly popular among students but also supported by adjustments to the institutional structure made by campus administrators. Changed exam schedules, classes not being held on Fridays, and other policy choices supported Party Pathway students. Because that Party Pathway is more accessible and more manageable for continuing-generation, upper-income students than for first-generation students, this has the effect of disadvantaging first-generation students at a structural level.

Scholarship also shows that campus programming can help mitigate some of these challenges. Research on institutional support program, particularly those that facilitate deep early connections such as pre-orientation and SB programs, as well as high-contact extracurricular activities, and dorm arrangements, can be highly effective in supporting first-generation students and students of color—that is, students who are minoritized on predominantly White, predominantly continuing-generation and/or affluent campuses.[36] Institutional structures provide important entry points that lead to different types of campus spheres and connections. Moreover, timing is critical as doors to connection close quickly, leaving students who have less access, knowledge, or interest in these types of opportunities with a much more difficult time finding connections and a sense of belonging.[37] Among other things, this suggests that participation (or not) in different types of campus programs during the first days or weeks on campus will lead to varied subsequent campus experiences and connections.

These examinations show us that students enter campus through different means, have access to different types of campus resources, and are differently located within the campus's demographic context. Although a small number of previous studies have considered variation, for example, in students' desires for class mobility[38] and the tools they bring depending on private or public high school backgrounds,[39] this research tends to focus on only one axis of variation.[40] This means that we miss the ways that students' experiences are conjointly shaped by class, race, and gender, as well as the ways college contexts reflect and reward different racialized, gendered, and classed positions. We take these variations into account as we consider both the institutional and peer contexts within which students and geographies are embedded. In the following discussion, we elaborate on our key concept of campus geographies.

Campus Geographies and Stratification

What do geographies look like and how do they work? To give the reader a more concrete understanding, let's start with a literal translation: Where do students spend time on or around campus? If, for instance, we gave each student a map of campus and the surrounding area and asked her to draw out where she goes on a typical day or in a typical week, what would we see? Some parts of campus would remain unmarked; others, heavily drawn in. Anthropologist Michael Moffatt, in his 1984 ethnographic study of students at Rutgers University, asked respondents to do precisely this: draw a map of the campus that reflected their lives.[41] Students included their dorms or off-campus apartments, classrooms, bars, and workplaces—even the train station where they caught a commuter rail home some weekends. What's immediately clear in these pictures, which are reproduced in Moffat's book, is that "campus" is different for each student. Engineering majors may spend a great deal of their time in the science building and labs and library; athletes spend time not only in classrooms but also on the fields, in the gym, and dining halls that accommodate their earlier or later eating times; campus newspaper editors spend many hours in newsrooms frequented by practically no one else. In part, campus geography captures *where* students spend their time.

However, we can also think about a social geography: *Whom* do students meet in these spaces? What kinds of interactions are taking place? Part of this, of course, is a question about how students form friendships and other relationships. But it is also a question of where students live out their social hours and how they connect to a broader constellation of peers. Some students spend time with friends on the soccer or Ultimate Frisbee field; others, in a student center lounge or dorm living room; and still others, in a fraternity house. Being part of these spaces, then, has the effect of putting students into contact with others who are also entering the space or already inhabit it. These cohabitants, in turn, shape students' time use and meaning-making. Peer norms provide guideposts about how to navigate campus life and what it means to be a "good" HC student. For example, does being a HC student include studying long hours, taking on leadership roles, partying with friends, and/or volunteering with community groups? Peer group influence is critical for understanding the meaning of theses spaces.

To identify campus geographies at selective colleges, we used NLSF survey data for both first-generation and continuing-gen students to uncover shared patterns of academic, extracurricular, and social activities and peer and faculty engagement at the end of the first-year of college.[42] Selective college students in the survey sample were somewhat equally divided into four campus geography types: Work Hard (23%), Disconnected[43] (31%), Multisphere (23%), and Play Hard (23%). Figure 1.1 provides a visual depiction of the constellation of attributes that characterize each geography and the differences between them.[44] Next, we describe the characteristics of each geography and the notable factors that differentiate them. In subsequent chapters, we take a closer look specifically at first-generation student

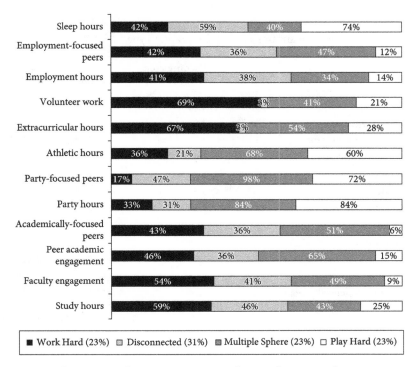

Figure 1.1 Percentage above mean across indicators by geography type ($n = 2,550$).

experiences within each geography, including entry points, peer culture, fit, and the benefits and costs of being embedded within each context, paying close attention to race and gender differences.

A Disconnected geography is characterized by the lowest level of campus connections. Table 1.1 shows that students in this geography are least involved in all social and extracurricular aspects of college life, spending less than half the combined hours in athletics, partying, extracurricular clubs, and volunteer work than those in other geographies. Like their Multisphere and Work Hard peers, Disconnected students work twice as many hours as their Play Hard peers. Finally, Disconnected students study the same number of hours each week (27) as their Multisphere counterparts, yet they are less likely to form academic connections with faculty and peers, suggesting they have made fewer academic and social ties in the first year.

Students in Play Hard geographies primarily organize their lives around partying and athletics—both recruited and intramural. Table 1.1 shows that

Table 1.1 Indicator Means by Campus Geography Type ($n = 2,550$)

	Work Hard	Disconnected	Multiple Sphere	Play Hard
Study hours	32.10[bcd]	27.03[ad]	27.23[ad]	21.03[abc]
Faculty engagement	3.57[bd]	3.03[acd]	3.47[bd]	2.21[abc]
Peer academic engagement	3.92[bcd]	3.26[acd]	4.58[abd]	2.62[abc]
Academically focused peers	7.07[bd]	7.01[acd]	7.46[bd]	5.78[abc]
Party hours	5.39[cd]	5.04[cd]	11.66[ab]	12.44[ab]
Party-focused peers	5.39[bcd]	5.31[acd]	7.56[abd]	6.45[abc]
Extracurricular hours	17.01[bcd]	5.62[acd]	14.98[abd]	9.71[abc]
Athletic hours	4.71[bcd]	2.96[acd]	8.28[ab]	7.51[ab]
Volunteer hours	3.28[bcd]	0.08[acd]	1.80[abd]	0.67[abc]
Sleep hours	46.83[bd]	50.09[acd]	45.43[bd]	53.59[abc]
Employment hours	4.86[d]	4.61[d]	4.01[d]	1.95[abc]
Employment-focused peers	3.81[cd]	3.64[cd]	4.22[abd]	2.17[abc]

Note: Means significantly different ($p < 0.05$) from Work Hard, Disconnected, Multisphere, and Play Hard.

[a]Work Hard.
[b]Disconnected.
[c]Multisphere.
[d]Play Hard.

Play Hard students devote a combined total of about 20 hours each week to these activities, and they have close peer ties who value the campus party scene. On the other hand, nonathletic extracurricular activities, such as clubs, volunteering, and working for pay, are much less central to their lives. Compared to those in Work Hard geographies, Play Hard students spend approximately half as much time in these activities. Moreover, Play Hard students fall at the bottom end of the distribution on every indicator of academic engagement, and they are the least likely to connect with faculty or surround themselves with academically oriented peers who value studying and achievement. Finally, students in this geography get the most sleep.

Work Hard campus geographies include students who are solely focused on academic and extracurricular pursuits. Compared to other geography types, Table 1.1 shows that students who inhabit Work Hard geographies study the most (32 hours per week) and rate their academic engagement with faculty and peers quite high. Moreover, they spend a combined total of 20 hours each week on nonathletic extracurricular activities and volunteer work. This is twice and three times the hours of those in Play Hard (10 hours) and Disconnected geographies (6 hours), respectively. On the other hand, Work Hard students exhibit low levels of engagement in the two main social hubs of campus life: athletics and partying. They spend less than half as many hours in these activities compared to those in Play Hard and Multisphere geographies. Finally, students in a Work Hard geography surround themselves with close friends who also value academics over party life and/or leisure.

Finally, students in Multisphere geographies are highly engaged across all domains—extracurricular, academic, and social; their close friends share this orientation to college life. While students in Work Hard and Play Hard geographies tend to focus their lives and connections around one or two domains, Multisphere students embody a "do it all" approach to college life. They are at the top end of the distribution along all indicators, except sleep, devoting large number of hours to each. Table 1.1 shows that each week Multisphere students spent on average 27 hours studying, 19 combined hours participating in athletics and nightlife, and 16 combined hours on extracurricular and volunteer activities. Multisphere students are also unique in that they have close bonds with faculty members and close friends who value both social and academic life. The students in Multisphere geographies resemble qualitative descriptions[45] of the typical prep school students who are socialized to excel with ease in all areas of student life, yet surprisingly, a portrait of students who excel in all areas of campus life is largely missing from higher education research.[46]

How do Geographies Function?

Geographies reflect larger patterns of where and with whom students spend time. Although it's tempting to think of these as merely individual lifestyle choices, they are central to campus stratification. Friendships and other connections provide not only emotional support and companionship, but also college-specific knowledge such as what clubs to join, what classes to take, and how (and whether) to use campus support resources. They also help students orient to college life, including what to prioritize: for example, should you study all weekend, or ease up on reading to go out with friends?

Campus geographies also shape first-generation students' access to resources for moving up the socioeconomic ladder. These include accumulated networks (social capital), interactional styles, tastes in clothing and food, and even ways of speaking (cultural capital), and orientations toward the future (habitus or worldview). Importantly, we show that acquiring and embodying the upper-class sensibilities that seem natural among class-privileged young adults takes practice to successfully pull off.[47] Sustained amounts of time with peers and faculty who have such cultural capital is one way of gaining that practice.

For first-generation students, however, such sustained cross-class social time brings its own challenges. Moreover, cross-class ties are by no means the only valuable friendships: as sociologist Janice McCabe shows in her book *Connecting in College*, friendships with same-class peers provide intimate and supportive emotional ties that stem from a shared background, as well as positive academic support. Like ties to friends and family at home, these friendships are less likely to provide new cultural capital. As we will show, campus geographies offer students different types of connections and resources.

Each geography is a *type* of space located within a larger, shared campus. Students select and are selected into these spaces, which then influence their campus lives and the tools they bring with them to post-college life. We refer to these geographies as types both because they are Weberian ideal types— archetypes that include some variation within them—but also to differentiate them from purely social cliques or groups of friends. Thus, we say that students participate in *a* Play Hard geography rather than *the* Play Hard geography. Because of the demographic and historic similarities across selective campuses in the United States, we suggest that these geographies will be similar across a wide range of colleges and universities. That our concept is derived from a multicampus national survey sample provides support for this view.

Finally, geographic participation rests on more than simply individual interest. Students both select into these geographies by virtue of their backgrounds and personal preferences—students who played high school sports may be inclined to keep playing sports in college—but also through prevalent social structures on campus among their peers. Gateways into geographies are supported by institutional structures, such as recruited athletic teams and SB and other types of pre-orientation programs. However, a student's success in participating in a given geography (i.e., finding affirmation or a sense of belonging) is not equally assured: geographies value and reward particular forms of classed, racialized, and gendered ways of being, shaping the way first-generation students from different race and gender groups are situated within the space. In other words, each geography has its own normative culture that is often supported by institutional structures. While some students are able to participate with relative ease, others struggle or feel disenfranchised. Those who struggled often described contorting themselves to fit the mold by changing everything from their clothing style to social habits and interactional styles. Moreover, both efforts to fit in and respondents' broader recounting of acculturation into their geography suggest that these are not merely pre-existing affinities or continuing on from high school choices—students are shaped by their geographies.

Chapter Outline

In the rest of the book, we unpack our argument about first-generation students' participation in varied geographies and how these sites provide access to different types of cultural tool kits.[48] Each chapter is framed by the findings from the NLSF and then fleshed out and illustrated with the interview data from HC.

In the second chapter, we compare first- and continuing-generation students, laying out the broad similarities among first-generation students along this first axis of comparison. We focus on students' high school backgrounds—the ways they get to college—and then discuss briefly the ways this background leads them into an initial institutional sorting process. While the rest of the book focuses on first-generation students and the differences among them, beginning with a comparison to continuing generation students allows us to highlight the ways that socioeconomic background matters and orients students to college, as well as showing the ways that continuing generations students are also sorted into the same geographies but with different distributions.

In the subsequent four chapters, we delve into differences among first-generation students, detailing the ways in which students both sort themselves and are sorted by institutional mechanisms into different types of campus geographies. Here we describe the characteristics of each of the four campus geographies—Play Hard, Work Hard, Multisphere, and Disconnected—showing how each leads to particular types of learning, activities, and peer and faculty relationships later in their college careers. Chapter 3 focuses on respondents who fit the Play Hard geography. We show that students in this geography arrange their lives around leisure, participating in high status social venues of parties, athletics, and/or GLOs. While respondents in this geography often indicated that their classes and academic work were important to them, their daily lives were more relaxed and more social than respondents in other geographies. Chapter 4 introduces respondents in the Work Hard geography. These academically engaged students made not only classes and homework central to their daily lives, but their friendships and social lives also were often rooted in either academic work and/or extracurricular interests. Chapter 5 discusses respondents who float between the Work Hard and Play Hard geographies, what we call Multisphere. These respondents incorporated elements from both, balancing serious academic work, strong extracurricular involvement, and social lives in high-status venues. There are few respondents in this geography, and we think of them in some ways as being outliers. Chapter 6 focuses on the experiences of respondents in the Disconnected geography. These students, while academically motivated and interested in a social life, were unable to locate comfortable spaces on campus or develop many substantial friendships and did not participate in many extracurricular activities like clubs or sports. These students are the largest group in our survey sample and represent the typical presentation of first-generation students at selective campuses.

In Chapter 7, we shift to focus on the ways campus geographies expose students to varied cultural models of success (or not) and accordingly shape their strategies for attaining that success. Play Hard students learn early not to prioritize academic outcomes above friendships and social life. Rather, they learn to focus on building powerful networks and are able to connect with more affluent friends through parties, team sports, and Greek Life. Work Hard students, by contrast, spent more time with peers from similar socioeconomic backgrounds. Their academic and social priorities remain geared toward building their formal resumes and having high GPAs, which guides their academically and extracurricular engagements. Multisphere students rely on both academic and network strategies and seem to be comfortable navigating each, while Disconnected students struggle to locate a clear and consistent route toward post-college success and plan to rely on themselves.

Finally, in Chapter 8, we recap our primary findings and show how they call into much more complicated question how it is that students from various racialized, gendered, and classed positions make the most of college and, in turn, how to support these students who all fit the institutional category of first-generation. We argue that the designation of "first-generation student"—increasingly the term of choice on campus and on the rise as a means of designing and directing student support services—is reductive, ultimately doing a disservice to students. We close by discussing the implications of this research for selective colleges wishing to support a range of first-generation students more successfully.

Conclusion

Highly selective colleges remain profoundly classed, dominated in population and practice by upper-income continuing-generation students. Scholars, editorial pages, and pundits increasingly call for these colleges to admit and support first-generation students. This is an important step, but we do not yet know enough about how to fully support these students after the point of entry. Although a growing body of work examines the experiences of first-generation college students at predominantly wealthy, predominantly White college campuses, scholars have largely treated first-generation college students as a monolithic group, focusing primarily on economic backgrounds held in common.

As Dan and Briana's stories show, first generation students have wide and disparate ranges of experiences, which, in turn, have implications for post-college outcomes. While many selective colleges and universities across the country are increasing student recruitment and support services for first-generation students, ranging from SB programs to dedicated offices to student clubs, these efforts may be ineffective without detailed understanding of variation within the first-generation student body. Utilizing the lens of campus geographies moves the question from whether students become integrated on campus to more holistic questions of with whom, in what contexts, and how—and at what cost. By looking at these smaller contexts of engagement, this book aims to identify the more specific and varied ways first-generation students find their way into and through selective college campuses. In the chapters that follow, we examine what happens for students like Dan and Brianna after they unpack their bags and start their new lives on campus.

Notes

1. We define first-generation college students in this book as those who grew up in households where neither residential parent nor caregiver graduated from a four-year college.
2. We use pseudonyms for all respondents in this book, as well as blurring, changing, or omitting other information that might identify them, such as majors, clubs, or hometowns.
3. Sociologists use both African American and Black, and we recognize that these terms shift in usage over time. We use both terms interchangeably in this book, and we capitalize all terms referring to racialized groups.
4. A number of scholars have written about these patterns, see the following works for examples: Martin, 2012; Stuber, 2009; Stuber, 2011a; Armstrong and Hamilton, 2013; Walpole, 2003; Aronson, 2008; Aries and Seider, 2005; Jack, 2019; Lee, 2016; Goldrick-Rab, 2006.
5. Jack, 2019.
6. Stevens, Armstrong, and Arum, 2008.
7. Attinasi (1989) also uses the term *campus geography* but employs it differently in referring to the overall physical, social, and cognitive dimensions of one campus.
8. Cultural and social resources are typically referred to using the terms *social capital* and *cultural capital* (Bourdieu and Passeron, 1990); our analyses include these as outcomes of students' friendships and other relationships.
9. Race and ethnicity are separate although often overlapping and conflated concepts. In this book we use race to refer to both, both for simplicity of writing and because racialization is widely experienced by both Black and Latinx/a/o Americans.

10. Many scholars refer to this as intersectionality. For seminal and in-depth discussions of this concept, see Crenshaw, 1991; Collins, 1991; Bettie, 2003. For a recent examination in higher education specifically, see Byrd, Brunn-Bevel, and Ovink.
11. A full description of our methodology is found in the appendix.
12. See Charles et al., 2009 and Massey et al., 2003 for full descriptions of NLSF.
13. See Appendix A for a discussion of time lag between the survey data and interview data collection.
14. Rothwell, 2015; McCabe, 2016; Wilkins, 2014.
15. A recent U.S. Department of Education report indicates that the racial composition of first-generation college students is 49% White, 14% Black, 27% Latinx, 5% Asian, and 5% other (Redford and Hoyer 2017).
16. At the time of this writing, HC does have any multicultural GLOs.
17. Wachen, Pretlow, and Dixon, 2018.
18. According to a recent Pew Research Center Report (2019), the percentage of undergraduates in poverty increased from 12% to 20% between 1996 and 2016, but it only increased from 10% to 13% at the most selective institutions. See Chetty et al. (2017) for a similar discussion of slow growth in the percentage of lower income students at the most selective colleges despite efforts to increase enrollment and financial aid.
19. Students from the lowest socioeconomic quartile are only one-third as likely to enroll in selective colleges as academically similar students from the top socioeconomic quartile (Giancola and Kahlenberg, 2016).
20. Bowen, Kurzweil, and Tobin, 2005.
21. For example, Martin, 2012; Stuber, 2015; Stuber, 2009.
22. Stuber, 2011a; Jack, 2019; Jack, 2014; Aries & Seider, 2005; Ostrove and Long, 2007.
23. First-generation students come from families with median incomes less than one-third of their continuing-generation peers (Saenz et al. 2007).
24. Rivera, 2016; St. John, Hu, & Fisher, 2011; Saenz et al. 2007.
25. Hurtado et al. 1998; Massey et al. 2003; Espenshade and Radford, 2009; Charles et al. 2009.
26. Feagin, Vera, and Imani, 1996; Willie, 2003.
27. Torres and Charles, 2004.
28. See also Eisen, 2015 and Wilkins, 2014
29. See also Ray and Best, 2015; Lerma, Hamilton, and Nielsen, 2019, and Feagin, Vera, and Imani, 1996.
30. Hurtado et al. 1998; Massey et al. 2003; Espenshade and Radford, 2009; Charles et al., 2009; Winkle-Wagner, 2010.
31. Torres, 2009.
32. Pager, 2008; Reskin, 2012.
33. Chase, 2008; Kimmel, 2008.
34. Stuber, Klugman, and Daniel, 2011.
35. For a rich discussion on this topic in the higher education, see Armstrong and Hamilton, 2013; Jack, 2019; Lee, 2016; Chamblis and Takacs, 2014; Stevens, Armstrong, and Arum, 2008.

36. Chambliss and Takacs, 2014; see also Stuber, 2015 on the role of institutional structure in shaping first-generation students' extracurricular participation.
37. Chambliss and Takacs, 2014; Tinto, 2010.
38. Hurst, 2010.
39. Jack, 2019.
40. Hurst (2010) includes respondents from multiple gendered and racialized positions but does not organize her analyses along these lines.
41. Moffatt, 1989.
42. The four campus geography profiles were generated using a statistical technique called latent class analysis that identified how respondents cluster together across indicators of student involvement, peer group values, and faculty engagement to form homogeneous subgroups. See Appendix A for a full description of methodology.
43. Scholars consistently document that lower income students commonly experience isolation and lack of fit, but what might be surprising is how prevalent this experience is for selective college students in general (31%). In Quadlin and Rudel's (2015) recent research on selective college student time use, they also find a substantial percentage (26%) of students are inactive, with low extracurricular and social engagement. Moreover, a recent large survey of college students shows that feelings of loneliness on campus are quite common, with nearly 30% reporting feeling lonely in the last two weeks and 60% in the last year (American College Health Association, 2016).
44. Figure 1.1 shows the percentage of students who scored above the mean across all academic, social, extracurricular, and relational indicators by geography type. This standardization allows the reader to easily observe differences across each dimension both within and between campus geographies.
45. Khan, 2011; Chase, 2008; Cookson and Persell, 1985.
46. While scholars have captured distinctions between academically and socially focused students and described students who are disconnected, no studies to date have identified a group of students in higher education who excel in academic, social, and extracurricular spheres.
47. Khan, 2011.
48. Swidler, 1986.

2

First-Generation Students
at Selective Colleges

This chapter places the experiences of first-generation students in context by describing how their early lives are both similar to and different from the "typical" student on highly selective campuses—namely, continuing-generation students. Here we provide a comparative portrait of what first- and continuing-generation students' lives look like in the years before college, how they choose to attend a selective institution, and finally, the types of campus geographies they found themselves in at the end of the first year of college. While the rest of the book examines differences among first-generation students further into the college years, this chapter outlines the specific ways that first-generation status matters for initial pathways into selective campuses. We argue that these early differences have implications for how first-generation students find a sense of belonging on selective campuses that tend to privilege and reward the experiences of continuing-generation students who make up the majority.

Selective College Students in High School

Family Life

Who are the first-generation college students that attend selective colleges? Consistent with previous research, Table 2.1 shows that fewer than one in five selective college students in the National Longitudinal Survey of Freshmen (NLSF) sample are the first in their families to attend a four-year college.[1] In addition to not living with a parent or guardian who graduated from college, Table 2.2 shows that first-generation students grew up in household contexts with significantly fewer economic resources, more household responsi- bilities, and somewhat stricter discipline practices than their continuing- generation peers. These students also had less access to middle-class cultural

Geographies of Campus Inequality. Janel E. Benson and Elizabeth M. Lee, Oxford University Press (2020). © Oxford University Press. DOI: 10.1093/oso/9780190848156.001.0001.

Table 2.1 Generational Status by Race/Ethnicity ($n = 2,550$)

	Black and Latinx Students (%)	Whites Students (%)	Entire Sample (%)	P value
Continuing Generation	65	86	82	
First Generation	35	14	18	
Total	100	100	100	<0.05

capital opportunities that are typically valued in educational contexts, such as traveling, attending plays, and visiting museums or libraries. Moreover, their parents were less likely to intervene in their academic lives than their more advantaged peers.

Consistent with other studies of class-based differences in parenting,[2] Hilltop College (HC) first-generation students described having independence in their high school lives, often making important decisions on their own without consulting parents for help. For example, Jack (Latino)

Table 2.2 Family Background of Selective College Students by Generational Status

	First Generation ($n = 718$) Mean/Percent	Continuing Generation ($n = 1832$) Mean/Percent	P value
Socioeconomic indicators			
Family income <35K	29%	5%	<0.001
Family ever received public assistance	14%	4%	<0.001
Applied for financial aid	94%	63%	<0.001
Received loans to pay for college	62%	32%	<0.001
Works for pay to finance college	47%	22%	<0.001
Household context			
Household labor (hours/ week)	8.14	6.15	<0.001
Middle class cultural capital	2.97	4.18	<0.001
Strictness of discipline	1.13	1.01	<0.05

described his mother's parenting this way: "She expected me to just like be on my own, doing my own thing because she had given me a lot of independence and freedom when I was younger to be a smart student. Like I never asked, or rarely asked her for help or anything like that." As Kerry Landers describes in her book on lower-income Ivy League students, "unlike the helicopter parents of their peers, the parents of low-income students do not call the school after their child fails a test, receives an undesirable roommate or dorm room, or is rejected from a top medical school."[3] Rather, first-generation students often make college search and other important decisions on their own without guidance from parents or other adults.

Although this chapter focuses primarily on differences by generational status, it is important to note that Black and Latinx students are overrepresented in the population of first-generation students attending selective colleges. In line with previous research, Table 2.1 shows that Black and Latinx students (35%) are more than twice as likely as their White counterparts (14%) to grow up in households without a parent or guardian that graduated from college.[4]

Academic and Extracurricular Engagement

The high school academic profile of first-generation students closely resembled the typical continuing-generation student who attends selective colleges and universities. Table 2.3 shows that both groups earned approximately a 3.7 grade-point average, and held similarly high educational aspirations, with over half of each group planning to pursue postgraduate education. On average, first-generation students studied a few more hours (22) each week than continuing-generation students (19.5). With the exception of foreign language, first-generation students rated their courses just as challenging as their continuing-generation peers, but they took slightly fewer Advanced Placement (AP) courses (2.5 vs. 3.3).

First-generation student narratives suggest these differences in course taking are more about opportunities than interest or ability. Nearly all of our first-generation interview respondents reported taking the most challenging courses available, often striving to be the best in their school. For example, Katherine (White) told us, "In high school I wanted to be valedictorian, so I was always really focused on academics and sports at the same time. I would always take honors classes if they were available and then AP

Table 2.3 High School Academic and Extracurricular Indicators
by Generational Status ($n = 2{,}550$)

	First Generation ($n = 718$)	Continuing Generation ($n = 1{,}832$)	P value
Student characteristics			
Grade-point average, mean (SD)	3.71 (0.02)	3.74 (0.01)	
Number of advanced placement courses, mean (SD)	2.55 (0.13)	3.33 (0.07)	<0.001
Hours studying per week, mean (SD)	22.07 (0.96)	19.51 (0.41)	<0.05
Aspirations			
Take college 1 year at a time, %	7	5	
Graduate college and then consider options, %	39	38	
Attend graduate or professional school, %	54	57	
Reported course difficulty (10-point scale)			
English, mean (SD)	4.38 (0.17)	4.43 (0.09)	
History, mean (SD)	4.32 (0.16)	4.28 (0.08)	
Math, mean (SD)	5.12 (0.20)	5.16 (0.09)	
Natural sciences, mean (SD)	4.77 (0.16)	4.71 (0.08)	
Social sciences, mean (SD)	3.72 (0.14)	3.78 (0.07)	
Foreign languages, mean (SD)	4.15 (0.18)	4.56 (0.08)	<0.05
Extracurricular participation			
Athletics, %	49	57	<0.05
Arts (drama, band, dance), %	34	37	
Student government, %	31	28	
Volunteer work, %	47	49	
Employment (hours/week), mean (SD)	10.15 (0.68)	7.59 (0.34)	<0.001

once they became available. So yeah I was always taking higher-level classes."
As Katherine explained, first-generation students attending selective colleges
were outstanding high school students who studied long hours and sought
out the most challenging curriculum available.

Table 2.3 shows that first-generation students' extracurricular engagement
also largely mirrored their continuing-generation peers. Approximately half
of each group reported volunteering, and about one third participated in

student government and the arts (drama, band, or dance). First-generation students, however, were somewhat less likely to play sports (49%) than their continuing-generation counterparts (57%), and they worked significantly more hours each week. Across the board, the first-generation college students in our HC sample described having overly booked high school lives filled with academics, extracurricular activities, and employment. For example, Aleyda (Latina) told us,

> I was . . . a student who tried to do everything and was really stressed out, so I was the student government vice president, was the yearbook editor. . . . I was just like president of everything, and I also worked and had like five AP classes my senior year so I tried to do everything.

For first-generation students like Aleyda, high school success was about balancing academic success, extracurricular engagement, and outside of school commitments, such as working for pay.

Neighborhood and High School Context

While it is clear that first-generation students are equally as ambitious in high school as their continuing-generation counterparts, they achieved their success by navigating through high school and neighborhood contexts that offered fewer high-quality resources and more potential distractions. Table 2.4 shows that first-generation college students (18%) are significantly less likely to attend private high schools compared to continuing-generation students (29%). In addition, they rate their school quality, reputation, and infrastructure (buildings, classrooms, and libraries) significantly lower than their continuing-generation counterparts. For example, nearly half of continuing-generation students rated the quality of their school as excellent compared to only one third of first-generation students. Moreover, first-generation students reported that their schools and neighborhoods felt much less safe than their continuing-generation counterparts. Table 2.4 shows that first-generation students witnessed significantly more disorder and violence within their school and neighborhood environment than their continuing-generation peers, ranging from peers cutting classes, talking back to teachers, and using illegal drugs to gang activity, physical violence, and weapons.[5] These patterns are linked to historical and present economic

Table 2.4 High School and Neighborhood Characteristics by Generational Status

	First Generation ($n = 718$)	Continuing Generation ($n = 1,832$)	P value
Public high school, %	82	71	<0.01
Private high school, %	18	29	
Rating each as excellent			
Infrastructure			
School building, %	23	34	<0.01
Classrooms, %	16	24	<0.01
Audiovisual equipment, %	27	32	
Library, %	23	33	<0.05
Computers, %	45	47	
Teachers			
Teacher interest, %	46	51	
Teacher preparedness, %	45	49	
Strictness of discipline, %	19	20	
Fairness of discipline, %	15%	17	
Overall quality			
School quality, %	32	49	<0.01
Public reputation of school, %	56	66	<0.01
School spirit, %	34	31	
High school context			
Exposure to disorder	33.90	31.80	<0.05
Exposure to violence	51.50	45.10	<0.001
Neighborhood Context			
Disorder Index	9.29	5.71	<0.001
Violence Index	27.70	13.71	<0.001

(and racial) segregation[6] that concentrate lower-income and Black and Latinx students into communities with underresourced schools and poor labor market and housing options.

Many of our first-generation respondents described a stark contrast between their motivation and aspirations and the resources available at their high schools to support them. When asked about their high schools, first-generation public school students often noted their shortcomings. Tommie (White) described his high school as "a poorer school, comically known as 'duct tape high' because when there's a tear in the carpet or whatever, they just slap a piece of duct tape down, and it's so common throughout the school." In addition to issues with infrastructure, HC interview informants told us that students in their schools were often disengaged and disruptive in class. For example, Jason (African American) recalled, "I would say 95% of the students there were not focused on their schoolwork. They were focused on looking cool." Although first-generation students in our sample were mostly tracked in smaller classes with more academically oriented peers, they described their mixed-population classes as chaotic and confrontational (in the words of Andrew, an African American respondent). For example, Angela (Latina) described one class in this way:

> There was a lot of yelling. A lot of like, there was so much yelling. There was a lot, a lot of general disrespect for the teacher, you know. Students talking back. Students on their phones and I just remember just, like, a lot of noise, like, and it was hard to control the class and I, and I just, like, I couldn't focus and it just—so I would just leave and go to the, um, college and career center and do other work there.

For many first-generation students like Angela, succeeding in high school meant learning how to manage potentially distracting environments, including identifying alternative spaces to work.

High School Friendships

Table 2.5 shows that first-generation students are just as likely as their continuing-generation peers to surround themselves with close friends who value both academics and extracurricular activities (volunteering, sports, and religious activities). This may be surprising given that first-generation students disproportionately attend public schools with fewer academically focused students. First-generation respondent narratives, however, indicate that they and their close circle of friends are typically outliers tracked in a high school pathway with small numbers of other academically motivated students. In this way, their high school experience occurs in a much smaller bubble separated from the larger study body. As Julie (White) explained, these smaller groups of academically driven friendships helped push students to work harder in school and apply to competitive colleges:

Table 2.5 High School Peer Group Characteristics by Generational Status

Peer Values	First Generation ($n = 718$) (%)	Continuing Generation ($n = 1,832$) (%)	P value
Close friends think it is very important to . . .			
Regularly attend classes	57	52	
Study hard	34	35	
Get good grades	59	52	
Finish high school	97	95	
Participate in religious activities	6	4	
Community and volunteer work	6	6	
Play sports	25	27	
Hold a steady job	10	5	<0.05
Have a steady romantic partner	4	3	
Be willing to party or get wild	11	17	<0.05
Most or some of closest friends have . . .			
Used Illegal drugs	24	34	<0.05
Used alcohol	51	68	<0.05
Have had sex	21	22	

I've always felt like I was more ambitious, you know, than kids I went to high school and, you know, I had a very close knit group of friends in high school but we all had similar interests in that we were ambitious, we were, you know, committed and dedicated, and our sort of goal was to get out of this town kind of thing. Like that was our aspiration. And, a lot of people at our high school didn't share those same beliefs and values, and so I wasn't really friends with those people.

These smaller circles of similarly academically engaged peers provided a functional community[7] or an alternative set of academic norms and expectations from the larger school environment.[8]

In fact, many first-generation informants point to their close group of academically engaged peers as one of their most valued assets, providing much needed motivation and encouragement. For example, Charles (Latino) names his peers as his primary source of guidance and knowledge about the college process:

My drive to get to college was probably like 100% with my friends. My parents . . . they like, don't know much about like, college and how to get there, they just know what it is. They always assumed I would be like, a doctor, or lawyer [laughs], you know, like that type of thing, and my guidance counselors, we were, like, on that No Child Left Behind program, but it sort of sucked because all of us, like, I don't know, smarter kids I guess, they never paid attention to us. So, it was 100% on us, we just motivate each other, and that's how we got here.

For many first-generation students, these smaller groups of academically motivated peers often provided important informal and formal compensatory resources,[9] helping to scaffold the college journey in public schools where guidance counselors and teachers are often overburdened.

First-generation college students' close high school friendships also buffered them from the potentially distracting high school party scene. As Table 2.5 shows, first-generation students are less likely than continuing-generation students to have friends who value partying, use drugs, and consume alcohol. In fact, many interview respondents explained that they strategically avoided peers engaged in the party scene. For example, Brian (White) explained, "In high school, I made a conscious effort to not hang out with any people who I thought would be damaging to my academics. I just worked my ass off in high school, and sacrificed my social life to be a good student." For many first-generation students, as Brian described, engaging in party culture presents role conflicts: Getting caught up with the party scene meant not being serious about your future.

When first-generation students described high school peers embedded in the party scene, it was almost always negative. As Kaelin (Latina/multiracial) told us, "kids in my high school just didn't do things that I, like, appreciated and, like, wanted to do in life. Like you know, like, a lot of them were like, they were, like, going out. I mean, that's like normal high school stuff. Drinking. Um, smoking." For Kaelin, like many first-generation students we interviewed, engaging in party culture did not mean having a fun time, but instead it meant choosing a life path that was directly at odds with upward mobility and success.

Interestingly, ethnographic portraits of affluent boarding school students highlight that participation in party culture is not something to be avoided, but rather a key part of education. Sociologists Peter Cookson and Caroline

Persell, authors of a seminal study in this area, write that "students must try to conform to the demands of two cultures which have little in common. Not only are they expected to be good students, they are also expected to drink, socialize, speak, and dress in the culturally approved manner."[10] As we will show in later chapters, these dual expectations—to work hard and play hard—are deeply embedded within HC's student culture, favoring students who know how to perform this delicate balance.

The greater exposure of continuing-generation students to drugs, alcohol, and parties in high school suggests they may already be internalizing these expectations. Most first-generation students, however, received the message that education was *the* ticket to upward mobility not only from their smaller peer groups but also from their parents who wanted them to have a better life than they had. This meant staying focused on academics in high school and avoiding the pull of the party culture. They learned the lesson early that they needed to avoid integrating into the larger peer culture found in their high schools and communities to achieve success. Despite their strong record of success, first-generation students may be less well primed for the campus climate found at selective, predominantly White colleges.

Choosing a Selective College

Next, we take a closer look at first-generation students' college selection priorities and application process. Research on the college selection process shows class-based differences.[11] For continuing-generation students, this process is a family affair that begins well before the senior year of college, with campus visits, detailed research about campus "fit," and ongoing conversations with school personnel and even sometimes outside hired counselors. For example, a recent study found that "affluent families often visited 5 to 15 colleges and universities in the final years of high school, as parents honed in on the right 'fit' between their daughter's aptitude and the academic and social programming on offer."[12] By contrast, first-generation students have a much more limited college search process. They have less guidance, visit few if any campuses, and often choose less costly colleges over more favored options.

First-generation students know that their families support their decision to attend college, but when it comes to the nuts and bolts of the application process, the student, not a parent, is in the driver's seat. For example, when asked about her family's involvement in her college search process, Katie (White) stated, "My mom knows nothing about the system except maybe some gossip she hears from co-workers or something like that. So I was really on my own and when it came to the decision, it was also my own choice. My mom didn't have much to do with it." Similarly, Brittany recalls, "My mom leaves that to me. She doesn't, uh, she wouldn't really know what to tell me." Without college knowledge and experience, parents of first generation students often leave the search process to their child and school personnel.

Unfortunately, with the exception of those who attended private high schools or landed slots in outside college prep programs, first-generation students often felt disappointed by the support available within their high schools. College counselors often had little knowledge of how selective colleges and universities worked and the financial support they could provide. Anna (White) felt frustrated by her counselor's lack of knowledge:

> One thing was our guidance counselor didn't know what was out there, like what's outside of [my state], like what there's to do. Also, being from a place with low socioeconomic status and not knowing about places that offer a lot of financial aid also I think kind of lessened the realization of what you can do.

Similarly, Emma (White) described her guidance counselor as "unsupportive," with little knowledge of schools like HC:

> I know at my school, like just with, usually like the caliber of students that we have, they tend not to like push people to like apply to more rigorous schools like HC. So when I initially told her that I was applying and wanted to go here she was like, "Well, I wouldn't get your hopes up. I don't think you're gonna get in. I really think [state university campuses] are a much better choice for you and that's really where you should go.

As Emma points out, very few students from lower-income high schools ever apply to selective colleges, leaving counselors with few examples. It's easy to see how even well-intentioned guidance counselors may lack the knowledge of the financial aid opportunities at selective colleges, steering them instead to public institutions.

These differences in access to economic resources and information about the college search process are also reflected in what first-generation students are looking for in a college. When asked what was most important in choosing a college, both first- and continuing-generation students ranked academic reputation and post-college placement as most important, but first-generation students rank factors related to financial aid and cost as substantially more important (Table 2.6). In fact, Table 2.2 shows that nearly all first-generation students (94%) applied for financial aid to fund the cost of college compared to only 63% of continuing-generation students. They are also twice as likely to take out student loans and work to pay for college than continuing-generation students. First-generation students also rated campus

Table 2.6 Importance of College Selection Criteria (0–10) by Generational Status

	First Generation ($n = 718$) Mean (SD)	Continuing Generation ($n = 1,832$) Mean (SD)	P Value
Cost	6.46 (0.21)	4.45 (0.11)	<0.001
Availability of financial aid	7.43 (0.22)	4.19 (0.12)	<0.001
Availability of athletic scholarship	0.83 (0.16)	0.80 (0.07)	
Sports opportunities	1.65 (0.18)	2.55 (0.11)	<0.001
Academic support programs	5.12 (0.21)	4.67 (0.11)	<0.05
Recruitment efforts by school	3.16 (0.22)	2.92 (0.10)	<0.05
Specific course availability	5.87 (0.24)	5.73 (0.11)	
Academic reputation	8.51 (0.12)	8.75 (0.05)	
Athletic reputation	2.47 (0.21)	2.93 (0.11)	<0.05
Social prestige	5.83 (0.18)	5.76 (0.09)	
Social life	5.39 (0.19)	6.10 (0.08)	<0.001
Theme dorms	1.46 (0.15)	1.54 (0.08)	
Distance to home	4.85 (0.22)	4.55 (0.10)	
Religious environment	1.78 (0.18)	2.26 (0.10)	<0.05
Campus safety	5.80 (0.17)	5.12 (0.10)	<0.01
Job placement record	6.04 (0.22)	5.69 (0.11)	
Graduate school placement	5.46 (0.26)	5.79 (0.11)	
Professional school placement	5.17 (0.25)	4.98 (0.12)	
Admissions' standards	6.74 (0.18)	6.85 (0.08)	
Size of school	5.57 (0.21)	6.38 (0.08)	<0.01
Parents' connection to school	0.89 (0.14)	1.46 (0.09)	<0.01
Parents' opinion of school	4.82 (0.21)	5.53 (0.09)	<0.01
Friendship with students or alumni	2.29 (0.20)	2.38 (0.10)	

recruitment and campus safety as somewhat more important. In line with the "fit" approach to college selection, continuing-generation students were more concerned about aspects of campus life, such as athletics, social life, religious environment, and school size. Moreover, they rated their parents' connections to and opinion of each college as somewhat more important than first-generation students, further highlighting the different types of roles parents play in the process.

Consistent with survey results presented in Table 2.6, first-generation Hilltop respondents told us that they choose HC primarily based on cost. When asked how they made their final decision to attend HC, respondents commented on the beauty of the campus, the school's prestige and rigor, conversations with faculty, and even having connected with other students on visits to campus. However, when push came to shove, respondents spoke about financial aid awards as what ultimately made the decision for them.[13] Jack, for example, a Latino student, told us, "I cried when I saw the financial aid bill, or the award. That was nice, and I knew that was the place to go out of the three I got into." Richard, a White respondent, recalled, "Honestly, I was looking at other schools. Hilltop wasn't my number one choice, but when I got the financial aid package, that's when I was excited about HC."

Respondents made these choices not only for themselves, but also for parents. Angela narrated her decision in this way, noting, "So, that financial aid was really, like, the deciding factor for me 'cause I didn't want to have to worry about loans, and I didn't want my mom to have to worry about trying to, like, help me pay for everything." While Angela was cognizant of avoiding loans, she also did not want her mother to "have to worry about . . . pay[ing]" for college costs. Similarly, John, a Latino student, told us, "Money was the issue; it's weird I didn't want my parents to have to pay a single dime for school for personal reasons, and to this day they haven't paid a single dime for it so that's 'cause of Hilltop."

In some cases, respondents chose Hilltop over a different, favored campus. Few respondents told us that Hilltop was their first choice,[14] but for some it was distinctly lower in their list of campuses. Katie (White) recounted that she "really had never had an intention to go to HC, but I don't know, I guess when the decision came down to it HC just seemed like a better school and I liked that it was smaller and it offered me a lot of financial aid that [my first choice] didn't offer." As we see in Katie's response, her award letter was not the only issue—a smaller campus and a strong academic reputation were important too. But being offered "a lot of financial aid" was significant. In fact, many respondents described having little if any knowledge about Hilltop as a campus, other than that it could offer financial aid and it's strong academic reputation. Similarly, Samirah (African American) had hoped to attend a different school and, in fact, received scholarships to four other colleges: "It was kind of sad because . . . my dream was always to go to the University of Michigan, but when it came down to it, I got accepted and they invited me to programs, but it was like you were gonna have to pay $30,000 dollars a year, and I saw HC and ended up choosing Hilltop. It wasn't my first choice, but you know." Indeed, Samirah's decision was not only about the tuition but also about being able to simply go and see the campuses in person and what that communicated to her:

> Really one of the biggest problems was the fact that I couldn't afford to visit schools. Right? So it was hard for me to make this decision and she was like you know you can come visit and we will pay for you. And that kind of, like, it kind of got stuck in my head like wow maybe they want me. You know like I never had a school offer to give me money to come visit them. Like I got the scholarship, but I never had them say we want you to come see our campus. And they paid for me to come and that's when I made my decision.

As Samirah's experience shows, selective colleges are able to capture the interest of underrepresented students and even woo them away from their favorite college with financial incentives from strong aid packages to all-expense-paid visits—known as fly-in programs—organized around students' interests and background.

Several African American respondents, in particular, reported hoping to attend historically Black colleges or universities (HBCUs). Most HBCUs— like most college campuses generally—are not able to offer the same kinds of financial aid as Hilltop, which boasts a substantial endowment and can provide a great deal of grant funding to its students. Brianna (African American), for example, recalled that she

> had a conversation with my mom about which will help me be more up- wardly mobile and while HBCUs like . . . Howard and Spellman are like Black Ivy, they still don't get the same um—the same like acknowledgement or respect as a Hilltop would. So even though I knew I would probably be happier and more comfortable in a place like Spellman or Howard, Hilltop

was it in terms of building social and cultural capital and the financial aid package didn't hurt too because it was almost a full ride.

Notably, Brianna felt she would be "happier and more comfortable" at an HBCU and didn't doubt that her education would be excellent. However, between the more widely known prestige of Hilltop and the large financial aid award, she chose pragmatically.

Perhaps this motivation is not a surprise: It seems logical that for students whose families are struggling financially, financial aid packages that cover more of the cost and/or offer a higher grant to loan ratio would be appealing. However, this orientation toward the college, the nature of that choice, was often very different from those of their continuing-generation peers. As sociologist Ann Mullen points out, many students attending elite colleges have always planned to attend such a campus. Their parents are highly educated, often being alumnae of the same college or of a peer institution, and choosing an elite campus or that specific campus had been presented as a virtually foregone conclusion since early childhood. Moreover, many attended selective private high schools or well-funded public high schools that routinely send their graduates to Ivy League and other highly selective campuses. As one Yale student interviewed by Mullen told her, "I had a [high school] graduating class of 62 and 7 are here. I think over a third of my class went to the Ivies."[15] Incoming students therefore arrive with very different ideas and expectations about college, different ways of seeing themselves in this space. This contributed to a sense of difference, particularly among the broader campus.

In some cases, respondents felt a sense not only of difference, but judgment or vulnerability. Lauren, a White student, provided the strongest example of this. She had become uncomfortable speaking about how she chose Hilltop, a seemingly neutral get-to-know-you conversation during orientation and new friendships. She discovered that admitting she'd chosen Hilltop "because they offered the most financial aid" was an answer that marked her as different and drew uncomfortable reactions not only from students but also from professors. She recounted these early conversations as follows:

This is a loaded question. It's the first question everyone asks you when you got on this freaking campus. I did the [pre-orientation trip]. My student leader's like, "So, why did you choose Hilltop?" And I said because they offered me the most financial aid, and he looked at me like I had just grown a second head. I realized that's not an acceptable answer and you know, I had a professor ask me the same question too, and I gave the same answer 'cause it's the truth. Why did you come to HC? And I said 'cause they offered me the financial aid and she said to me, I'll never forget this. She said to me, "Oh, so you're an investment? Be sure to live up to our expectations." I was like thank you. I really like her but I just was like blown away by that.

These responses communicated very clearly to Lauren that choosing a college for the money was an inappropriate response, an inappropriate motivation. This reaction calls to mind the excerpt from Tobias Wolff quoted by Mullen, describing how the upper class "turn[ed] cold at the mention of money, or at the spectacle of ambition too nakedly revealed."[16] For Lauren, such responses indeed had a chilling effect. Following the exchanges she described, she told us, "I don't tell people that anymore. It's like, when you get comments like that, you're not gonna say anything, you know?" Already early in her campus life, she has strategized that the best way to make her way through college is to stay quiet about her background or comments that might give clues about it.

Initial Impressions: Connection and (Multiple) Marginalization

As Lauren's case showed us, social class differences immediately emerge in "getting to know you" conversations where students are looking for quick points of connection. For many first-generation students like Lauren, these class differences created barriers to social connections with affluent students. On a campus that feels so different, then, how do first-generation students identify friendships and locate a sense of belonging?

While most of our respondents were excited to come to HC, some realized more quickly than others how their family backgrounds differed from most students on campus by observing the luxury cars in the parking lots and preppy dress of their new, mostly White peers and their families. Nadya (Black), described,

I was really self-conscious and not because of my race but because of my class, I guess. I realized how rich everybody was and everybody, like, honestly looked the same and had the same things that I couldn't afford. Um, and it was hard fitting in because first of all, I've never heard of a lot of the brands that people were wearing and nor did I have the money to buy that stuff. So, it was, I was a little bit intimidated.

Similarly, Jay, a Latino male student noted,

I'm not saying you can't be friends with somebody who's from the higher income, but I mean, let's be honest, there was some kids [in my dorm] going to the Superbowl and I'm watching the Superbowl on a TV screen, and if he were to invite me to go there's no way I would be able to pay for it anyway. So there's just like, the things that he may like to do as a friend, I simply just can't do, so therefore I can't be his friend.

For Nadya, Jay, and others, other students' levels of affluence presented at least potential difficulties in trying to make friendships or envision spending social time together.

As students navigate college for the first time, dorm life, and especially roommates, are critical sites of peer connection and belonging. They provide someone to sit with in the dining hall and explore campus social activities. First-generation students often face barriers to connection with more affluent roommates and dorm peers and described awkward moments and silences that limit their ability to develop relationships beyond acquaintance-level. As Phillip (Latino) recounts, "we really don't have anything to talk about." Rico, an African American student-athlete at HC, avoided spending time in his room because of similar friction with more affluent roommates. He spends most time with and feels the most comfortable with his teammates because as Rico explained, it's "where you can just be you."

Although all first-generation students felt at least somewhat out of place, students of color had more negative initial impressions of campus life. For example, Victoria (Black) described campus as a "sea of White people," highlighting the lack of students of color on campus. White students initially perceived campus as more friendly compared to African American and Latinx first-generation students, suggesting that racial majority status provides at least some tools for managing class marginality, in particular by being able to "pass" or remain (visually) unmarked as different. As Rebecca, a White respondent described, class differences are easier to hide, making it ostensibly easier to assimilate into campus culture—at least temporarily. When Rebecca arrived on campus, her initial thoughts were "Oh my god I am at the preppiest place in America. I swear, I don't know what I am going to do. I don't fit in here." However, in reflecting back, she then decided that "it wasn't that serious" as a hurdle: "I mean, like, I still had a certain level of comfortability because being poor is something you can hide, so that was something where I was like I just won't talk about money and we'll be fine." Being White allowed her to fit with relative ease into the majority space of the dorms and social venues on campus, provided she could manage the key issue of class successfully. Rebecca felt that this was a workable strategy.

By contrast, Beth, a Latina student, described her first days on campus as follows:

When I first arrived, I saw no Black people. No light-skin people. No nothing. Nothing of color. I just saw White faces. So, a typical Hilltop student on my first day here: boots, leggings, sweater, a little jacket, whatever. The scarf. Blonde hair, blue eyes, brown boots. Boots, boots, boots.

For Beth, the "typical" student was both unlike her in style and racialized appearance and preponderant: there were "no [students] of color" with whom Beth might identify. Beth's impressions also tell us about gender: there are particular ways to be feminine, to be a young woman, that don't match her style choices and/or financial capacities. Students of color, and particularly women of color, often experience multiple forms of marginalization. Even students of color who came from predominantly White precollege environments feel the ongoing drain of being the only person of color in academic and social spaces. For example, Zendaya, an African American student, reported, "I had less of a time like getting into the culture than other people, 'cause I always been around White people. So I just like didn't care. But I feel like it gets tiring. 'Cause like I miss home, and I miss being around people that look like me."

For first-generation students broadly and first-generation students of color especially, differences from campus peers were clear early on. White first-generation students' racialized position allowed a potential measure of comfort and anonymity and seemed to blunt their "culture shock;" this was not available to students of color who struggled to manage both forms of marginalization concurrently. As students made friends and became involved on campus, however, more complicated variations unfolded—a topic we look at in subsequent chapters.

Generational Differences in Campus Geographies: Within-Campus Stratification

Given this somewhat rocky start, how do first-generation students find a sense of belonging during their first year? In this section, we examine whether first-generation students are situated in similar campus geographies as their continuing-generation peers. Table 2.7 shows that the majority of first-generation students are located in Disconnected (41%) and Work Hard (25%) geography types, with smaller percentages of students in the more socially oriented geographies, Multisphere (17%) and Play Hard (17%). Continuing-generation students, however, are more evenly distributed across geography types, with 25% in Party Hard, 25% in Multiple Spheres, 29% in Disconnected, and 21% in Work Hard. These patterns suggest that first-generation students are less connected to the mainstream areas of campus life and are less able to create a life that balances both academics and social engagement compared to their continuing-generation peers. The contexts they disproportionately find themselves in tend to be lonely and/ or solely focused on academic and extracurricular activities. Although some continuing-generation students follow these same pathways, they are much more likely to inhabit worlds filled with connections to the central social hubs of campus life.

In subsequent chapters, we examine race and gender differences among first-generation students within and across campus geography types. We end this chapter by taking up the question of whether these generational differences simply boil down to race. Table 2.8 shows generational differences among nearly all race-gender groups. White first-generation women are less

Table 2.7 Percentage of Students in Each Geography Type by Generational Status

	First Generation ($n = 718$) (%)	Continuing Generation ($n = 1832$) (%)	Entire Sample ($n = 2,550$) (%)	P Value
Work Hard	25	21	23	
Disconnected	41	29	31	
Multisphere	17	25	23	
Play Hard	17	25	23	
Total	100	100	100	<0.01

Table 2.8 Percentage of Students in Each Geography Type by Generational Status and Race and Gender

	White Women (%)		Women of Color (%)		White Men (%)		Men of Color (%)	
	FGEN	CGEN	FGEN	CGEN	FGEN	CGEN	FGEN	CGEN
Work Hard	26	24	36	29	9	17	33	18
Disconnected	45	30	38	35	44	27	26	29
Multisphere	16	24	16	25	20	24	22	34
Play Hard	13	22	10	11	27	32	19	19
Total	100	100	100	100	100	100	100	100

Notes: FGEN = first-generation students; CGEN = continuing-generation students. All generational differences are statistically significant, with the exception of White men.

likely to be situated in the more social Play Hard and Multisphere geographies than their more affluent continuing-generation peers. The largest difference among White women, however, is in the Disconnected geography: Forty-five percent of first-generation White women are located here compared to only 30% of White continuing-generation women. We find a similar gap between White first- and continuing-generation men, but due to the relatively small number of White first-generation men in the NSLF sample, we must be cautious when interpreting results for this group.

In constrast, first-generation men and women of color are just as likely to find themselves isolated in a Disconnected geography as continuing-generation students of color. We do, however, find generational differences among students of color in the other geographies. First-generation men and women of color are more likely to find themselves within the academically focused Work Hard geographies and less likely in the more social Multisphere geographies compared to continuing-generation women and men of color. In addition, first-generation women of color are also less likely to inhabit a Play Hard geography than their continuing-generation peers, but this generational difference does not exist among men of color.

While it is clear that generational status shapes the contexts students inhabit during the first year of college across racial-ethnic group, these results also suggest that class advantage—having a parent who graduated from college—is more likely to protect White students, especially White women, from isolation. In subsequent chapters, we explore how maintaining a position in these geographies is more or less challenging for some race/gender groups than others.

Conclusion

This goal of this chapter was to describe the characteristics of first-generation students attending selective colleges by providing a portrait of their high school lives, college application process, and initial experiences during their first year of college. We do so by juxtaposing first-generation students with continuing-generation students, the dominant demographic at selective colleges, to highlight the important ways social class matters. Like their continuing-generation peers, we show that first-generation students are highly accomplished both inside and outside the high school classroom, but they developed their strategies for success within somewhat different neighborhood, school, peer, and family contexts.

Once in college, we find that these differences carry over into how first- and continuing-generation students find a sense of belonging. First-generation students are less likely than their continuing-generation counterparts to be located in Play Hard and Multisphere, the more social campus geographies. This pattern is in line with research showing that first-generation students perceive the more social aspects of college as less important than and as a distraction from their coursework.[17] Moreover, these generational differences in engagement in socially oriented geographies largely hold across race and gender.

First-generation students are also much more likely to find themselves in a Disconnected geography, with few connections to campus peers and staff, than their more class-advantaged counterparts. These generational differences, however, are most pronounced among White students, with Black and Latinx continuing-generation students just as likely to find themselves within a Disconnected geography as their continuing generation peers. Regardless of social class, Black and Latinx students often experience selective, predominantly White institutions as hostile contexts, marked by racial harassment and microaggressions, making it more difficult to identify places of belonging.[18]

Why is it important to understand these early steps? Simply put, educational progress is cumulative: We need to look at the beginning to understand what happens along the way and at the end. Students' first impressions help shape their sense of belonging, a key concept in higher education. This is especially important for thinking about the adjustment of students from different demographic groups: students in the majority may feel an immediate sense of fit, campus makes sense to them,[19] while students who are less so may feel less at ease, have greater difficulty making friends, or feel less comfortable participating in class. These, in turn, may lead to different types of opportunities during and after college. For example, feeling too uncomfortable to speak with a professor can shape students' grade point average and access to different types of scholarships, honors, or faculty reference letters.[20]

While many students, regardless of background, may struggle to get used to college-level work or the experience of living away from home, students who see college as a space in which they belong are more likely to stay enrolled and, ultimately, to graduate. Finally, looking at first steps helps us understand how students develop friendships and get involved in activities later in their college careers. These early friendships and engagement in college life help shape students' sense of belonging and also lead to different kinds of social niches, choices about classes and activities, and even job- or support-seeking. We take up these latter points more specifically in the coming chapters, where we turn our attention solely to first-generation students and the larger questions guiding our analysis.

First, we look carefully at how first-generation students navigate each campus geography type—how they got there, their impressions, and who they met. Although many first-generation students are unable to plug into the extracurricular and social activities on campus, as shown in previous research,[21] this is not the entire story. Other students find ways to connect into social circles characterized by academics, social life, or both. We explore the ways that institutionally facilitated access points, such as Summer Bridge programs, recruited athletic teams, and pre-orientation programs, may influence how students are oriented toward campus life, creating routes into some types of engagements and away from others. We examine how these institutional practices structure student engagement while also recognizing that students themselves select into different types of contexts based on demography and precollege experiences.

Second, we meet students midway[22] through college to examine the quality of student experiences within each campus geography and, importantly, what students learn in these spaces about upward mobility. We pay close attention to the normative peer cultures found within each geography and how they shape the ways students from different racialized and gendered identities experience college life, with both short- and long-term implications. In answering those questions, we expose deeply rooted organizational practices that shape students' engagement on campus and the ways that engagement in social, extracurricular, and academic spaces is profoundly influenced by class, race, and gender.

Notes

1. Giancola and Kahlenberg, 2016.
2. Calarco, 2014; Lareau, 2003.
3. Landers, 2018.
4. Fischer, 2007. Analyses not shown indicate that these racial and ethnic differences are consistent across gender. The sample includes the same percentage (35%) of Black and Latinx first-generation students.
5. Exposure to disorder and violence in schools and neighborhoods was assessed using a severity-weighted index developed by Massey and colleagues (2003). A full description of each index is found in the appendix.
6. Reardon and Owens, 2014; Massey et al., 2003; Jack, 2019.
7. Furstenberg et al., 1999.
8. See Crosnoe (2000) and Crosnoe, Cavanaguh, and Elder (2003) for a larger discussion of the social embeddedness of peer relationships and how the protective benefits of academically-oriented peers are often context specific.
9. Erickson, McDonald, and Elder, 2009.
10. Cookson and Persell, 1985: 163.
11. Hoxby and Avery, 2012; McDonough, 1997; Hamilton, 2016; Landers, 2018.
12. Hamilton, Roska, and Nielsen, 2019: 6.
13. Torres (2009) and Lee (2016) also find that financial aid packages were central to lower-income students' decisions to attend selective colleges.
14. Chambliss and Takacs (2014) argue that is common among selective college applicants in general who tend to apply to a large number of schools. Moreover, they find that students who ranked the college they attended as their first choice were more satisfied with their college experience than those who did not.
15. Mullen, 2010: 99.
16. Mullen, 2010: 18.
17. Bergerson, 2007; Stuber, 2009.
18. Hurtado and Carter, 1997; Massey et al., 2003; Espenshade and Radford, 2013; Charles et al., 2009; Fischer, 2007; Torres, 2009.

19. See Smith, 2015.
20. For a more extensive discussion, see Jack, 2019, Chapter 3.
21. Martin, 2012; Stuber, 2011a; Lee, 2016.
22. In Chapter 3 to 6, we measure academic, extracurricular, and social outcomes using Wave 3 NLSF data collected at the end of the sophomore year. We refer to this as midway because it approximately marks the halfway point in traditional selective college student's career. See the appendix for full detail of measures.

3

Play Hard

Introduction: What Does a Day in the Play Hard Life Look Like?

Todd, a White basketball player, greatly enjoys his time at Hilltop college (HC). His typical weekend is largely devoted to basketball practices or games and social time. Days are given to his team and some homework, and during the evenings, "I'll hang around or go to the fraternity house or downtown at night on the weekends . . . probably party, drinking and just having some fun." He is not involved in other types of extracurricular activities, instead balancing time between his team, his friends, and getting academic work done. While he has academic commitments, fun and social life play larger roles in his time on campus.

Rick (African American) is on a number of intramural athletic teams. He describes typical weekday and weekends as substantially formed around leisure activities. Rick told us that a weekend day might be "dedicate[d] to work, sometimes I wake up, go to the gym, eat, hang out, maybe play basketball, or football. Play squash. Or something like that. And I don't know, then drinking kind of starts, I mean, once dinner starts, or after dinner, start drinking." While Rick reports that he "definitely parties," he describes his primary activities as intramural or pick-up sports games or practice with his team.

Like Todd, time playing is also time with friends and the source of many friendships for Rick: Among his friends on campus, "We like sports, we like hanging out and, like, drinking . . . extracurricular stuff. We like working out, we like going to the gym, playing basketball, playing football. We like watching football games. We just have similar interests." Friendships are built around these shared social pursuits, and time with friends is built around relaxing, playing, or partying.

Rick and Todd's campus lives fit popular images of college for traditional-aged undergraduates: fun with friends, the best four years of your life.

Geographies of Campus Inequality. Janel E. Benson and Elizabeth M. Lee, Oxford University Press (2020). © Oxford University Press. DOI: 10.1093/oso/9780190848156.001.0001.

Students who fit a Play Hard geography squeeze more leisure into their college lives and meet more friends through social pursuits than students in other geographies. They spend more time in places on and near campus that revolve around play, including fraternities and sororities, bars, and both intramural and recruited athletic teams. Although academic achievement is important for many Play Hard students, it is less of a driver in these students' lives than for those in other geographies. Similarly, extracurricular participation beyond Greek Life and athletic pursuits was minimal for Play Hard students.

This version of college life is associated with popularity and high social status on campus; respondents across all four geographies described its prominence within HC's social scene. Like the "Party Pathway" identified in sociologists Elizabeth Armstrong and Laura Hamilton's research on White women at a large public university, this geography is highly visible on campus and primarily inhabited by socially oriented, class-advantaged White students. As Armstrong and Hamilton explain, class-advantaged students in these spaces "associate with similarly privileged others, in exclusive contexts, and in ways that allow them to expand their circle of similarly privileged acquaintances."[1] First-generation Play Hard students therefore meet more cross-class peers through these geographies, even when they themselves are not members of Greek Life or athletic teams. Black and Latinx respondents in Play Hard geographies also made more friendships with White students than their same-race peers in other geographies, an outcome linked to stronger sense of belonging on campus.[2]

Play Hard geographies are not easy to access or manage for first-generation students. While only 17% of first-generation students in the National Longitudinal Survey of Freshmen (NLSF) sample find their way into Play Hard geographies (compared to 25% of continuing-generation students), it is here where we observe the greatest variation of experience along gendered and racialized lines. Social norms for Play Hard students are set by the majority group, and successfully conforming to the classed, gendered, and racialized expectations of interaction takes work. Moreover, because cross-gender contact, including dating and/or hookups, are central to what many heterosexual students seek in a Play Hard geography, racialized and classed norms around gender performance are especially heavy. Play Hard students reported varying levels of comfort and satisfaction, often participating at a steep cost to their senses of self-esteem or enjoyment.

Entry Points: Early Connections
to Cross-Demographic Others

Entering a Play Hard geography is less challenging for first-generation students who are relatively more comfortable in the predominantly White, predominantly upper-income demographics that already shape those spaces. Students who arrived from private high schools in which they had formed friendships with wealthier others and/or, in the case of students of color, White peers had a head start here. For these students, campus could still be overwhelming or feel uncomfortable, but they felt less of the culture shock that students who arrived from homogeneously low-income and/or African American or Latinx high schools. We also find some evidence that Play Hard students in the NLSF sample are slightly more economically advantaged than first-generation students in other campus geographies (Table B.1), which might also suggest more comfort or exposure to the dominant campus demographic.[3] A second factor that helped students enter this geography was sharing extended activities with cross-race and/or cross-class others, typically through sports teams.[4] Each of these pathways speaks to the power of existing student body demographics and, as previously described, of the college as an institution.

Respondents who had attended private schools, in particular, reported a sense of familiarity with campus—Hilltop worked like and to some degree looked like their high schools. Echoing sociologist Anthony Abraham Jack's "Privileged Poor," respondents who attended private high schools, these students already learned some of the "rules of the game" and "did not experience the strangeness, unfamiliarity, and isolation that entering elite college brings."[5] Mike (Black), for example, who attended a preparatory high school, recalled that his first impression of Hilltop was that he "thought it was a lot like the prep school: small place, and a lot of White people around . . . button down shirts, khakis, came from money." Similarly, Selita (Black) reflected on her first impression of campus: "These are a lot of rich White people, I remember thinking. But I went to school with a lot of rich White people so it's fine." By comparison, Jeff (Black) noted that many first-generation students "have never interacted with people like the Hilltop student and the Hilltop administration, so they have a hard time adjusting and fitting in."

Having attended private school was not a panacea, however: Lebron and others also noted that although Hilltop was similar to their high schools—which helped—the student body at HC was Whiter and wealthier, which necessitated some adjustment. As Bernard, who attended a predominantly White private high school, commented,

> when I first stepped onto the Hilltop campus, I was originally overwhelmed. I had previously known that HC is a predominantly White school, but I was actually shocked by the lack of minorities on campus. I first noticed this during orientation, as I was the only African-American in my [orientation] group. It felt like more than half of the students were draped in pastel shorts, Sperry, and Vineyard Vines.

Although attending high schools with affluent White students tends to buffer the culture shock for first-generation students, students of color on predominantly White campuses often have Bernard's uncomfortable experience of being the one and only person of color in campus spaces.

Like the experience of private high school, athletics also serves as a bridge for first-generation students to more easily connect with cross-class peers in Play Hard settings.[6] When recruited athletes arrive on campus, they begin training with existing team members, either through an extended pre-season for fall sports or once classes begin for other seasons. This provides an immediate connection to other students through a shared focus and/or a high-status identity. Crucially, athletic teams at selective colleges like Hilltop College largely comprise affluent White students, and many of the peers new students will meet are already enmeshed in Play Hard geographies. Sharing intense practice and weight room sessions as well as fun times getting to know the social world allows—or even forces—respondents to interact with peers around them with whom they might otherwise have felt uncomfortable. Play Hard students who did not enter as recruited athletes often participated in intramural sports teams that facilitated similar kinds of connections and buffers.

These facets were important in allowing Play Hard respondents to settle into campus quickly as they acclimated among peers who shared something important in common. Gretchen (Latina) provides a strong example here. Gretchen arrived on campus with an athletic scholarship, one she had been thrilled to receive. Her early impressions of campus and her new peers were shaped by her time getting to know her teammates and other athletes on campus for fall training. She recounted one interaction, in particular, that was emblematic of this:

I had a . . . random, like, [encounter] when I was watching the [team] practice inside, there was a football player running around the track. He came
and introduced himself to me and my dad and was just talking to us about
the whole Hilltop community and everything. So it was kind of nice to
just to see this guy that didn't know us at all and he just came up to us and
started talking to us and telling us about HC and stuff like that. . . . Everyone
seemed pretty nice and friendly.

Unlike many first-generation respondents, especially Black and/or Latinx
respondents, Gretchen told us that it was easy to find students with whom
to identify, because "a big aspect of it was the athletes. It was easier to connect with them because we all were athletes so it's kind of similar, you know."
Having the shared focus on athletics helped first-generation students like
Gretchen wade through initial discomfort and find commonality with her
more affluent peers.

Another important function of athletic preseason was that they provided
buffers from the campus as a whole through team comradery, lessening feelings
of alienation faced by many other respondents—especially respondents of
color. This is most directly expressed by Rico (African American), who told
us that being on a team with so many others who share things in common
allows him to feel "typical," rather than the exception or an outsider. This is
in strong contrast to most respondents, who told us that they felt atypical because of their race, ethnicity, and/or socioeconomic background. Rico told us
that "actually, since there are a lot of athletes on the team, I do feel like I am
the typical Hilltop student. Maybe not the regular students that go to class and
that's it, but the athletes I do feel like we all can relate to each other." Because
his teammates are all working to balance school and sports, just like he is, he
feels typical among them. And because he spends the majority of his time with
those teammates, that goes a long way in making campus more comfortable.
Respondents on teams thus eased into campus their first fall, having developed friendships with both demographically similar and different peers and
with greater comfort and more positive impressions.

There were also Play Hard students who did not enter through either
pathway. Notably, among our interview sample, all those who were neither
private school graduates nor athletes were White, suggesting that belonging
to a racialized majority on campus may facilitate joining this geography
without needing an institutionalized set of connections. We discuss this in
the variation section.

Commonalities

Academics: Pulled into Fun

While some Play Hard respondents listed academics as an important focus for them in their campus lives, they generally placed schoolwork equal to or lower than social and/or athletic time. Midway through college, Play Hard students continue to score lower than all other groups on indicators of academic engagement, connection, and effort. Table B.2 shows Play Hard students in the NLSF sample study the fewest hours per week (19 hours) and rate their academic effort a full point lower than all other groups. They have the lowest levels of faculty engagement, and they are nearly half as likely (36%) to have a college mentor than Work Hard students (65%). Play Hard students also make few academic connections with their peers. They rarely study with peers outside of class, and their studying is often interrupted by peers listening to music, watching TV, or partying. Moreover, Table B.3 shows that Play Hard students are about half as likely to make friends through their classes compared to those in other geographies. Overall, while most HC Play Hard students report that schoolwork is important, they are pulled into social time with Play Hard friends who both distract from academic work and also reinforce a Play Hard philosophy in which academics are not the first priority.

Much of this focus on fun stems from the social construction of a Play Hard geography. While students at academically selective campuses are academically capable and motivated by virtue of the competitive selective process, those who participate in a Play Hard geography are surrounded by peers who place lower importance on academic work and who pull participants into shared fun even when they intended to be studying. Even students who intend to focus more on academic work end up being distracted by friends. Brian (White) told us that even going to the library or doing homework could end up pulling one into a social situation, which meant he had to be strategic and intentional about academic work:

> My roommate would go and he would go to the library just to be seen at the library. Just so that like other people would be like, "Oh, yeah. [He] was there." And, and that like, that made me so, it weirded me out. Like how is that? Yeah, how is that conducive to your studying? Just like always looking over your shoulder and making sure that that girl you've been, you know, eyeing, sees you? You know, like that's so ridiculous.

Brian tried to find a balance between the two, managing to do both studying and socializing at the same time, but spoke about how ultimately the lure of social time overtook his attempts to study:

> Like you have a paper due and you feel really accomplished because you got something done, so it's just like, "Oh, great. I'll have a beer." And then that leads to oh, your friend sees you drinking, "Come drink in my room." "Okay." And then after like creating an outline to a paper due on Monday, you have, that's all you have done, and then you're hungover the next day, and it's a real, it's a real pain.

Similarly Charles (Latino) talks about how a weekend day might include "pretend[ing] to do some work when we're all chillin'," describing the way that collectively not doing work can be a form of social togetherness. It's easy to imagine that even when a student has planned to get some schoolwork done, the shared "pretend[ing]" but instead "chillin'" might mitigate that activity.

Despite this lower focus on academics, most HC respondents in this geography describe feeling both busy and stressed about balancing their activities. This likely tells us something about the overall culture of Hilltop, as well as the academic focus and skills of respondents: Even those least focused on academics are still at least somewhat stressed about their work. Rico (African American) is a good example here. Rico says he feels pressed for time, "constantly on a schedule." However, he also says he spends most of his time "in my bed, resting. Probably in the weight room, practicing." Moreover, weekends for Rico are spent with his fraternity brothers off campus, "chilling" and going to parties. Thus, as we see in Rico's accounting, descriptions of daily life on campus include much more social time and much more relaxation time than respondents in the Work Hard geography. However, we also see that even those students who spend a significant amount of time relaxing or socializing at this highly selective campus are neither immune from stress nor fully disengaged from academic life.

Faculty Connections

As described earlier, NLSF survey results show that Play Hard students have the lowest levels of faculty engagement and mentoring. The qualitative interviews with HC students reveal that Play Hard students have very different types of expectations and connections to faculty than their Multisphere and Work Hard peers. Overall, Play Hard students have minimal contact with faculty and typically only see faculty outside of class for required advising appointments or meetings scheduled by faculty. For them, these relationships are pragmatic, not personal. For example, Rico (Black) explains: "It's very professional relationship; it's really like 'how are you doing professor.' We talk about the grade or my advisor will talk about my classes and what requirements I have to take and fulfill and that's pretty much it." This boundary between academic and personal was common among Play Hard students and is markedly different from students in the Work Hard and Multisphere geographies who describe close-knit and sustained relationships that extend beyond the classroom.

Some described their lack of engagement simply due to time constraints (e.g., varsity athletes), to feelings of intimidation, or to a sense that faculty are not interested in forming relationships with them, but part of the reason for this disconnect is that Play Hard students have few opportunities to learn how and why to engage with faculty. Although small in number, we find that Play Hard students who did have an institutional link to faculty through working as a research assistant, participating in the Summer Bridge (SB) program, or studying abroad had substantially closer faculty relationships than other Play Hard students. This finding is consistent with other research that shows that frequent and meaningful contact, especially time outside of class, is critical for the formation of a successful faculty–student mentoring relationship.[7]

Extracurricular and Social Life: Prioritizing Fun and Limiting Campus Engagement

Leaving recruited athletics and Greek Life aside, respondents in a Play Hard geography are far less engaged in extracurricular activities midway through college than most. Table B.4 shows that Play Hard students in the NLSF sample have the lowest involvement in all nonathletic extracurricular activities: 21% volunteer, 13% cultural group, 11% religious group, and 8% arts group. They spend about one-third as many hours on extracurricular and volunteer activities as Work Hard students. Moreover, Table B.3 shows that Play Hard students are the least likely to meet their closest college friends through clubs (7%). As we will discuss, most HC Play Hard respondents did not view non-athletic pursuits as meaningful parts of their college lives.

Instead, respondents in a Play Hard geography prioritize leisure and time with friends, disproportionately engaging in the more social aspects of college life, including partying, athletics, and dating, and many of their friendship connections come through these engagements. Table B.3 shows that Play Hard students spend the most weekly hours partying (11) and using media (29). They are most likely to be involved with Greek Letter organizations (GLOs; 37%) and to identify close friends through this venue (29%). Nine out of 10 students in this geography are engaged in campus dating culture. Play Hard students are also heavily invested in athletics, with nearly half playing a varsity or intramural sport. Finally, Table B.4 shows that Play Hard students get the most hours of sleep each week (50). Even HC Play Hard respondents who are on recruited athletic teams, who spend significant portions of their time in mandatory training and practice, describe more leisure and social time than students in Work Hard geographies.

Among our interview respondents, both athletes and members of GLOs report spending the majority of their time with others in those spheres. Both groups also report that their social lives revolve around drinking, cross-gender romance, and—especially for men—exercise[8] and video games. For example, Jason, an African American man on a recruited sports team, decided to join a fraternity because he "knew that most of the social events were revolved around that." Jason has a lot of friends, both on and off his team, and is heavily involved in his fraternity, and he attributes his full social life to these memberships: "I'm in the social scene quite often. I'm always meeting new people and always talking and going out and stuff." Indeed, there's a great deal of overlap between his team and his fraternity, and he spends most of his time with friends who share one or both of those spaces. He reports a typical weekend night is "party with a sorority, and then another party with a sorority, and another party with a sorority," and asked what he spends most of his time on outside of classes, he indicated, "I spend most of my time working out or drinking."

Jason's narrative highlights that these social worlds often overlapped. Many athletes also joined GLOs and/or had friends who did, who in turn invited them to parties, and vice versa. One especially important function of athletic teams is that they often served as a pipeline into other elite campus venues, especially Greek Life. Although most first-generation respondents entered unsure about participating in GLOs, those that did rush reported being "pulled" in by friends on the team. As Dan, a White male athlete described, "the decision to join was made for me. [My frat] is known as the lacrosse fraternity, a lot of lacrosse players join the fraternity. So to be a member of the lacrosse team, was to be a member of the fraternity. So I just followed my friends." For students like Dan, athletics therefore not only provided an instant network of friends with a shared interest; it also helped students gain easy access to new social opportunities. Other student athletes described the same experience. For instance, Tommie (White) told us that his first friends were teammates whom he met during his SB orientation:

> I had [SB] with one guy who was on the team, and a lot of the [team] guys who lived in town for the summer, they kinda come up and kind of bail me out of that place for a little bit. I go hang out with them, so I kinda met the lacrosse guys, and camp came around right after that, and you just get in this niche with all the [team] guys, and that gives you good social jumpstart for sure.

This bond and "social jumpstart" still holds for him, as he told us, "it's just the whole being on the team, you kind of have like a brotherhood there with all those guys, and that's real nice, that's huge." Respondents who were on athletic teams were very explicit with how important this was to a social life.

Whether they participated in athletic teams and/or Greek Life or not, most Hilltop students across all geographies agreed that GLOs served as the gatekeeper to mainstream, high-status social life. A large number of students in Play Hard geographies were or had been members of GLOs because these organizations represent such a significant and iconic part of the social life at Hilltop. While cost is often an issue for first-generation students, many of Hilltop's GLOs offer a limited number of scholarships to students who cannot afford dues. This meant that at least *joining* a fraternity or sorority was financially accessible to respondents. Notably, HC does not offer multicultural GLOs, so these groups are all predominantly White. Despite this, Greek life is so central to popularity, friendship, and dating at Hilltop that decisions about whether or not to join a GLO seemed to be a choice that all students have to make no matter how briefly they thought about it. Moreover, because GLOs tend to demand a large amount of time and are associated with behaviors viewed as either very positive or very negative, the decision to join or not join may be polarizing. One asks, "Am I a Greek person or not a Greek person?" This simple yes-or-no question becomes a defining characteristic, what students stand for and who they are, even though participation is voluntary.

Decisions about joining Greek Life also shaped access to the romance and hookup scenes at HC. Greek parties are where the action is for students at HC, and students who are hoping to meet someone for either a short- or long-term connection—particularly heterosexual connections—learn early on that this is an important potential market. Men often described meeting women, either through sororities or through fraternity parties, as a primary reason to join a GLO. Women mentioned this less often as a reason to join but spoke about how looking for romantic and/or sexual partners shaped their day-to-day social lives around partying. As we will see at the close of this chapter and in others, this does not mean that students necessarily enjoyed these party spaces or thought of them as fully safe. We discuss issues around gender and sexual marketplaces later.

Even for respondents not in a GLO or athletic team, the culture of partying at HC seemed both alluring and hard to avoid. Some respondents told us that they started drinking to make friends, while others told us how difficult it was to avoid drinking when they had decided to stop. Richard (White) was one of the latter and provides an especially interesting example of the importance of drinking in Play Hard respondents' social worlds. Having developed an illness during his junior year, Richard could no longer drink. This was a serious change to his social life. He told us, "I had a big friend group freshman, sophomore, and junior year, and a lot of it was predicated on alcohol. . . . I remember the only days we didn't drink were like Sunday and Tuesday, you know?" While Richard participated in this part of college life, he saw himself as by no means one of the heaviest drinkers—he'd learned to drink safely at a young age, and he compared himself to friends and peers who "got blackout drunk."

After he got sick, however, Richard stopped drinking entirely. This changed his friendships, changed the way he interacted and the events he could participate in: As he noted, although his friends were superficially supportive, alcohol was such a part of social life that it was impossible to avoid. As Richard related, he would tell friends, " 'I kind of want to have a chill night,' and they're like, 'Alright, sure.' And . . . then like 14 more people show up and then everybody else wants to, you know, either drink or do another thing." Richard's account tells us both about how much drinking takes place and how important it is to many social interactions—how to be social without drinking?—but it also tells us about how nondrinking social situations can effectively become parties. The evening may begin with a small group, but others join and soon you have a larger group, and it's harder to maintain the low drinking level. Students who stop drinking (or never drank in the first place) are effectively pushed out of the scene by this spilling over of virtually any social event into a party.

Alternately, this social scene may pull students into choosing to drink. Brooke (White), for example, told us that when she enrolled in college, she had not planned to drink. However, she began to feel that she was missing out on the fun that others were having. Brooke told us that "when I came here, I didn't drink. [laughs] And then I quickly learned that you don't meet people if you don't at least go out, you know?" Brooke recounted how early potential friendships seemed to be stalled by her nonparticipation in this part of campus life: "Cause I'd meet people in classes and they'd be, 'Oh, you're really cool. Let's do this.' And I'd be like, 'Oh, I don't do that.' And then like every starting of a friendship would stop there. And then, so I was like, 'Okay. I need to start going out.'" Brooke's experiences adjusting to college life highlights the role that peer culture plays in decisions about drinking: Rather than being simply an individual choice, it is contextualized within the larger social structure of available options.

Making Space on Campus

We asked respondents to talk about places in which they felt both most comfortable and least comfortable on campus. Play Hard respondents had wider ranges of places in which they reported feeling comfortable than students in other geographies—indeed, several Play Hard respondents told us that they felt comfortable everywhere on campus. This feeling of comfort on campus was often linked to the groups of people among whom Play Hard respondents spent the most time: large friend groups and especially athletic teams and Greek Life co-members. Play Hard respondents were enmeshed in venues that by nature have broad-reaching networks and high status—a fraternity or sorority may have 50 to 100 members across multiple years of students, while an athletic team might have up to 100 people on its roster. Those who were not members of either such configuration often had similarly large networks of friends and acquaintances through their social activities.

Respondents who were part of a team or a GLO described feeling most comfortable among that group—others with whom they shared a social identity and many hours of time spent in common. Todd, a White male, reported he is most comfortable in his fraternity, the locker room, and his apartment "because . . . I've been around [the students who share those spaces] for three years, for the most part. They know when I am joking or if I'm serious and I never have to explain myself." Notably, all three of those spaces comprise many of the same friends and peers across spaces: Todd practices with teammates who are his friends and, conversely, lives and parties with friends who are his teammates. As we see in Todd's narrative, these friendships served as a social buffer through which male respondents, especially, could be themselves. Many spoke about the comfort of not feeling judged and the vulnerability along class and/or race lines they felt in other spaces because of that risk of judgement.

For male athletes, these buffer friendships and senses of understanding were deepened by sharing so much required time on the field and in the locker or weight room or even working in the same segment of the team (e.g., defense), providing not only familiarity. Dan (White), for example, seems to equate his comfort level with his friends and teammates with the comfort he feels being alone. Asked where he feels most comfortable on campus, he first listed his own apartment, "definitely number one," because he can "sit on the couch, and throw a movie on." However, he "also feel[s] comfortable in the company of my friends . . . I feel comfortable in the locker room; it's a bunch of guys with the same mentality as me."

Like their male peers, female athletes described their teams as the people with whom they were most comfortable. Like men, women spoke about teams as being like family. Katherine (White), for example, is effusive about the closeness of these friendships: "I feel really close to them. They are almost like sisters and like from the first year here. . . . I felt almost closer to them than I was from my, like, best friends from home." However, they were less positive about Greek Life settings, and in contrast to men, women in Play Hard geographies were more likely to mention extracurricular spaces and classrooms—places where they share a mindset or viewpoint—as comfortable spaces. We discuss gendered and racialized variation more fully toward the close of this chapter.

Finally, those who were members of neither type of organization described being comfortable with friends and sometimes in academic spaces (although this answer was rare). Somewhat surprisingly, women often reported feeling uncomfortable in fraternity party settings, much like respondents in other campus geographies. That they continued to participate in a Play Hard geography may speak both to the importance of this social setting and the lack of commensurable options for fun, as well as to the emotional costs of participation. For those who wish to participate in a Play Hard geography while feeling uncomfortable in these types of party settings, maintaining this lifestyle is difficult. We turn to the question of what is required to be part of the geography and whether all respondents had equal access next.

Variation: Fitting in Through Friends and Romance

While Table B.5 shows only a small number of first-generation students in the NLSF fit a Play Hard geography (17%), we see the greatest levels of variation along racialized and gendered lines within this small group, both in terms of who ends up in this geography and their experiences there. Twenty-seven percent of White men are located within a Play Hard geography compared to 19% of men of color, 13% of White Women, and 10% of women of color. This reflects the ways that students' demographic statuses shape their likelihood of entering and staying in different geographies. However, even within Play Hard geographies, respondents' relative levels of comfort and ease varied substantially.

In this final section, we explore two defining features of a Play Hard geography, friendship and romance, as a means of understanding this variation in access and fit. These spheres of campus life have cultural scripts and rituals that are tied to particular constructions of femininity and masculinity, which in turn influence the ways in which first-generation students from different backgrounds can access and engage in these spaces. Generally, White male interviewees exhibited the most comfort in Play Hard geographies, followed by men of color and White women; women of color had the most difficult time, reporting that they were stressed and unhappy and, in some cases, wishing they had chosen another campus altogether. These variations highlight the costs of participating in this idealized and high-status geography and that those costs are unevenly distributed. We return to this discussion in greater depth in Chapter 7.

Campus Friendships: Greek Life, Athletics, and Other Informal Spaces

First-generation HC men were more likely to participate in Greek Life than women, and the structure of fraternities and partying on campus facilitated heteronormative performances of masculinity. For both White men and men of color on HC's campus, fraternity life provides access not only to a popular party scene but also romantic or sexual opportunities with women. The structure of Greek Life on campus builds in particular social practices that lead to advantages for men, such as control over alcohol and party themes and locations.[9] Men learn early in their college lives that access to these opportunities are restricted if they are not connected to the fraternity scene. For example, Jason, an African American male, told us he joined a fraternity because he "knew that most of the social events were revolved around that." While women often described Greek Life and local bars as potentially uncomfortable or even threatening, men were less likely to do so, rather seeing them as locations for fun.

Within their friendships with other men, male Play Hard respondents reported a social life based around hanging out and casual talk and activity. Despite often small numbers of close friends, male respondents of color and White male respondents both reported being able to find downtime around shared scripts of masculine activity that did not hinge of class- or race-specific past-times. Jokes, pick-up or intramural sports, video games, TV, and partying and/or "the girl hunt"[10] all provided activities around which to build friendships and common time. Their social time is therefore centered around casual activities that provided a widely-shared cultural script for friendship.

Crucially, these scripts crossed race and socioeconomic lines and did not wholly rest on spending money, so that the barriers to joining in were relatively low. Dan (White), for example, told us that,

> besides [the team sport], we kick it, we play video games a lot, we watched sports event together, we party, that's about it. . . . We enjoy the same activities; I feel that is how friends are really made. You enjoy the same things like music, having the same tastes and preferences.

This seemed to allow men to bridge gaps across race and socioeconomic status to a great extent and to have a purchase on social interactions with others who might be very different from friends at home. Dan mentioned that while "things get personal sometimes," overall, conversation is kept light.

Because of this shared cultural script of masculine taste, men's friendships—and especially those located through athletic teams and Greek Life—seemed to provide an important source of downtime and a space in which men could at least temporarily avoid feeling vulnerable, judged, or demeaned. This also meant that men could spend time together while avoiding difficult subjects, including talking about how they come from different backgrounds. For many Play Hard respondents, this allowed a level of comfort across not only socioeconomic status but also to some degree racialized and ethnic statuses. Rico (African American), for example, feels most comfortable with his team, because everyone gets each other: "In the locker room with my teammates, that's where you can just be you. You can relate to everybody there. Everybody is a [team] player, everybody's going to look out for you so I feel like those are my closest friends so that's where I feel the most comfortable." Although the rest of campus may feel judgmental or alienating, male respondents located an important context of belonging among other men who shared their tastes.

While women's friendships, whether through teams or GLOs or outside them, also provided an important source of comfort and relaxation, there were indications that this was also varied. Women in Play Hard geographies often described activities with friends as focused on talking and their shared party scenes—getting ready to go out, pregaming, and going to parties together, much of which was organized around hook-ups or relationships. While Play Hard men also focused on cross-gender interactions and parties, female respondents described these social processes as more emotionally and financially taxing because the stakes were higher in terms of normative expectations about relationships versus hooking up, judgmental standards about women's appearances and personalities,[11] and fears about personal safety.

Moreover, as other scholars have found, even women who are not initially interested in romantic relationships find themselves "pulled in" to romances or hook-ups because they are the dominant topics of conversation and activity among female friends.[12] As Julie (White) told us, "it's tough to have a good time with your girlfriends if they're just like standing around looking for guys, and texting people and, you know, not really paying attention to what's goin' on." As Julie highlights, social time with friends may be waylaid by the search for partners and/or performing femininity. The pressure women felt to conform to heteronormative gender scripts in these settings were both financially and emotionally costly. We return to this topic in greater depth in Chapter 7 as we discuss the ways respondents changed over time.

Although shared social contexts, especially athletic teams, were often able to facilitate friendships across racialized lines, race still deeply shaped respondents' experiences on HC's predominantly White campus. Although Play Hard students all participated in high-status settings, had wide-ranging friendship circles, and led active social lives, respondents of color were much more likely to differentiate between a few real friends of color with whom they shared close ties and a broader range of more superficial friendships. By contrast, White respondents simply spoke about friends.

John provides an especially clear example here. A Latino student, John was one of only two students of color in his sophomore house of 16 men. He described them as a "bunch of frat boy type of students." John spent some social time with them: "So like go down and drink with them and what not." In his recounting of that time, John stressed that he felt comfortable there:

> I mean I didn't have a problem being the only Latino or student of color in my sixteen-person house, because I was. My friend, he was Asian so we were pretty much the only students of color in the house, or as you would say a different ethnicity than White. And like these guys would sit in the living room like ten of them at a time and watch a show and like I would sit down and not have a problem. I'd interact with them, I'll crack jokes with them, you know—normal.

However, in junior year he moved into a new house with more men of color. This made a substantial difference to John, providing deeper connections:

> I don't know why, I don't know how it happened, but I just feel like these friends and these people these relationships are more meaningful than the relationships I had with other, White students. I don't know if that makes any sense, but it was a huge transition. So I went from like White to students [of color] and now my close group of friends are students of color because I can be myself with them more than I can [pause], I'm more comfortable basically.

He added that although he does the "same thing" with his new friends that he did with his old friends— hang out, crack jokes, drink—these relationships also nurture deeper connections and conversations:

> I can do the same thing now with my friends now, I feel like with my friends now I can talk with them, and actually talk about different issues and have hot debates about hot topics and what not. Get mad at each other, but you

know it's all part of the discussion. But I feel like I can't do that with my first two-year friends like they were more into "oh what did you do last night? I have so much work," like very superficial and there was never a point where I feel like I got close with them. We would never sit down and be like "hey how's your day going, what's going on? Are you alright man?" you know? Like get personal, and build actual relationships. And like I don't know it sounds corny, but that's important, like a huge part of my life. I'd rather have three good friends than have ten people that I can say I would call friends, but not really be friends, more like acquaintances.

These activities allowed him to spend comfortable time with very different groups of peers.

Indeed, this low-key masculine social script allowed John, like many other male Play Hard respondents, to enjoy his time on campus. Ultimately, the tool kit for this particular type of masculine friendship helps men to make connections with others but, as John suggests, may not be enough by itself to form deep bonds. Within this predominantly White space and among White friends, students of color may feel pressured to resist prevalent race-gender stereotypes that links Black and Brown bodies with being angry, aggressive, or hypersexual.[13] Students of color must therefore carefully manage their self-presentations, emotional displays, and interactions on campus;[14] respondents of color who attended private high schools were often already accustomed to this emotion work.

This differentiation between superficial fun and deeper, real connections was part of a larger narrative among Black and Latinx Play Hard respondents. Although they participated in the high-status party spaces of campus and had wide-ranging friendships, they also described the ways that overall, in Rick's words, "the social part [and the] people here kind of suck." Play Hard students of color were not the only respondents to point out that "the social part . . . suck[s]," but respondents of color in Work Hard and Disconnected geographies largely avoided these dominant social areas, opting for smaller numbers of closer and more similar friends.

While Play Hard respondents had bigger groups of friends, some described their friendships with White students as temporary rather than close ties, as we saw in John's case. Indeed, John differentiated between "acquaintances" and "good friends" who really understand him. Maggie (Black) echoed this sentiment:

I'm definitely closer to, like, my friends who are, like, I'm, I'm very close with them. . . because of, like, the SB experience. I definitely saw how our identities are very different in the [dorm where I live], which is great I think because it's a learning experience for all of us, I think. But I'm definitely closest to, like, my roommate in the house and, like, my other roommate who I did SB with.

Like John, Maggie described friendships with peers from different backgrounds and described spending social time and even shared living space with them. She highlighted the ways that "getting to know these other girls who, like, come from, like, different, like, perceptions and, like, those things can be frustrating but, like, I also, like, value other parts of our friendship." While Maggie framed those friendships as "interesting [and] fun," her friendships with similar peers are closer.

This schism seems even more complicated for female respondents of color than for male respondents of color for a number of reasons. First, male respondents of color reaped greater rewards, or at least fewer sanctions, from the party and hook-up scenes that were often the focus of Play Hard social life. Second, as we have already seen, male respondents relied on gendered social scripts that were less punishing and easier to adhere to than those available to women. Finally, male respondents of color especially conceptualized Hilltop as where they *needed* to be, a place that would bring them success—in part, through contacts with wealthier White peers who shared team, Greek, and/or social spaces. Lebron, for example, reflected that the "first two weeks coming back [to campus]" are always very difficult as he readjusts after being home—ultimately, however, he reported that "I like going back to school because I need to be here, I know I need to be here." Although men of color are not entirely comfortable and happy in Play Hard geographies alongside more affluent, mostly White peers, they do not face the same challenges as women of color, and they are more likely to see the benefits of engaging in these spaces.

By contrast, White respondents, especially men, seemed to have an easier time accessing and finding belonging within in a Play Hard geography. Being White allowed respondents to pass through campus relatively less visually marked as different. Within this majority-White campus, first-generation White students were able to capitalize on their majority status—they could be "normal."[15] Although their class differences made them uneasy initially connecting with wealthier peers, White first-generation students were still able to capitalize on shared interests and norms of casual fun that did not rely on large amounts of spending money—especially in the early years, when going out to bars was less likely to be part of a night's social plan. This made informal and individual approaches to forming friendships more manageable, rather than needing to rely on institutionalized settings.

Richard provides an example of this. His first friends were in his dorm and his classes. He did not do a precollege orientation, but told us that he made early friends easily:

> The first couple months I kept my door open, not just unlocked but physically open, so that I could meet new people. Generally, they were amicable, sociable, mostly White, mostly smart. I took early classes that semester, and I noticed many students would come to class, myself included, hungover. I would recognize many students in my classes just by walking around campus, and there was a sense of everyone knowing each other even if you hadn't had an introduction. Most people seemed approachable, except those who made themselves out to be unapproachable.

Richard's ability to develop these friendships, based around shared taste in music, a preference for partying, and shared hangovers, was facilitated by his majority-racialized status. He did not feel a sense of discomfort or difference around race, and his majority peers did not categorize him as different. Similarly, Dan (White) recalled that he and his roommate "were homebodies freshman year, we spent a lot of time in our room. We had quite the popping spot, so we had a lot of visitors come to my room. We played a lot of video games, watch a lot of TV, stuff like that." He recalled that campus was friendly—when walking around campus, he would "flash a smile and people flash back." It was easy for him to make friends not only on his team but also in his dorm—"If you walk around the halls, there will always be someone eager trying to make new friends. Everyone was in the same boat and a lot of people just clicked and I met a lot of people from different places, sports teams, and lifestyles." This ease of making friends with a smile and an open dorm room door is partially facilitated by being part of a majority group. Connecting with others is often easier when not managing the complications of interaction across racialized lines, and class is often less immediately visible than race.

However, there were trade-offs to this majority status and normality. Certainly, being White did not mean that there were no challenges for White students. First, despite this racialized commonality, as Brian noted, "there's like being the guy who buys shots at the bar, or buys . . . dinner or something like that. That I wanted to do but . . . I never had the means to do it." As respondents got older, these challenges and discomforts may have gotten even more difficult for students who formed friendships with primarily or only wealthier peers.[16] Moreover, in the absence of a targeted support system for first-generation students, White first-generation students lacked a clear route to finding others who shared their backgrounds and with whom they could connect around shared experiences.[17] We return to the costs of joining a Play Hard geography in Chapter 7.

Participation in and Access to Hook-Up and Dating Markets

Like respondents in other geographies, Play Hard respondents described campus as being dominated by the hook-up culture. Most women indicated that they had hoped to have romantic relationships on campus when they started college. They found the campus hook-up culture problematic or at least not of interest to them. Despite this, many pointed out the way that campus norms push students—even those who hope to find long-term partners—into hookup scenes. For example, Julie (White) reflected back that while she participated in hooking up for the first few years of college:

> The goal for me was to eventually have a stable relationship. I didn't really enjoy like behaving in that sort of, like, making out with a bunch of different guys, kind of thing. I didn't really enjoy it. But it was something that everyone was doing . . . and I felt like I wasn't gonna get anywhere, or ever get close to my end goal if I didn't participate.

Like Julie, female Play Hard students attempted to use romance and/or hooking up work as a tool for participating in social life and for obtaining longer-term relationships that they desired.

White women in a Play Hard geography described the hook-up culture as largely unappealing, and most participated in it, if at all, only long enough to find a longer-term partner. Compared to women of color in

Play Hard geographies, White women were more likely to frame their engagement in the hook-up culture as a choice, and they were more likely to identify romantic relationships in these contexts. Eventually, all four White female interviewees in Play Hard geographies, however, had had boyfriends, whether on campus or long distance. These relationships then provided a buffer from the critical eye of the hook-up scene.

While most women of color in Play Hard geographies also did not enjoy campus dating market dynamics, they were more likely to attempt to participate than women of color in other geographies. All but one participated in hook-ups or what Selita (African American) called "situationships." However, although these women were enmeshed in mainstream social spaces and party life, they did not necessarily feel comfortable or included. Selita goes to fraternity parties, yet she describes her chances of making a romantic or sexual connection as low because no one is looking for someone who looks like her:

> I feel like no one is checking for me and I'm just here drinking liquor and, you know, standing out because it's mostly White women there and all the men are checking for White women and I'm obviously not White, so I'm just standing there, like, in the way more or less.

While she can access the party culture as a woman, she remains outside the hook-up scene as a woman of color. Moreover, only one woman of color in a Play Hard geography was in a committed relationship, underscoring how women of color struggled with both types of dating markets. While White women were able to transition hook-up participation into relationships, this was less of the case for women of color in our interview sample.

By contrast, men in Play Hard geographies described having a romantic partner either on campus or off as a barrier to participating in the party aspect of a Play Hard geography. This suggests that the possibility of hooking up was a key aspect of a Play Hard geography for many. Rico (African American), for example, told us that "I have a girlfriend, so I don't really go out that much, but I do go out sometimes, I go out with a couple teammates, go to [a] frat house, go downtown and have a good time." Rico's phrasing, "I have a girlfriend *so* I don't really go out" suggests that the "going out" is very much oriented around what sociologist David Grazian calls "the girl hunt."[18]

Indeed, many male respondents' descriptions of weekends spent with male friends include mention of spending time with women. Male Play

Hard respondents sometimes characterized students seeking relationships as being emotionally needy, almost aberrant. This interesting and common response seems to fit well with the idea of a particular performance of masculinity: In this setting, men are not supposed to be emotionally needy or interested in a partner. As we saw with Rico and with other respondents in a Play Hard geography, men who did have steady relationships characterized them as very unusual. These findings echo a substantial amount of sociological scholarship on contemporary hook-up culture, most pervasive among middle- and upper-socioeconomic status White students.[19]

One explanation for the varied level of satisfaction and participation is that women continue to be stigmatized for sexual behavior. Indeed, some male respondents in a Play Hard geography expressed concern about women who participated in hook-up culture, framing them unsuitable for dating: Since HC was a party- and hook-up–centric campus, guys should be wary of the kind of women they might meet. However, since the same men making this critique also participated in the party culture in which hook-ups take place, it suggests that their concerns were about female sexuality and not about the concept of hooking up. Another possible explanation is that while men see relatively few costs or risks to their participation, women must balance potential rewards of participation[20] with risks associated with the marketplace: Women are frequently reminded that they must keep themselves safe in bar and GLO party settings and of the risks of physical and sexual harm that may come to them.

Overall, men have low risk in the venues in which hook-ups are located, while women have relatively higher risk of negative outcomes, including sexual violence and slut-shaming from both women and men. That women continued to participate in these social settings despite their feelings of unease speaks both to the emotional costs of participation and to the strength of the normative peer culture that prioritizes these social venues.

Conclusion

In many ways we might think of Play Hard geographies as a classic version of elite college attendance, and in some ways what Hilltop and peer colleges and universities were designed for. When institutions like Hilltop began, they were intended to serve the young men of wealthy White families who could earn a "gentleman's C" and then join a family business. College years were for sociability and—through that sociability—connecting with the other young, White, wealthy men on campus. Indeed, those who strove to excel academically were seen negatively as too obviously striving, an embarrassing characteristic.

To a great extent, these same rules continue to apply to many current students. As sociologists Elizabeth Armstrong and Laura Hamilton found, students at the top of the socioeconomic ladder do not reap substantial consequences either in or after college when they perform at a mediocre academic level and when they prioritize fun over studying or work.[21] They can rely, just as previous generations did, on the connections and financial support of their families. Although this option is not available to their less economically advantaged peers, these wealthy students nonetheless set the norms of dominant (i.e., Greek Life and party-centered) campus social life.

Moreover, as in past generations, adult observers on and off campus largely turn a blind eye when affluent White students engage in Play Hard behavior because college as a time for fun—the "best four years of your life"—is so deeply ingrained in our ideas about higher education and because White youth are generally understood by authority figures as nonthreatening. (By contrast, students of color who engage in similar behavior are more likely to be tightly regulated, with varied consequences. This was not voiced by our interview respondents but is clear in both the news media and sociological research.[22]) This version of college life, of effortless fun, is played up in media and students' own folkloric accounts of college life.

Finally, participating in a Play Hard geography is not simply about deciding to go to parties or spending time relaxing. Importantly, it is also about learning the Play Hard ethos of leisure that is marked by a classed and racialized performance of ease[23] or effortlessness. As we discuss in Chapter 7, learning to "chill" with affluent and largely White peers is central to how the informal or hidden curriculum of college feeds into students' plans for the future.

Notes

1. Armstrong and Hamilton, 2013: p. 10.
2. See, for example, Johnson et al., 2007.
3. All tables referenced in this chapter are found in Appendix B. Table B.1 shows that students in Play Hard geographies were somewhat less likely to receive public

assistance, apply for financial aid, and receive student loans compared to those in other geographies.

4. Table A3 in the appendix describes the school type, entry point, and campus geography for all qualitative respondents. Nearly half of Play Hard respondents attended a private high school and/or entered HC through an athletic program.

5. Jack, 2014.

6. In other work, we also show that Play Hard students were more likely than those in Disconnected and Work Hard geographies to participate in high school athletics and have friends involved in the party scene.

7. Chambliss and Takacs, 2014; Jack, 2019.

8. This included participation in intramural, club, or varsity sports teams and going to the gym with friends.

9. These practices are detailed by other sociologists, so we will not delve into deeply here. For excellent discussions of the Greek system and gender inequality, see Armstrong and Hamilton, 2013. While HC did not have Black fraternities or sororities, many other campuses do, and these are often afforded fewer advantages than White GLOs, making this institutional relationship quite different. For discussions of these variations, see Ray and Best (2015) and Ray and Rosow (2012).

10. Grazian, 2008.

11. See here excellent work by Stuber, Klugman, and Daniel, 2011.

12. Holland and Eisenhart, 1990; Armstrong and Hamilton, 2013.

13. Jackson, 2018; Wingfield 2007. Research also suggests that White admissions counselors weed out students of color who seem likely to be too activist. See Thornhill, 2019.

14. Jackson, 2018.

15. Wilkins, 2014.

16. For a discussion of how some of these dynamics may play out, see Lee, 2016; see also Stuber, 2011b for a discussion of White first-generation students' varied interpretations of economic inequality.

17. For more on this interplay between Whiteness and class, see Stuber, 2011.

18. Grazian, 2008.

19. See, for example, Allison, Rachel, and Barbara J. Risman. 2014.

20. Although research suggests that these may be few and far between: See Armstrong, England, and Fogarty, 2012.

21. Armstrong and Hamilton, 2013.

22. For immediately relevant examples, see Ray and Best (2015) and Ray and Rosow (2012).

23. Khan, 2011.

4

Work Hard

Introduction: What Does a Day in the Work Hard Life Look Like?

Like many college students, Brianna is very, very busy. A Black senior, Brianna's weekdays revolve around academic work and meetings for five different campus clubs. She told us, "Most of my time is spent in the classroom and when I'm not in the classroom it's attending various lectures offered on campus or group meetings." Asked about the groups she is involved with on campus, she reels off a list ranging from student government to a campus feminist organization and several focused on race, wondering if she has even remembered all of them. Rebecca, a White senior, also spends her time on campus rushing from commitment to commitment, studying, and catching up with friends where she can: a typical weekday is "classes . . . and a lunch either meeting or just lunch and then afternoon class and then meetings, club meetings, that kind of thing in the evenings." Both of these young women prioritize their studies and extracurricular activities, folding their friendships into these two spheres and steering clear of the party culture on campus.

Students located in a Work Hard geography, the second most common for first-generation students,[1] place a high priority on academic achievement and on extracurricular involvement. For many Work Hard students and their friends, academically oriented activities are important elements of their social lives. Rebecca (White) described spending time with friends as regularly including academically oriented activities: "We go to lectures, we watch movies, we have ridiculously long conversations about random things." Samirah (African American) told us that she and her friends "do homework together, you know watch a movie together, go to the store together, pregame or like go to a party together." That she includes doing homework together in the same list as going to a party together is strongly illustrative of the ways that respondents in a Work Hard geography framed academic life as a primary venue for friendship, and friends as part of their academic life.

Geographies of Campus Inequality. Janel E. Benson and Elizabeth M. Lee, Oxford University Press (2020). © Oxford University Press. DOI: 10.1093/oso/9780190848156.001.0001.

Like Rebecca, Samirah, and Brianna, Work Hard students organize their campus lives and extracurricular activities primarily around their academic interests. Their campus friendships—typically within a small, close-knit group—are also rooted in those areas. Work Hard students generally avoid high-status social hubs of campus, including downtown bars, Greek life, or athletics Accordingly, within Work Hard geographies, students often form strong friendships with same-race, same-gender, and/or same-socioeconomic status others that they often met through Summer Bridge (SB) pre-orientation or extracurricular interests. This is especially the case for women of color; among White respondents, we see more cross-race friendships, and for male students, more female friends.

While respondents located here report strong friendships and robust academic and extracurricular campus lives, they are also lonely outside those spheres. Much of their campus engagement is in reaction to the racism, classism, and sexism they feel and observe on campus and to the predominant campus culture that affirms White, male, and upper-class identities more than others.[2] Although these students are not forming the same types of connections with cross-class peers as Play Hard students, we should consider friendships with similar others against the backdrop of an otherwise homogeneous campus and what students gain or risk by trying to join that mainstream space. On one hand, scholars have argued that becoming socially integrated into campus life is one of the key elements of college success. As students adjust to campus, get involved with friends and extracurricular activities, and gradually loosen ties to family and home community, they become enmeshed in the life of the college and are more likely to stay enrolled and ultimately graduate.

However, this pattern speaks more to students in the majority on their campuses—on most selective campuses, White and middle- or upper-income students from continuing-generation families. Students who are minoritized, including students of color and first-generation students, reap fewer benefits from acclimating to mainstream campus life and, in fact, often experience difficult challenges in settings with majority peers, leaving students unhappy or disconnected altogether. On the other hand, joining co-ethnic campus clubs and other organizations can buffer these experiences, providing respite from micro- and macro-aggressions.[3] Moreover, friendships with similar others provide Work Hard students with emotional intimacy and academic reinforcement.[4] These spaces allow students to find ties with others who share important things in common, but may also mean giving up on or opting out of the dominant social world of campus.

Entry Points: Early Connections to Similar Others

While all first-generation students grew up in significantly less-resourced families than their continuing-generation peers, Table B.1 shows that Work Hard students in the National Longitudinal Survey of Freshmen (NLSF) were somewhat more economically disadvantaged than those in other geographies, growing up in families that were most likely to ever receive public assistance.[5] Most interview respondents in this geography came through the SB program—13 of the 18 Work Hard geography students in our interview sample attended this program.[6] As noted in Chapter 1, HC's SB program provides a highly selected group of underrepresented students—predominantly lower-income students of color who have overcome significant challenges—with a rigorous, month-long academic and social orientation experience to prepare them for life at HC. The SB experience does not end at the end of the summer: SB aims to provide a supportive community for SB students that extends through all four years and includes social and academic programming and mentoring provided by faculty, staff, and upper-level students.

The SB program was central to Work Hard students' friendships and subsequent patterns: respondents formed immediate close bonds with others who shared important aspects of their identities, aspects that marked them—often visually—as different from the "typical" HC student. This was particularly the case for students of color, virtually all of whom across the sample attended SB programs and most of whom fit a Work Hard geography. Notably, Victoria (African American), the only Work Hard woman of color who did not attend SB, nonetheless mentioned SB as a key factor in her friendships by extension: all of her friends had already met through the program, and getting to know one helped her meet others.

Because of these close ties and because of the way that students attending SB are a very different population than the Hilltop campus at large, respondents often described it as having been significant to them, a place in which they could easily make friendships and feel at home, and that these connections would have been harder to accomplish without this institutional structure. Manesha (African American) told us,

I think people in SB don't have that hard of a time usually. I think people that aren't in SB and they are students of color have a hard time because they don't have that initial community that they come in with and the majority of people that they do see they can't identify with.

Similarly, Smokey (Latino) described how when he arrived on campus to participate in SB, "I thought the campus was really beautiful and I really liked [it] and the people were cool, especially liked the SB people because it was a lot of people from similar backgrounds so it's like, 'oh there's people like me [here].'" He contrasted that to the rest of campus, the more "typical" HC student, as follows:

Advice I got in SB was from [the counselors], like they basically just told us it was going to be different, it's not going to be anything like this. So yeah my perception of the campus completely changed [when fall started], a complete culture shock. . . . I guess I had never been in a place where I was aware that I was, like, a "minority." Like I had never been in a situation where I was like, wow, there were so many White people and so much White privilege. Like I've been to banquets and things like that [on campus] and I've felt left out, but this was a place I was supposed to be included in and living in and I just felt completely excluded, you know?

As both Smokey and Manesha observe, students of color are in the minority on campus and the transition during one's first year can be difficult. Participating in SB was therefore an extremely important base of friendships and continued connections on a campus that was often uncomfortable and even unwelcoming.

Smokey's narrative highlights an important contrast with the Play Hard students: rather than feeling "normal" or "typical," Work Hard respondents, both students of color and White respondents, learn early that the space created by SB friendships is an oasis from a larger, dissimilar campus. For men and women of color, these ties were primarily with peers who were demographically similar in terms of both race and socioeconomic minoritization; for White respondents, these close ties were more often with peers who shared their socioeconomic backgrounds but not necessarily their racialized positions. In this way, these friendships with similar peers are protective, but do not necessarily help them connect with others who are in the majority on campus.

Work Hard respondents' early friendships often not only stayed constant over subsequent years but also served as links for students into academic and extracurricular participation with like-minded others. Respondents' friends brought them along to meetings or encouraged them to join groups, making extracurricular activities shared spaces for friendships. Manesha, who is African American, told us,

> [T] two of my closest friends are Latina. They formed through Summer Bridge at first, then through science class together and then once two of us dropped the science major, we all were the chairs of MFU [Multicultural Feminist Union] and we continue to be the base of MFU and that kind of shaped our friendship along with our majors and, like, our activity on campus.

As we see in Manesha's words, friendships and clubs are reciprocal, with one leading to the other, and then back again—and both shape her academic pursuits.

Commonalities

Orientation to Academics: Central and Interwoven

One distinguishing feature for students in Work Hard geographies is a strong central focus on academic work. Students in a Work Hard geography rank at the top end of the distribution on all measures of academic engagement, connection, and effort midway through college. As Table B.2 shows, they study about 29 hours each week, on average, which is 10 hours more than those situated in a Play Hard geography. Work Hard students also rate their academic effort as a 7 out of 10, a full point higher than Play Hard students. These students continue to exhibit strong faculty engagement both inside and outside of class, and they are most likely to have identified a college mentor (65%) compared to those in other geographies. Work hard students often study with peers outside of class (Table B.2), and they are more than twice as likely as Play Hard student to meet at least one of their closest college friends through classes (Table B.3). Finally, they are least likely to report that their studying is interrupted by social distractions compared to those in other geographies (Table B.2).

We see these patterns strongly reflected in the narratives shared by our Work Hard interviewees. Coursework and studying are a central feature of their daily lives. Respondents' description of a "typical weekday" often sounded like Victoria's (African American), who told us,

> I have class, like one to two classes a day. I don't really eat because sophomores don't get into [the dining hall] until 11 so I don't really eat. Then I probably either go to like a brown bag or like some type of a thing, and then in the evening hours or before there's like a club meeting, or some type of lecture for a class. Then at night I try to do my work and then try to go to sleep.

What is emblematic in Victoria's narrative is that it starts with classes but includes brown bags—lunchtime academic talks—and evening lectures as well, before ending with homework. Other activities, like eating and socializing, barely figure in. Like Victoria, most Work Hard geography respondents described being active and engaged from morning until night, and doing homework until even later. As Aleyda recounted,

> I usually get up, get some breakfast, go to class and then after class I usually go to work. And then spend my time making posters or organizing events and then after that I usually go to dinner, go to the gym, and then spend the rest of my night doing homework.

As we see in these narratives, each hour seems to be accounted for during the day, and downtime or socializing are rarely included in these descriptions. Moreover, while many respondents across geographies spoke of spending time on their classes, Work Hard respondents were the only group to describe engaging in other academic activities like brown bag lunches, lectures, and studying with friends as a social activity. While this may seem typical for students at a highly selective campus, data from respondents who fit the Play Hard geography and others show that this is not the only, or even the dominant, way students organize their campus lives.

This linking of academic and social speaks to a second distinctive element of Work Hard geographies: respondents' academic foci were often intertwined with social and extracurricular interests and activities. Students' *formal academic* activities, like classes and majors, and their *informal, out-of-class* activities centered on the same topics and often overlapped. Indeed, this included not only interlinked academic and extracurricular interests, like being an environmental studies major and a campus leader working on climate change issues, but also social life, the ways that respondents spent time with friends, as we began to see in our previous discussion. Angela (Latina), for instance, spoke about how her major related to the activities she participates in and how she spends time with friends:

> I'm a Gender and Sexualities Studies [GSS] major. Um, I'm a double major and GSS is one of them and so I know a lot of the professors who teach GSS courses. I know a lot of the students who take them and, like, GSS also houses groups like Multicultural Feminist Union, African American Students' Alliance, and, um, Rainbow Coalition, which I work for now. Um, so, that's kind of just an area that, you know, where I can go and there'll be, like, people [who] will talk about different things that pertain to me, you know, like the Black Lives Matter movement or something like, things related to women's studies and feminism and stuff so it just really helps with my interests. Like, it's really geared towards my interests. That's why I feel comfortable there.

Angela describes the academic department in which she majors as not only intellectually engaging or connected to a future career. Rather, this is a space that hosts the clubs to which she belongs and in which people are talking about the social justice movements and topics she cares about. This space is more than merely academic for her; it is something that affirms and supports not only her interests but also her identity—an identity otherwise marginalized on campus. Here, in contrast to other places on campus, she can find "people [who] . . . talk about different things that pertain to me." In this way, these types of spaces are where Work Hard respondents were able to be themselves because peers in those spaces share their views, making such venues important as backstage and sheltering spaces of comfort—a theme we return to later. While this was common among Work Hard respondents, it was unusual among respondents in other geographies.

Perhaps, not surprisingly, given their strong academic focus, respondents in Work Hard geographies prioritize their identities as students. Although virtually all of our respondents felt underprepared by their high schools, the implications were different for students in a Work Hard geography who understood themselves as star students first and whose identities were predicated on this type of achievement. Respondents in a Work Hard geography therefore not only reported *working* hard at college, but also *worrying* hard. Carlos (Latino) is emblematic here. He told us, "Well I mean, at least in high school I was always an A student. No matter what, I was usually always in the upper tier of like my class, just 'cause I don't know, I always had a natural affinity for getting things done." At Hilltop, however, his placement in the top tier had shifted:

> I mean here, it's a whole different level. Especially like not being prepared by high school like so many other kids were like, so obviously prepared when they were here, like going to private schools and all this other stuff. They were leagues and bounds ahead of me. I remember when I was taking, even some basic statistical classes and like other things, just the wealth of knowledge that these kids had. I remember I was taking astronomy and like people were like "oh yeah, you guys have learned this," and like everybody in the room except me and like one other person had learned that concept. And I was just like, "Well alright, I feel very disadvantaged right now!" [laughs]

Similarly, when we asked Samirah (African American) about balancing her coursework and other campus commitments and whether she ever felt stressed, she responded: "Oh hell yeah! Every week I struggle with like making it to a meeting or you know reading, doing my reading before my next class because it is so easy to be ignored on this campus." Like Manesha, Work Hard students felt a lot of pressure to be outstanding students and campus leaders. Success in these areas was not only central to their identities as HC students, but also as we discuss in Chapter 7, how they planned to get ahead after college.

Faculty Connections

Consistent with survey results described earlier, qualitative interviews with HC students show that Work Hard students have incredibly close, almost familial relationships with faculty. In contrast to typical twice a year advising appointments described by Play Hard students, Work Hard students had deeply caring, consistent, and personal relationships with faculty and staff on campus. Nearly all Work Hard interview respondents were closely mentored by faculty as part of the SB program and/or worked as faculty research assistants. Both of these opportunities facilitated Work Hard students to connect with faculty beyond their coursework.

In contrast to Play Hard students whose expectations for faculty relationships were quite low, Work Hard students described sustained "close-knit relationships" (Briana) that included interactions beyond the classroom, such as invitations to faculty homes for dinners and holidays.[7] As a group, Work Hard students warmly responded to questions about faculty relationships and described genuine and deep connections. For example, Katie (White) told us, " I feel comfortable with them and I know they got my back." These connections to faculty members and perceptions of faculty as caring serve as protective elements against campus challenges.[8] Moreover, these connections help students to develop not only support structures but also a sense of ease around authority figures, which may help students access help when they need it in college and also develop skills useful in job-related networking.[9]

The closeness of faculty–student relationships was most pronounced among those who were part of the SB program. Students in the SB program describe support staff as their go-to people on campus for academic and emotional support, ranging from picking classes to navigating personal issues. For many SB students, SB support staff were like trusted family members. For example, Zendaya (African American) described her SB faculty mentor as her "school mom" explaining:

> She's a big part of my life, and I always go to her for advice. . . . I can just talk to her about whatever like if I'm feeling stressed, like when I was changing my major, like I spoke to her when I was trying to tell my mom about my boyfriend. I just feel comfortable talking to her about whatever it is. . . . It's just like a nonjudgmental zone.

As Zendaya explained, SB support staff provide much more than simply academic support. They also help students deal with the social and emotional stressors that can derail many first-generation students. The early and sustained faculty relationships provided by the SB programs show that institutional initiatives can promote the types of close mentoring relationships linked to student retention and success.

Orientation to Extracurriculars, Social Life, and Leisure: Shared Interests, Shared Social Life

Midway through college, Work Hard students' extracurricular engagement far exceeds those in all other geography types. Compared to students in other geographies, Table B.4 shows that Work Hard students in the NLSF invest at least twice the number of weekly hours in extracurricular activities (10.8), and their participation rates in most nonathletic extracurricular groups is nearly double that of other groups, with 49% engaged in volunteer work, 48% in cultural groups, 31% in arts related groups, and 31% in religious groups. In addition, three out of four Work Hard students hold jobs, the highest percentage of any geography. They also sleep five fewer hours each week compared to Play Hard students, and Table B.3 shows that they are most likely to report meeting at least one of their closest college friends through clubs (30%).

This level of participation is clear in our interview sample: While a few respondents participated in only one group at the time of their interview, most participated in four or even five. Manesha (African American), for example, described her days as taken up by and arranged around extracurricular groups: in addition to classes, her days are spent "attending group meetings, events that groups throw, brown bags . . . and homework and the gym and work." Angela (Latina) also provides a strong example here. She spoke about how much time she spends on activities for the clubs she's involved in, likening them to "more of a job that I don't get paid for" because the commitment to participate is not limited to just a meeting or two per week, but often includes events, subcommittees, or collaborative projects to support other campus groups. Students were often stressed and tired from balancing these commitments to extracurricular life, academics, and (typically) paid work that often also reflected their academic and extracurricular interests.

The ways in which Work Hard respondents arranged their extracurricular activities were deliberate so that their academic and extracurricular lives were complementary. For example, a student might be a member of the African American Students' Alliance, the Social Justice League, and the Voting Rights Coalition. Sarah (Latina), for example, recounted that she is involved in "so many things. I get lots of emails. I do things with lots of feminist centered things around campus." Victoria (African American) is active in three clubs and an internship, each of which is centered on her social justice interests: "I'm in Multicultural Feminist Union, Caribbean/ West Indies Students Club, African American Students' Alliance, [and] I am an intern in the Multicultural Center." Being involved in a club focused on personal interests and shared with friends allowed respondents to carve out or construct spaces around important shared interests and identity points alongside others, making a safe and affirming geography for themselves beyond the classroom. Joining and participating in clubs provides an institutionalized means of spending time with like-minded others—for students feeling excluded, this is important, and for students who choose to avoid or feel excluded by the mainstream social culture, this allows the creation of an alternative social culture. For Work Hard respondents, clubs are therefore more than just hobbies, fun, or just something to put on a resume.

Despite their heavy extracurricular activity, they were not very involved in the two high-status social hubs of campus: athletics and Greek Letter Organizations (GLOs). Survey results from the NLSF presented in Table B.3 show that midway through college those situated in Work Hard geographies spend nearly half as many hours each week engaged in athletic- and party-related activities compared to Play Hard and Multisphere students. Moreover, they are about half as likely to participate in GLOs and intramural athletics, and very few report meeting their closest college friends through these venues. Finally, Work Hard students are least likely to be involved in the campus dating scene compared to those in other geographies.

Overall, HC respondents in Work Hard geographies described their social lives as being on the quieter side, avoiding the "party hard" area of campus life, such as Greek Life, sports, and bars. Work Hard respondents, especially women of color, tended to avoid GLO parties populated by and oriented toward upper-income White students and often toward male interests. HC's campus does not offer any multicultural GLOs, and sororities are not permitted by their national chapters to provide alcohol at parties—this means fraternities control much of the party life on campus. When Work Hard respondents did go to parties and social events, they usually went to smaller parties organized by clubs they or their friends belonged to, or free events put on by the campus. Angela (Latina), for example, described weekends as

like usually I go to parties at [the Multicultural or LGBT Centers] or at MFU. So, and then, you know, I'll go out, I'll have fun, you know, with the people at the party or usually my friend group . . . like interacting with people more socially but there, it's a private party so it's very limited.

In this way, Work Hard respondents avoided some of the pressures to "keep up with the Joneses" that respondents who hoped to participate in that mainstream party structure confronted on a daily basis. They also did not have a lot of social contact with students outside a Work Hard geography, including those who were demographically different from themselves.

Respondents in the Work Hard geographies, especially women, often described their lives, either ruefully or self-deprecatingly, as dull. These students spoke about being "room rats" and having quiet evenings in dorm rooms with a small group of friends or going to smaller events on campus. Weekend nights were spent with friends catching up from the week, watching a movie on someone's computer or TV, having a glass of wine, or calling family. As Kaelin (Latina/multiracial) described, "my social life is pretty boring and it's pretty, you know, like, chill." While many Work Hard respondents described this quiet social life as enjoyable—at least while on campus—not all were happy about their choices. Victoria (African American) was among the most frustrated. When asked what a typical weekend looks like, she responded:

> Like Saturdays, [I] wake up for brunch, do some work, or don't, I just sleep. And then Sundays it's [club] meetings, homework, sleep, it's like I just feel like as soon as the weekend comes, it's over. Like, there's nothing to do.

The rural location of Hilltop's campus is one aspect of this feeling that "there's nothing to do," and many respondents described social options as constrained to the few bars and restaurants in the nearby town or to parties on campus.

Students in a Work Hard geography shared these quiet social lives with small groups of close-knit friends. Like the "tight-knitters" in sociologist Janice McCabe's work,[10] Work Hard respondents reported that their friendships were extremely close. These small circles formed a kind of oasis in which respondents could duck some of the pressures and discomforts of the larger campus. As Brianna (African American) said, "I believe in quality over quantity." She continued, "I would say I've formed some great relationships with great people . . . and I'll say it's very limited. I wouldn't consider myself to have many friends but . . . not having superficial relationships [is] what matters to me the most." Respondents described their friendships using words like "unit," "nuclear," "bubble," and "core." As Britney (African American) reported, "I can talk to them about pretty much anything."

One reason these friendships were so close and protective is that they were based not only on shared interests but also shared demographic backgrounds, including class and/or race or ethnicity, that are minoritized on Hilltop's campus. Smokey, for example, noted that he and his friends are "similar because we come from lower socioeconomic backgrounds, first-generation, and like most of us are of color." Likewise, Ed (African American) told us, "My close, close friends, we have very similar financial situations, . . . as I talk to them, as I get to know my friends, very similar." Brianna also noted that her close friends share important things in common, noting, "I would say they are similar to me." She clarified that generally her friendships are "typically with Black individuals or people of color in general. Like Latino individuals or Asian individuals. But not too many White individuals." Thus, her friends on campus tend to share the experience of being a person of color on this predominantly White campus.

Notably, White respondents in this geography were more likely to have friendships with people who were racially different from themselves than most other White respondents, perhaps because they attended SB or made early connections with others who did. Rebecca (White), who told us that she connected with her first-year roommate's friends from SB, reflected that among her closest friends, "I have different experiences, different lived experiences: I am from a rural community, a lot of them are from cities, umm I'm White so I haven't had a hell lot of racial and ethnic discrimination in my life that they've had."

These friendships were not necessarily exclusive; indeed, some students in a Work Hard geography spoke about managing friendships with wealthier friends. However, in these cases respondents often distinguished between friends with whom they felt *real* comfort with, and those whom they held at some distance. For example Sarah (Latina) differentiated between the ways she could speak with similar and dissimilar friends:

At Hilltop, I have—[pause] it's more selective who I'm able to talk to because I've also made friends that are not from similar backgrounds as me, being here at HC. So, I feel like with that, it makes it harder for me to bring stuff up with them and, no, it's not the same thing with them here. Like here at HC, I have defined who I will be able to feel comfortable with, talking about any emotional or class issues or, I mean, academic issues, or any political issues. I feel like at HC I have to look further to find those people who I feel extremely comfortable with on different aspects.

As we see in her narrative, being a student at Hilltop has placed Sarah into connection with peers from a wide range of backgrounds, including those who are wealthier than she. While she formed friendships in those circles, she also found that she did not necessarily feel comfortable talking about "emotional or class issues," among other topics, with these friends. For that kind of trust, she has to "look further" and find people who have similar backgrounds. Overall, however, respondents in a Work Hard group were more likely than students in other geographies to have friendships with similar others.

As we also begin to see in Sarah's narrative, respondents often framed these friendships in contrast to the mainstream of the campus or to the "typical" Hilltop student. Sarah went on to tell us that in some ways, being surrounded by upper-income White peers makes her feel more at home with the community of economically similar peers of color at Hilltop: "I kind of feel more at home because of the fact that we're surrounded by a student population that's very much one demographic, which is White and like high income. I feel like the communities of low-income, first-gen, or non-White students [are] closer." Indeed, Zendaya (African American) mused that in some ways it seemed easier to locate similar others for her as a woman of color, than for low-income White students:

> For me I just thought, like, even because there were so few people of color here it was so easy for us to all link up and be friends, so I feel like I had an easier time finding a group of friends, of people I wanted to be with than even like some of the White people I knew because they had trouble, like, finding people they thought cared about them. Whereas I felt that I automatically had that in a sense.

For at least some respondents, being different in a way that felt visible helped located peers who shared at least some characteristics and provided an underlying assumption of shared interests.

Although phenotypically similar to the majority of their peers, White respondents in Work Hard geographies also understood themselves as outside of the campus mainstream, which they defined in largely social and economic terms. Rebecca, a White respondent, spoke about herself as outside the "White rich privilege" of Hilltop. Most of her friends are students of color or "allies," and most share her economic background. She found these friends through her first-year roommate, who had attended a SB program:

I would say I connected with the Black girl that I lived with from the same socioeconomic status as me, because she had been in the SB program. Umm and so a lot of her friends were also of the same socioeconomic status and I was like, oh you already have friends huh, that's cool, we could all get along really great. So then I ended up kind of being absorbed into their friend group, already distinguished, and that was really awesome my first year because I had this kind of already shaped friend group of people who were already kind of comfortable in their identities within that friend group and being able to be comfortable with my identity within that friend group was really cool.

As a student who did not participate in SB, Rebecca considered herself lucky to have found this friendship group:

If I hadn't been in that room, I would've struggled so hard. And I've seen other students struggle with that who don't kinda go into a [pause], don't find that, that community that will actually support them when they get here. So I'm very cognizant of how luck played into kind of my experience.

Overall, Work Hard respondents avoided the mainstream social life spaces and focused instead on smaller peer groups formed with others who shared interests and demographic backgrounds. These centered on academic and extracurricular activities, which themselves were often related. While they defined themselves as apart from mainstream campus and "typical" students, they found respite in friendships. However, that also meant that they did not form many close connections with wealthier peers or engage in networking—we'll return to this in Chapter 7.

Making Space on Campus: Constructing Community

For many Work Hard respondents, their choices about where and with whom to spend time are the result of feeling uncomfortable with a domi- nant mainstream feeling of what Rebecca (White) called the "White male voice" of the campus. Their feelings of relative comfort and discomfort in campus spaces were related to their racialized, gendered, and classed senses of self. Work Hard students also saw themselves as very different from their peers. Aleyda (Latina) gave the example of her roommate, who she feels is more typical of other students on campus: "Her older sister goes here and her mom and dad graduated from here. So she's a legacy and it's like, and I know her cousin got recently accepted and he's coming and her other cousin got accepted and she's coming here too." Angela (Latina) shared the feeling that wealthier students would not understand her experiences, detailing the ways that much of campus can feel uncomfortable to her:

> I don't feel comfortable in classrooms where I don't really know people, you know. Like in my Spanish class, I don't really feel comfortable, which is strange. There's a lot of, like, um, not to stereotype but there's a lot of, like, there's like two frat boys and the rest are, like, um, sorority girls and there's just, like, the conversations they have just, I just don't have the same experiences as them, I should say.

Work Hard geography students therefore shared a critical sensibility toward the mainstream of campus life and a sense of differences from campus as a whole, in which they often experienced micro-aggressions. As Victoria (African American) phrased it, she dreaded "all the things I know I'm gonna have to deal with in the space" each time she came back to Hilltop from home.

To manage all of this, they formed communities that provided oases of support within the larger campus. Their friends shared their focus on academic work and a critical take on campus life, and they formed closer connections to academic and institutional staff and spaces. Moreover, their friendships were organized around shared priorities and not having to hide one's identity, politics, or emotional response to campus. Rebecca (White), for example, described her feelings of comfort as being based on the presence of "likeminded people I guess." She also pointed out that the spaces in which she feels the most comfort are those that are institutionally designated, designed to speak to and encompass students who are in some way not the stereotypical Hilltop student:

> I guess a lot of the points of these spaces is acceptance of like intersectional identities. So like those are spaces I don't feel like I have to live up to any other identity than my own. So I don't have to hide the fact that I'm poor and I don't have to, like, down the fact that as a woman I feel, like, afraid on this campus, like I'm allowed to express those, I'm allowed to be umm, like, angry at institutionalized—[pause] I won't swear—[pause] dumb things

that occur on this campus. Like that's what's nice, being able to express frustrations in a place where people are also frustrated but, like, in a very cathartic way.

Being in spaces that allowed her to be open about her background was important, and in which she did not feel she needed to "live up to" expectations of Hilltop student identity formed around wealthy White male students. Moreover, in this space she could openly express her emotional and critical reactions to other aspects of campus in which those White, wealthy, and male-oriented views were more dominant.

These spaces were extremely important to students, often serving as lifelines, not just casual hangout spots. Jack (Latino/multiracial), for example, spoke about how he has been able to stay in college through "this tiny little community" that he had formed, which was outside the mainstream of the campus: "Meeting new friends, making new friends, and studying interesting stuff and getting to know my professors and people at the Multicultural Center, just you know, tiny little community that I've kind of surrounded myself by." He talks about how he has stuck with this little niche and that's helped him avoid being stereotyped or other negative social outcomes.

Notably, respondents in Work Hard geographies were much more likely to include academic and formal campus spaces—such as academic departments, the library, and the multicultural and women's centers—as spaces in which they felt comfortable than respondents in the Play Hard geography, providing another example of the ways that academics were deeply important to them. Although respondents in other geographies described close friendships and spoke about how they could rely on their friends emotionally if need be, this explicit characterization of friendships as lifelines to people who could understand one's problems was far more important for students in a Work Hard geography than in others.

Variation

Table B.5 show that a quarter (25%) of NLSF respondents are located in Work Hard campus geographies, but the distribution of students in this campus context varies by race and gender. Approximately one-third of women and men of color in the NLSF sample are located in this geography compared to 25% of White women and 9% of White men; this may reflect the greater proportion of first-generation students of color in SB programs. While respondents in Work Hard geographies placed academic life—classes, grades, studying, and other forms of academic work—at the center of their campus lives, they had varying levels of success in locating friendships and partnerships.

Friendships: Connection and Orientation

Despite entering through SB or other academically oriented pre-orientation programs like Work Hard women, men, especially White men, in these geographies had a more difficult time locating male friendships around their academic interests. While men in the Work Hard geography found a few male and more female friends with a similar academic focus, they did not describe the same wide-range of opportunities to connect with these types of peers as women in this geography, suggesting that there are fewer ways for academically-oriented men to connect on campus. For example, Ed (African American) told us,

> At first, I thought everyone was just here to do the best they can . . . have fun outside of learning too, but have fun learning. And I feel like over time, I got a little more cynical and realized that I think people just care more about fun in general, and use college as a means to get to like another stage in life. Like, "I'm only here to have fun and to get a diploma so I can get a job."

Like Ed, men in this geography seek out friends through their academic interests rather than the mainstream party scene. As Carlos explains, "I don't care about partying, so much as I care about having meaningful social relationships . . . with people who share my desire to learn." Men in Work Hard geographies preferred connection and "intellectual stimulation" (Ed) to beer pong or sports.

Several respondents highlighted these preferences as a disjuncture within Hilltop's predominant culture of masculinity, one that prioritized "going downtown, and getting really drunk and things like that," in Smokey's words. As we saw in Chapter 3, Play Hard geographies disproportionately draw in men, even those initially uninterested, through large onramps located in intramural and varsity sports and party culture.[11] As Jack described, "people who are not, I guess, for men, people who, guys who are not like typical heteronormative alpha male types, you know, ones that are more sensitive, and quiet and introspective" have a more difficult time connect. He continued,

> Those people are kind of like, scooted to the side a bit. And you can kind of tell, there's like this franticness with the beginning of the year for guys to make their little groups, and you know, some people just don't fit the cast that Hilltop kind of provides.

Overall, Work Hard men found fewer social connections on campus and were less satisfied with their friendships.

While women had an easier time connecting than men did, there were nuances along racialized lines. Friendship groups organized around shared identities had heightened importance as oases for women of color who experienced micro-aggressions on a predominantly White, predominantly wealthy campus. For women of color, then, friendships with others who share that social space means affirmation and simply being seen without the pressure of needing to represent a community or worrying about racism. Samirah spoke to this very directly when she reflected,

> I feel, like, this pressure to always prove White people on this campus wrong. Prove to them than I'm more than just some random Black person. I'm more than just a disposable body. I'm super intelligent so that's why I push myself to take these hard ass classes and I'm in all these fucking clubs because I'm trying to fight the stigma that has been placed upon me.

Samirah makes clear just how much of her life is driven by this concern of being perceived as "just some random Black person."

Research shows that her worry is well-founded: White students often assume that students of color are less capable than themselves and admitted under affirmative action policies.[12] This presumption, whether conscious or subconscious, shapes students of colors' lives substantially. They may feel both hypervisible and at the same time invisible, unseen as an individual but showcased as a representative example of communities of color—an effect amplified when one is the only person in a social gathering, classroom, or other setting. This is made more burdensome by the emotional and interactional work needed to navigate stereotypes in majority-White spaces, such as being too angry or too emotional.[13]

Moreover, friendship ties to demographically similar others who share key experiences may be especially important for students involved in the kinds of campus-oriented social justice work that many Work Hard students of color do because of the emotional exhaustion involved in this effort.[14] These accounts fit with broader literature showing that friendships with similar others are especially important for Black and Latina college women at predominantly White universities, who often name co-ethnic peers as crucial to their campus successes. Similarly, the presence of and connection to co-ethnic peers on predominantly White campuses is important to these women's feelings of college satisfaction. By contrast, Black and Latino men's college satisfaction is not as related to co-ethnic peer connections[15], and they are more likely to connect successes to individual efforts.

White women in our interview sample participated in extracurricular activities at roughly the same rate as women of color. These respondents were more likely to express allyship with friends of color than to be involved in racial justice groups. Rather, their campus involvement was equally likely to be around gender and/or sexuality or career-oriented. This involvement seemed to have a different meaning for White women respondents: While they may have been critical of campus policies, critiques of the campus in terms of gender and sexuality politics arose less often in interviews, suggesting this was less prominent in shaping White women's campus experiences.

Romance and Hooking Up

As with students in the Play Hard geography, Work Hard respondents exhibited mixed outcomes in terms of dating and romance. Although all respondents in a Work Hard geography prioritized academic work above social life, women of color were more likely than others to report being left out of the dating market. Like many other respondents, they viewed the available dating scene as being more about hooking up than forming long-term relationships, and they viewed White women as having a much higher likelihood of getting both hook-ups and dates. Unlike women of color in the Play Hard geography, they had a critical take on this issue and understood it to be emblematic of larger patterns of racist exclusion on campus. Moreover, the spaces in which most students engaged in cross-gender interactions were spaces they felt uncomfortable joining—namely, fraternity parties and bars. This lack of availability shaped how their lives unfold on campus and how they think about themselves in this setting. While none of the respondents in a Work Hard geography reported *wishing* to participate in the hook-up scene, women of color described feeling even more marginalized from the dating market than White women or any men because of the perceived lack of availability: Even if they wanted to hook up, they would be excluded. This simply amplified the perception of feeling invisible or excluded on campus.

Victoria (African American) spoke to this as she reflected on the racialized dynamics of the hook-up market:

> I think that people to some extent are attracted to things that are similar to them, or most comfortable rather than similar to them so when I think to myself about who is hooking up or who I see hooking up actually, it's like a lot of the White students have access, and that might not be fair for me to say, but it's true, and when I go to these spaces I see the White students engaging with the White students. I see a lot of men of color engaging with the White students. So it's like certain people don't have access, even if it's not explicit.

Similarly, Angela (Latina) told us,

> I think race plays a lot into it. So it's easier to find a partner if you're White and you're straight but if you're not, it's really hard . . . it's just not something people talk about a lot but it's a real issue on this campus and, and it's, like, a larger social issue.

She elaborated further to connect the ways that the mainstream party culture was also a racialized one that largely served straight White students:

> [The] image is the hook-up culture, which is like get drunk, go to a party, find some random [pause] it's very heteronormative. So, like, if you're a guy, you get drunk, go to a party, find a girl and if you're a girl, you get drunk, go to a party, find a guy and then you go to each other's rooms and you have sex and you just ignore each other after that. Um, if you're a person of color, if you're queer, or if you're in a relationship, it's not really suited for you and there's, like, a silent minority of students who would prefer to be in, who would prefer more of a dating, like, scene than the hook-up scene but, like, for some reason, hook-up culture is what image is portrayed and it's the most dominant one.

As Angela highlights, this system pervades the mainstream party scene. Students who don't fit well into that market, or who simply don't wish to participate for any reason, by extension also feel left out of the party scene altogether. Moreover, she continued, dating and hooking up are largely circumscribed by one's social connections and remain homogenous: "people, I guess, rely on their own social circle... but there's not really, like, a lot of going out of that circle." Interestingly, while these experiences were largely shared with women of color in the Play Hard geography, Work Hard respondents' interpretations were more critical. While Play Hard respondents expressed frustration or disappointment, they seemed to experience rejection as individual rather than institutionally located.

The situation was no better with dating. Although several women of color told us that they had hoped to find boyfriends on campus, few had been able to do so. Brittney (African American) told us that she hoped to find a romantic partner at college: "I came and I was like I'm gonna find a nice mature man. Like who's gonna have a future and all this stuff and I got here and I was like these guys are made of plastic, look at the outfit." Again, respondents understood this as one aspect of the larger classed and racialized social mechanics on campus. Brianna, for instance, indicated that

> White individuals are more likely to be involved in romantic relationships than Black individuals but when it comes to Black individuals, Black women in particular or, like, women of color in particular are less likely to be involved in romantic relationships than like, um, their White women counterparts.

Zendaya (African American) was another student who had hoped to find a boyfriend when she came to college. She had attended a mostly White high school and did not have a boyfriend there: "and then I came here and like other people of color they were like . . . you're not gonna find anyone here. So I was like, ok cool, just do my schoolwork then." As we see in Zendaya's words the lack of availability in romantic markets often pointed women more firmly toward academics. Thus for many women in a Work Hard geography, each activity (or lack thereof) reinforced the centrality of academic work.

There were many fewer male respondents in our interview sample who fit a Work Hard geography. Men who did so were more likely to report having female friends and often described having found dominant standards of masculinity a turnoff—what Ed referred to as the "Hilltop culture. . . . The more so, downtown drunkenness, the Greek Life type thing." He continued, "I don't really find that interesting, in the slightest." Similarly, Jack described what he saw as "a lot of misogyny and, you know, there's always talk of sexual violence, which is, you know, always associated with [fraternities], or drugging drinks and stuff."

Men in Work Hard geographies also associated Play Hard and Greek Life cultures with social power and specifically with high socioeconomic status. Jack told us, "I feel like they run the social climate here, or they're at least the most vocal." Ed mused further that Greek Life social spaces are those in which class and particular ideas of masculinity seemed to become intertwined:

> I think the highest thing on this campus that you can be in is a frater-
> nity. Greek Life gives you power, it gives you a certain like, like a card
> that gives you access to a certain type of lifestyle that a lot of people
> don't get to enjoy. . . . So you have these people, and then you have
> the others, and the others being the non-Greek life people, so when it
> comes to like women . . . they intermingle a lot with the mixers and the
> parties in general, a lot with the uh, fraternities, so they get to know
> each other more.

Moreover, as Ed reflected, women may be able to access those spaces easily, but men who are not part of the Greek Life system or don't have close ties can not, which creates gendered—and perhaps raced—lines of exclusion:

> And then also, just thinking about it freshman year, that really one awkward
> time when you have your friend and you just met this girl that becomes like
> a friend of yours who becomes maybe an interest, and you guys try to go to
> a party, a fraternity party, and the girl goes in but you don't, and that already
> makes you feel like you need to have that type of access to get to what you
> want, which could be a girl or whatever.

Overall, men in Work Hard geographies found mainstream party spaces sim-
ilarly unappealing as women in the Work Hard geographies did. However, unlike women in Work Hard geographies, they struggled to find alternate routes to friendships with other men that were based on academics and/ or clubs.

Conclusion

Work Hard students represent a scholarly ideal at a campus like Hilltop: they are focused on academic accomplishment, engaged in leadership and civic work, and deeply personally motivated—in many cases, by the idea of giving back and social change. Moreover, they have formed strong relationships with faculty and identified peers who share their academic orientations. Ironically, most students in a Work Hard geography feel excluded on campus and have had to work hard to create friendship communities that provide affirmation and support. Indeed, these students are exhausted—worn out from making their own spaces of belonging, pressing for campus change, and experiencing racism, sexism, homophobia, and/or classism on a daily basis.

In making campus work for them, Work Hard respondents prioritize academic work and extracurricular involvement. Their friendships are largely organized around these two poles, and the three—social life, academic life, and extracurricular life—are typically intertwined. Even parties and other social events are organized by the clubs (usually social justice) in which they or their friends are members. Moreover, because their friends are very similar, they draw one another into largely analogous social spaces and shared orientations to academic work. While this provides strong support within friend groups, it does not help them necessarily feel more comfortable on the rest of campus, and even their academic focus does not mitigate feelings of discomfort in the classroom or academic worries about doing well enough. Ultimately, their focus on academics and extracurricular engagement with similar friends provides a buffer but does not connect these students to wealthier peers. As we will see in Chapter 7, this may have long-term implications for post-college life.

Notes

1. Twenty-five percent of first-generation students are located in Work Hard geographies compared to 21% of continuing-generation.
2. For long-standing discussion of campus culture on predominantly White campuses, see for example, Feagin, Vera, and Imani (1996), Willie (2003), and Charles et al. (2009).
3. Baker, 2015; Nenga, Alvarado, and Blyth, 2015.
4. McCabe, 2016.
5. All tables referenced in this chapter are found in Appendix B.

6. Table A.3 describes the school type, entry point, and campus geography for all qualitative respondents.
7. Chambliss and Tackas (2014) found that a single visit to a faculty member's home
   significantly increased college satisfaction and whether students would choose the
   college again, controlling for GPA, race, gender, and other factors.
8. Chambliss and Takacs, 2014.
9. Jack, 2019, Chapter 2.
10. McCabe, 2016.
11. Wilkins (2014) also found that partying and athletics were important gateways for
    male collegiate friendships.
12. See, for example, Torres and Charles, 2004; McCabe, 2009.
13. See e.g. Wingfield, 2007.
14. Lerma, Hamilton and Nielsen, 2020. See also Aleman (2000) on the importance of
    friendships among undergraduate women of color.
15. Baker, 2015.

5

Multisphere

Introduction: What Does a Day in the Life of a Multisphere Student Look Like?

Akeira, a Black first-year student, works two jobs and spends much of the rest of her time on her passion, theater. She's involved in the arts community on campus in other ways as well, both as a member of a group that brings after-school programming to local teens, and as an avid painter herself. For fun on the weekends, she might go to a party hosted by friends in a social justice club on campus, or she might stay in to watch TV with friends. She might also go to a bar near campus to party. Unlike many respondents, Akeira has friends across a wide range of activities and she told us, "I'm invited to a lot of stuff. I don't know why but people literally invite me to, like, everything." She tries to balance her time and be smart about sleep, but it is a challenge to manage her wide range of commitments. She told us about her first year at Hilltop:

> At first, I was really into going to everything. It was like, "OK. I'll just go to this and this," but it's like, after the first semester of literally almost dying because I was trying to force myself to go out every other night, I was like, "Maybe I'm not gonna do that. I'm going to pick and choose."

Socially and in her extracurricular activities, Akeira cuts across geographies with social connections and patterns that match both Work Hard and Play Hard patterns.

Multisphere geography students like Akeira embody a do-it-all mindset, what students in our interview sample described as a "work hard, play hard" orientation toward college life. While some were still early in their college lives at the time of their interviews, others are juniors and seniors who have worked out how to maintain this balance over the years. As shown in the survey results presented in Chapter 1,[1] Multisphere students are able to navigate across different campus spheres. Unlike other respondents, they participate in the mainstream party culture of the Play Hard geography, and they

Geographies of Campus Inequality. Janel E. Benson and Elizabeth M. Lee, Oxford University Press (2020). © Oxford University Press. DOI: 10.1093/oso/9780190848156.001.0001.

also participate in substantial extracurricular and leadership activities like those in the Work Hard group. Also, like the Work Hard group, students in a Multisphere geography have strong academic achievements, have friends who value academics, and rate academic achievement as a high priority.

Compared to those in other geographies, Multisphere students are generally happier at HC and report that their expectations have been largely met. Where they have not been met, respondents often understood those disappointments in personal, rather than structural and symbolic terms; they also don't seem to perceive setbacks as indicative of larger problems. Friendships and clubs are therefore not sources of refuge—us against the world, as in the case of Work Hard geography students—but simply social or goal-focused. Most notably, unlike students in all other geographies, these respondents seem to be able to avoid many of the costs of participation in mainstream campus life and trade-offs between spheres.

Students situated in these types of geographies, however, are quite rare—only 17% of first-generation students in the National Longitudinal Survey of Freshmen (NLSF),[2] raising questions about how campuses welcome first-generation students into both their academic and social spheres. Overall, Multisphere students resemble qualitative descriptions of prep school students who are socialized to perform perfection with ease in all areas of student life.[3] In this way, their college lives are very different from most sociological presentations of first-generation college students; indeed, this group has received little attention in higher education research.

Entry Points: Branching Out

Most respondents in Multisphere geographies arrived on campus through targeted pre-orientation programs, organized in some cases around identity, such as Summer Bridge (SB), and in others around academic interests, such as writing, environmentalism, or music.[4] While many participated in club or intramural athletics, none of the Hilltop College (HC) students in our qualitative sample entered through a preseason athletic program as a recruited athlete.[5] While these entry points led to early and lasting friendships, as we saw in other geographies, Multisphere respondents' campus acclimation processes are distinguished by a pattern of branching out. Rather than only following similar friends into shared pursuits, like the Play Hard student athletes, Multisphere students made friends across varied interest areas. Moreover, they developed close friendships with affluent students as well as those who shared their background; while these cross-class ties are by no means the only or most important for first-generation students, they may provide opportunities that peers with similar backgrounds cannot offer. While some might assume that students in this group were among the most economically advantaged, Table B.1 shows that this is not the case.

Some, like Philip (Latino), connected to new friends through SB, or like Emma (White), through a pre-orientation program for writers. These initial friendships were important and, as we saw in other geographies, often led to long-term close ties. In talking about her pre-orientation program, Leslie (White, female) told us, "With that, I was very lucky because a lot of the people I'm still very close friends with. And it was a good community to branch out with other people in the dorm." As we see in Leslie's description, respondents in Multisphere geographies met people early on with whom to connect, joined clubs quickly, and from those two sources created new connections that sustained them.

However, respondents in a Multisphere geography also *kept* making new ties, usually by joining additional clubs. Kyle (White, male), for example, told us that he "immediately . . . tried to get involved in a bunch of different clubs, so I immediately started connecting with people and making friends. However, I think I'm a pretty social person. Like, I'm able to pick up a conversation with anyone pretty quickly and pretty easily." Grant (White) similarly described,

I was a pretty extroverted individual so meeting students, for me, was very, was simply usually just saying, "Hey, do you want to get food?" I remember for the first semester, I went to all sorts of movie nights and brown bag events and campus meet-ups, get-togethers, a ton of clubs, I found people that had similar hobbies in regards to reading, and games, and athletics, and entertainment.

A number of Multisphere respondents described similar processes of putting themselves out there and a sort of personal determination to connect with new peers. This is the clearest in Jordan's (Black) narrative: Worried that he might not be "accepted," Jordan told us that his strategy was to "excel in things so much that I can't be denied. So by virtue of me focusing on myself and being so visible, it came to the point where people want to know who I am."

These friendships also helped Multisphere students to move beyond their first impressions of campus and new peers. Like respondents in other geographies, many Multisphere respondents had reservations about their new peers and the campus culture they perceived as largely White, wealthy, and unfamiliar. Philip (Latino), for example, recalled his first impressions of Hilltop students as White and very preppy, describing the "salmon shorts" that everyone seemed to be wearing. Jordan (Black, male) worried that, "I didn't have the same life experience, I don't look like them, and there's a good chance I won't be accepted because of it." However, unlike Work Hard and Disconnected students (and in common with Play Hard students), Multisphere students mitigated these negative impressions through friendships that cut across demographic differences.

This ongoing creation of new friendships to both similar and dissimilar others is key: by contrast, while respondents in the Work Hard geography also made early connections, they primarily kept to close friendship circles with others who shared their socioeconomic backgrounds (and, in many cases, also their racialized or ethnic statuses). Respondents in a Multisphere geography hit the ground running, meeting people and joining clubs early, and spring boarding from those early connections into new and widely varied friendships and other activities. Moreover, as we will see in the discussion of their social lives, Multisphere geography students formed connections to both mainstream and non-mainstream peers.[6]

Commonalities

Orientation to Academic Life: Central and Satisfactory

Overall, Multisphere students exhibit strong academic effort and make meaningful academic connections with faculty, staff, and students across campus. Midway through college, Multisphere students in the NLSF resemble their Work Hard geography peers in that they rank at the top end of the distribution on all indicators of academic engagement (see Table B.2). On average, Multisphere students study nearly 27 hours a week—this is 8 hours more per week than their Play Hard geography peers. Multisphere students also outperform their Play Hard peers on measures of self-rated academic effort and engagement with faculty both inside and outside of class. Moreover,

Multisphere students (57%) are significantly more likely to identify a mentor in college compared to their Play Hard peers (36%).

Students situated in this geography, however, differ from their Work Hard peers in terms of the role peers play in their academic life. On one hand, Multisphere students are similar to Work Hard students in that they often study with peers outside of class (Table B.2) and identify the classroom as a place where they met many of their closest college friends (Table B.4). On the other hand, Multisphere students report the most distractions in their study spaces, such as peers playing music, having conversations, and partying (Table B.2). The social nature of their studying and study spaces is not surprising given that this geography is composed of students' whose peers value both academics and social life and are equally invested in both areas.

Multisphere students described themselves as serious students, yet they did not express the same pressures around academic performance as their Work Hard peers. They were less likely to judge their satisfaction with their academic work and with themselves as students by grades alone. Grant (White), for example, told us a number of ways that he is pleased with his performance as a student:

> I'm patient, I like to ask questions, I like to get involved in discussion. I generally thrive, like in terms of motivation and work ethic, I'm probably average to maybe slightly above average than the HC student. I generally see myself as a positive contribution to the classroom.

Similarly, Phillip (Latino) told us that although he is "pretty vocal" in his classes and "diligent" with his coursework, he has found the right balance between his activities and his studies and that, in fact, his studies have become more meaningful to him over time:

> I kind of value doing a lot of extracurriculars and kind of occupying myself a lot in that sense. But I think now that I'm in college, I value being a little bit more thorough with my work than I was in high school, just because I feel like it--not that it does, but I feel like it counts more now that I'm in college.

Philip has found a balance that feels fulfilling to him, though he knows that some other HC students may put in greater effort and get better grades. He does not compare himself negatively to others, and (like Jordan, quoted previously, and others) talks about his academic work as personally meaningful.

Overall, Multisphere respondents seem satisfied with how they have prioritized their academic and social lives on campus.

Faculty Connections

Like Work Hard students, Multisphere students developed close faculty relationships through institutionally supported programs. While a few Multisphere respondents formed strong faculty relationships through SB, most developed these relationships by participating with faculty on research and/or off-campus programs. Because many of these types of opportunities happen after the first year, Multisphere students took longer to learn how to connect with faculty compared to Work Hard students. For example, when Anna (White) was asked about her relationships with HC faculty, she explained, "I would say the first couple of years were not very good because I just didn't understand the concept of networking and meeting people. But now I have multiple advisors and people who I can go to chat about stuff." Anna links this change to her new faculty research opportunities: "Now this year doing research is continuing the relationships." While all Multisphere students have developed at least one close faculty relationship during their time at HC, they did not report the same level of intimacy or support as SB participants in the Work Hard geography who often described long-standing, family-like relationships with faculty mentors that began in the first few months on campus.

Orientation to Extracurricular and Social
Life: Balanced Joiners

At the midway point of their college lives, Multisphere students exhibit moderate levels of extracurricular engagement across a range of activities, with the most involvement in athletics. As shown in Tables B.3 and B.4, over half of Multisphere students in the NLSF sample participate in varsity or intramural athletics,[7] 44% work for pay, 35% volunteer, 20% participate in a cultural group, 14% participate in an art-focused group, and 11% participate in a religious group. This investment across activities is also clear in time use, with Multisphere students spending approximately 6 to 8 hours each week on athletic activities, working for pay, and extracurricular and volunteer activities.

In all but athletic activities, their participation rates are considerably lower than Work Hard students but higher than Play Hard students. Moreover, athletics and extracurricular clubs are key venues where Multisphere students connect with their closest college friends.

These participation rates and outcomes tell us that, like students in the Work Hard group, these respondents spent a great deal of time on extracurricular interests. Also like students in the Work Hard geography, their social and extracurricular activities often overlap. However, unlike the Work Hard students, respondents in a Multisphere geography seem to have branched out to new and different activities across several areas. This not only allowed them to make friends across different interest areas, but also to form varied connections, often with peers who were not demographically similar to themselves. Roy (Latino) and Phillip (Latino) are good examples here. Both joined clubs, including pick-up athletic teams that were new to them. Roy joined the hockey team, and Phillip, the rugby team. While both had left those after a year or two, both considered them important elements of their acclimation process—they still had friends on the team, which had exposed them to new kinds of people, and they discovered that they could get along well with those people. Roy (Latino) told us, "I played hockey. These were like the frattiest kids I've ever met in my life. Crazy kids. But no, I just ended up meeting more people." Despite leaving the team, he told us that he was "still really passionate" about it. From that experience, he learned that "HC's a lot more diverse than it lets on, I think. I have friends in all sorts of circles, we get to go to each other's parties and stuff like that."

Similarly, Phillip (Latino) spoke about continuing friendships from the team he had joined:

> I was like, "Well, I didn't play a sport in high school but I think I'll join the rugby team." I don't know why I made that decision. I didn't know what rugby was 'cause that's not really much of a thing where I'm from. It ended up being a very intense sport, so I did it and . . . I met those people in that area of the school, and then that led to me meeting other people that are more in like the athletics department and that kind of thing, so I know people from [those areas].

This was exactly what Phillip had hoped would happen. When he enrolled in college, he planned to seek out many kinds of experiences: "Coming into college, I kind of told myself I wanted to get involved in a lot of like different things and things that I never done before. So I kind of immersed myself in different parts of the school." He made friends and connections in each of these areas, spanning a number of new interests. He told us,

> I feel like my social life has been impacted in that and just that I have a very broad friend spectrum, you could say. So I have a lot of different experiences with a lot of those people and I tend to have a lot of social interactions with a lot of different people.

Importantly, as we see in Phillip's and Roy's accounts, Multisphere students formed important new communities at HC that were not necessarily based on demographic background or around one group, such as a specific team or GLO. Anna (White), for example, joined the theater club after seeing a performance on campus during her first year, recalling that it looked fun, and she could not continue in her previous extracurricular focus from high school, soccer, because of an injury. She'd found friendships fairly easily, although she noted that she did not meet many students who shared her background. Her foray into theater led to substantial involvement with and friendships through the three groups of which she was a part when we spoke with her. At the time of our interview, Anna told us that her social life was diverse:

> I'm in three arts clubs so I spend a lot of time with those groups. I spend time with my boyfriend and his group of friends. I have a lot of friends who I just randomly hang out with, so the weekends are pretty chill, like go to a pub at least just one night.

As we see in these respondents' recollections, their pattern of branching helped respondents in Multisphere geographies both generate a sense of belonging on campus, while also helping them develop friendships with people who shared a variety of their interests, even if not their demographic background.

Multisphere students' extracurricular choices thus allowed them to try out new experiences, just something exciting, and therefore introduced them to others not necessarily like them, forming weak (or bridging) ties. While this kind of social capital is important in post-college outcomes, Multisphere respondents also illustrated more immediate gains. Jordan

(African American, male), for example, told us about how a casual pick-up sports team led him to join Greek Life, which, in turn, led to friendships and to a leadership position in his fraternity:

> Initially, I wasn't going to join. I was playing basketball, I also didn't have an understanding of how White fraternities worked; I still didn't until I actually joined. A lot of my friends was gung-ho for joining fraternities, that had a heavy influence on me, because those are the people who know me best. It was a situation where I didn't feel bad for doing this because my friends are, because this is my HC experience, these are my brothers, these other people really know me and where I'm from. Since then, I don't regret it all.

As we saw for other respondents, Jordan's friends in one area helped him branch into a new area, in which he immersed himself, while also maintaining strong connections to his first group of friends.

In many ways, Multisphere students' social lives resemble those of our Play Hard respondents midway through college. They are heavily involved in the two mainstream social scenes on campus: Greek Letter Organizations (GLO) and athletics. As we saw earlier, over half of Multisphere students are involved in varsity or intramural sports, and Table B.3 shows that 25% are affiliated with a GLO. These athletic and GLO participation rates far exceed those in the Work Hard and Disconnected geographies. Moreover, Multisphere students spend twice as many hours (10 hours) each week partying compared to those in Work Hard (5 hours) and Disconnected geographies (5 hours), and 9 out of 10 report dating or having a steady partner.

We see this multiplicity and balance in respondents' narratives of their social lives. While they also took their studies seriously, they spent time participating in high-status party scenes, like bars and GLOs, as well as more low-key or close-knit circles. Leslie (White, female), for example, who is a member of a campus sorority, described her social life as follows:

> The person I spend the most time with is probably my boyfriend or my roommates. A typical weekend for me—I have close friends who live in an off-campus house, so I might go over there and play beer pong and then go downtown. And sometimes I have a formal for [my sorority] or something. If I'm not going out usually I'll get dinner and do homework or something like that.

Leslie's mention of beer pong, going downtown, and her sorority all differentiated her from the Work Hard and Disconnected geographies, who only attended parties thrown by specific student organizations (Work Hard) or did not attend at all (Disconnected and some Work Hard students). Most respondents fitting a Multisphere geography had similar responses: some quiet time with friends or romantic partners and some time spent going out to a more stereotypical college party setting.

Phillip (Latino) is perhaps the quintessential Multisphere respondent. He told us that a "typical weekend night, probably, I would say it's half and half of me going out and staying in . . . just like to hang out with my friends a lot, you know, in the dorm or whatever, you know?" Like Leslie, Anna, and other Multisphere respondents, he spends time with students from the numerous extracurricular activities in which he participates:

'Cause I like to relax after, especially if it was a hard week, but if there's things that are going on, especially if I'm involved in it, like I'm in the Hispanic Student Council, so a lot of times, you know, especially if we're having some special event, they'll have an event . . . so I'll go to things like that, and then my friends tend to go to that too.

Moreover, Phillip spends time at social events for activities that he is not involved in, to spend time with friends:

I'm friends with a lot of computer nerds, I guess you would call 'em, and I mean I'm one too—we like to play games a lot and that kind of thing. So I'm not into like PC gaming so, but I'll come with them if they want to, "Oh, let's go play [an online game] in the library," and stuff, so I'll come with them and just kind of hang out. It doesn't matter what I'm doing. And that's kind of what I've been doing a lot this year is just kind of playing games with my friends or we'll go to [a local café] and play like board games and that kind of stuff.

Finally, Philip also spends time with friends who like to go out, either to events held by student clubs or to parties:

But then we'll also go out, too, sometimes, like my friend likes to go to the parties at the Multicultural Center a lot, just because they're kind of friendly and that kind of thing. He likes to dance and that kind of stuff. So we do, you know, various things. And then if I was hangin' out with my friends at, 'cause I still hang out with some of the guys that were on the rugby team last year, and if I'm with them, we'll hang out and we'll watch like the fight that's on or, you know, like we were watching baseball the other time, or we'll go out and party, and it just depends who I'm with, you know, and what we do.

One key element of Philip's narrative is that he has friends with varied social habits, all of whom Phillip feels comfortable with. What he does socially depends on the friends he's spending time with, and ranges from a night playing board games to a night out drinking or dancing.

While all Multisphere respondents engaged in mainstream social life, their level of participation varied. Jordan (African American, male) told us, "I go out every weekend" and also reported that a typical weeknight includes "going to a bar in town, and maybe having two drinks with my friends." By contrast, Emma (White) balances her social life with campus commitments to the campus newspaper, but still notes that "normally, I would maybe like go out once on the weekends or so, not both nights. My friends and I joke that we're kind of like old grandmothers. . . . So, yeah. [laughter] So we normally like hang out at our apartment or something. Just do something like low key movie night." While Emma's experience is different than Roy's or Leslie's, the commonality is that respondents fitting a Multisphere geography were happy with their social lives and that their social lives connected them to peers in varied locations, typically including at least some mainstream partying and also more low-key activities with close friends.

This latter form of socializing is also an important difference between Multisphere respondents and those in the Work Hard and Disconnected geographies. These respondents' narratives included many more mentions of casual low-key social time with peers, neither studying nor drinking nor focused on a clubs but rather just spending time together and relaxing. Emma (White), for example, talks about how her apartment, shared with friends, is a good social and homey place:

> I'm rooming with another one of my good friends and two girls that I lived with last fall on campus and then we all lived together during our study [abroad] program. We just kind of made the space like really nice and homey, and it's like a really nice place to like do work but also like hang out friends and have social things. So it's kind of like a really great mix of both worlds.

She also talks about little excursions she takes with friends to get ice cream and downtime with friends:

> We also like, I'm a big fan of [a local] ice cream [place]. It's like this huge . . . thing. Yeah, so the nearest one's like a half-hour away, so sometimes we'll just kind of take these impromptu road trips just to go get a milkshake or something, things like that. And then normally like Sunday's my dedicated work day. Like I sleep in but mostly just kind of hang around the apartment, get work done for the coming week, and then we all have like a TV show we like to watch together on Sunday nights, so like group viewing, and get ready for the week.

While respondents in the Work Hard group talked about studying with friends, Emma's social downtime with friends is more purely social—she does "get ready for the week," but it's through a regularly scheduled "group viewing" of a favorite show.

Most Multisphere students had close ties in GLOs, and were regularly invited to their events. Here again, we see some of the important differences between Multisphere and Work Hard or Disconnected students: whether Multisphere students participated in Greek Life or not, their comfort on campus and, in some cases, connections to peers allowed them to see GLOs as nonthreatening and their nonparticipation as neutral rather than evidence of exclusion. Overall, Multisphere students had more favorable views of fraternities and sororities than Work Hard students. Those who did not belong still saw benefits to the GLO system, and those few who rushed but were not admitted did not see this as personal or indicative of exclusion.

Grant (White), Akeira (African American), and Anna (White) are all examples of respondents who had not joined a GLO but saw them as positive. Akeira, for instance, told us that she had a number of older friends in various sororities and that she had considered joining—indeed, she still sounded on the fence:

> I've considered joining but then, also, in the same sense, kind of, like, I want—I want to join. Like, if I had to decide, I'd probably say I wouldn't join though only because, like, the Greek organization is a beautiful thing but it's, like, also, I've heard so many about the problems, which is sad.

The problems she specifies here are about gender: women, and sororities as organizations, being "kind of treated like second-class," and that at some parties, fraternity brothers often try to get women drunk. Despite this, she sees many of the benefits that students get from these groups as important and desirable:

I know, like, some of the big benefits is that you get to meet more [people] that you wouldn't have seen in general because, say your scheduling or your timing and everything because they have a lot, like, good events. Like, you have a lot of philanthropic events that you have to work together on or you have a lot of the . . . bonding dinners that you have to go to and everything. But one of the limits is kind of, like, once you get in . . . it's kind of, like, almost having a household in itself because there's a lot of events you have to kind of go to as a part of the sorority.

By contrast, Philip (Latino) and Emma (White) each hoped to join a GLO, but neither was selected. Both described themselves as somewhat disappointed, but both went on to enjoy their social lives on campus. Philip told us,

I just, for one, it's kind of a thing to do here a little bit. Not that everybody does it. But I kind of always wanted to do it and, you know, I wanted to see how it was, and I'm super glad I did it 'cause it was really fun. I feel like the rushing experience itself is worth doing even if you don't particularly want to be in a frat or anything.

Philip connected this experience to something new to try out in college and to part of a broader social experience—and, most important, to meeting new people:

It's just kind of cool to experience goin' to all the houses and hangin' out with a lot of people, you know? It was a really fun week. So I wasn't bummed that I didn't get a bid. I mean, I would have been happy if I got one but I just wanted to rush, that was kind of just what I wanted to do.

Emma for her part told us that after she was not selected to join a sorority,

I kind of like sat down and I was like, "Okay, like you can choose to be bitter about this and like angry for the rest of the year or you can like get over it and like move on and like be happy again." So I like, I chose the second option and like I think in the end it like worked out better that I didn't get in. Like it gave me more time to like, you know, pursue leadership roles in different organizations.

Ultimately, Emma felt that the opportunities she gained by not joining a sorority were worthwhile tradeoffs. Unlike respondents who spoke about the reasons they could not join in terms of costs, Emma did not frame her rejection as being about her socioeconomic status and, therefore, did not see it as a mark of being an outsider or of being excluded. She was more easily able to "move on and . . . be happy" because it was not symbolic. Moreover, because Greek Life was just one among a number of engagement avenues, not being selected was not a loss socially.

Interestingly, the three respondents who had successfully rushed GLOs each had critical takes on these groups. Jordan (African American, male) and Roy (Latino) felt strongly that their organizations were important in their current and future lives and reported friendships within them but also leveraged social critiques against the GLO system. Jordan described the decision to stay in the GLO, which he had joined at the urging of friends, as strategic. Once he had been admitted, he observed "how things work socially in the world," and he saw the ways that being part of this group could help him realize long-term goals:

> It makes me understand how powerful a network is in general, it really opened my eyes to how things work socially in the world. I think it was a valuable life experience [for] me in a different way. . . . It's a good network for my HC experience as well, it allowed me to navigate myself in different avenues and social spaces by virtue of having that attach to my name.

At the same time, he recognized that this system was not available to everyone—and specifically not to other Black men from first-generation backgrounds—and that this system did not operate as a form of merit. He asked rhetorically, "Is that fair? I would say no, but I definitely use that to my advantage." Roy had similar but more short-term goals for joining, namely, having a social niche as a man on HC's campus. Asked why he joined, he responded: "Uh, because I'm a guy. . . . You can't *not* be affiliated and be a guy on this campus." From Roy's perspective, the social costs of not joining are too great—a testament to the dominant nature of Greek Life on campus, especially for those who want to find hook-up or romantic partners.

A final striking difference in these students' social lives were that virtually all of the students in a Multisphere group were supported by a steady romantic relationship or had been during their time at college. Phillip (Latino), Roy (Latino), Kyle (White), Anna (White), and Leslie (White, female) all had romantic partners on campus or at home. Gabby (White), Grant (White), and Jordan (African American, male) did not have partners currently, but each had at least one relationship since enrolling. Akeira (African American) had not looked for a relationship in college because she maintained an emotional tie to "someone at home that [she] really miss[es]." Only Emma (White), who had hoped to have a boyfriend, had been unable (so far) to find a stable romantic partner. This profile is quite different than respondents in the Work Hard group and Disconnected group, who (especially women of color) often hoped for but were unable to find partnerships, and from those in the Play Hard group who were more likely to participate in the hook-up scene than to find steady romantic partners or who desired steady partners but could not find them in the party scene.

Making Space on Campus: Varied and Happy

Like respondents in Work Hard and Play Hard geographies, Multisphere respondents described feeling comfortable with friends and in places they could be themselves. For Multisphere students, this was in more than one location, and most mentioned that they felt comfortable in both their dorms or apartments and the clubs to which they belonged. These might be, for example, focused on dance or women's health or board games or a wide range of other topics, but clubs—and typically more than one—were mentioned by most Multisphere respondents. For example Gabby (White), explains how her social life is made up of friends she has met through her campus activities:

> My social life revolves a lot around like the, like a lot of the activities that I do, that's where I found some of my closest friends. So like a lot of times, if I'm doing something social, and by social I mean not academic, it's probably revolving around some organization I'm in. That's been really awesome

because it's allowed me to meet a ton of people and so I know a lot of people on campus which I really like, but outside of those sort of things I have a core group of probably like nine or ten people.

As Gabby described, her social world is more than just one group. Her campus activities provide pathways into varied friendships and social scenes. Moreover, Multisphere students also mentioned academic spaces, whether classrooms, departments, or the library, as comfortable. That Multisphere respondents felt at ease and that they could be themselves across a range of spaces is a marked difference from Disconnected students, who often described their rooms as the only place they felt comfortable, and from Work Hard students who also often listed a smaller range of spaces.

Multisphere students are also different from Play Hard students, who were often uncomfortable in academic spaces and whose social lives were mainly situated within the two mainstream social hubs of campus, athletics and GLOs. While most Multisphere respondents socialized in these spaces, these spaces did not make up their entire lives. Their descriptions of night life often included partying in different locations, some nights with their club friends, other nights at a downtown bar, and sometimes at a GLO, and their descriptions of daily life include varied forms of campus engagement. Gabby, for example, whom we met previously, was involved with residential life, an honors society, two theater productions, and several campus clubs focused on safer sex and sexuality, including as chair of one. The spaces she is comfortable in on campus include each of those and a number of social justice-oriented places, such as the Multicultural Center, and academic spaces like the Women and Gender Studies department offices. However, her social life also includes mainstream campus events, as she told us in recounting a typical weekend:

If it's a Friday night I'm probably definitely going out, and if it's a Saturday night I'm maybe going out. Depending on how much work I have to do for that weekend. [I usually go] to some kind of party, whether it's like a house party or a frat party . . . or like a bar downtown or something.

Multisphere students' social lives therefore take place in more varied spaces and often are contingent on academic pressures and deadlines. This is true even of those involved in GLOs. For example, Leslie (White, female), told us that she "has not gained a lot of close friends" through her sorority, and while she likes seeing them around campus, her closest friends are those she met through her club and academic interests.

One final and especially important difference between Multisphere students and others is that they were overall more satisfied on campus. Beyond being comfortable in several spaces, they were simply happier with their time at Hilltop. This level of satisfaction suggests that their discomforts, while certainly still present, did not overwhelm or taint their broader experience. Emma (White) says HC feels more like home than home and that she has been happy on campus since the very beginning. She recalled that when she would talk about college with friends from home, their experiences were quite different:

> I was always like really happy at Hilltop and, you know, went home and talked about how happy I was, but a lot of them like had a lot of disappointments and kind of like, almost like resentment toward their school in a way. Like they weren't that happy and kind of couldn't wait to get out of there. And I was like, "Oh, gee. Like I don't want to leave Hilltop. Like it's been great.

This has made her feel even more strongly that she belongs on campus and heightened the contrast to her life at home:

> Hilltop's definitely become home. Like I love my group of friends that I've made and kind of created here and everything. And it's, I really like kind of being around like the group of people that I have as my friends here and just kind of having people to constantly do stuff with as opposed to being home kind of, you know?

Grant (White) similarly told us. "There was never really a time that I really wanted [pause], that I really wished I didn't come to Hilltop. I've always either liked the school [or been] content in being here."

Variation

Like the Play Hard geography, Table B.5 shows that very few first-generation students (17%) in the NLSF sample find their ways into Multisphere geographies. Twenty-two percent of men of color and 20% of White men are situated in this campus context compared to 16% of White women and 16% of women of color.

Previous research and our qualitative data contextualize these patterns. As we saw in the Play Hard geography, mainstream social life is organized around Greek Life parties, bars, and to a lesser extent friendship networks facilitated by team sports (spaces that are also predominantly White and predominantly wealthy, reflecting the campus demographic as a whole). Participation in these activities reflect broader scripts for masculinity that boys begin learning early in life. These scripts are also broad enough to provide some commonalities across class, such watching or playing sports, or partying . In comparison to performances of affluent (and White) femininity, men face fewer class-based expectations about their physical appearance, clothing choices, and personalities. In short, it is easier for men to access and feel comfortable in these social locations and to find connection there.

Conclusion

Even more than the Play Hard students, Multisphere students are idealized among their peers as those who seem to balance it all: extracurricular participation, academic success, and social lives that often include partying. They also benefit from having friendships with both demographically similar and different peers. Moreover, Multisphere students are happier with their campus lives along each of these lines and more satisfied with their achievements.

The way that Multisphere students float among different academic and social spheres, able to be comfortable and successful in each, might lead some to argue that Multisphere students are the most fully "integrated," reflecting what some higher education scholars have argued is key for students' success in college.[8] This line of thinking proposes that students are most satisfied with their campus experiences and ultimately graduate if they engage in the life of the campus, both academically and in extracurricular activities, adapting to the campus culture and separating from their families and home communities. This model of integration, however, has been critiqued for assuming students are effectively homogenous and campus is a neutral space into which each student can acclimate with equal ease and comfort. Moreover, as critics have noted, this view places the onus on the student to change rather than the campus.[9] Rather, scholars have argued, this model works best for students who are in the majority at selective campuses— White middle- and upper-income students.[10] Students who are minoritized face challenges trying to acclimate to a campus in which they face micro-aggressions and may do less well if they cut themselves off from friends and family at home.

While we agree that campuses should do more to welcome students from diverse backgrounds, Multisphere students highlight what may be possible when campuses provide more effective gateways to a range of meaningful connections, both socially and academically. As we discuss in Chapter 7, Multisphere students gain particular benefits from their strong ties in multiple campus locations that orient them toward postgraduation plans. Like Play Hard students, this includes gaining new cultural capital such as the performance of ease that may support them in seeking white-collar jobs after college. Like Work Hard students, this also includes strong study habits and friends who reinforce academically attuned choices as well as shared backgrounds. We take this issue back up in Chapter 7.

Notes

1. See Table 1.1.
2. See Table 2.8.
3. Khan, 2014; Cookson and Persell, 1985; Chase, 2008.
4. As described in Chapter 1, SB participants are required to attend as part of admission to HC. To participate in interest-focused pre-orientation programs, students submit an application and, for some programs, a small fee; financial aid is available.
5. Table A.3 describes the school type, entry point, and campus geography for all quali-tative respondents.
6. In other work, we show that Multisphere students were somewhat more likely than those in Disconnected and Work Hard geographies to participate in high school ath-letics and have friends involved in the party scene who valued being popular and well-liked, suggesting these students may be somewhat more primed and/or com-fortable engaging in more social spheres of campus.
7. As Table B.4 shows, 41% of Multisphere students participate in intramural sports and 12% participate on varsity teams. These differences are important in terms of time in-vestment and preseason opportunities before the first year of college.
8. Tinto, 1987.
9. For example, Johnson at al., 2007; Museus and Quaye, 2009.
10. See, for example, Attinasi, 1989; Museus and Quaye, 2009; Museus and Maramba, 2011; Tierney, 19991; Rendón, Jalomo, and Nora, 2000; Guiffrida, 2003, 2006.

6

Disconnected

Introduction: What Does a Day in the Life of a Disconnected Student Look Like?

Ian, a Latino second-year student, describes his social life on campus in straightforward terms: "I don't really talk to that many people." Ian has few campus friends. A typical week revolves around classes and time in his room:

> Monday, Wednesday, and Friday, I go up [to campus] from nine o'clock to four PM. I read a little bit until dinner time, go to dinner, come back to my room, watch the computer, do homework, and then just sleep. And then on like Tuesday/Thursday, I just basically work on stuff that was left to me during Monday, Wednesday, and Friday. And yes, Saturday/Sunday, just spend my days in my room just doin' nothin'.

He lists no extracurricular activities because the single club that Ian joined disbanded, and he has not joined a new one in the year that has passed. He also does not describe having met friends through that group. Although he would like to locate friends to study with, he has not been able to do so. To say that he lacks meaningful social connections on campus is an understatement. Despite spending a lot of time on campus, Ian is largely removed from the life of the campus.

Erica (White) also spoke about her isolation on campus. She recalled that when she arrived on campus, she loved the beauty of the place and the "awesome" classes, but could not get comfortable with other students:

> I had this problem where I just never felt like I deserved to be here. Like I deserved to like, like I was good enough to be friends with anybody. I just thought that everybody was so cool, like well educated, and, like, witty, and they cared about things that people at home didn't care about. Like they knew about world events and . . . politicians and I don't know, they actually cared about things.

Geographies of Campus Inequality. Janel E. Benson and Elizabeth M. Lee, Oxford University Press (2020). © Oxford University Press. DOI: 10.1093/oso/9780190848156.001.0001.

Erica is an environmentalist and "cares about things" too, but she felt extreme discomfort around her new classmates. Although she says she has come through the worst of it and "acclimated" a bit, this lack of connection has not changed. On a typical weekday, she goes to class or work and studies on campus "until probably about two or three [o'clock] on average. Sometimes I stay up longer to do work in a computer lab or something. But, then I just come back home and, like, study. Like, do random stuff in my room." On weekends, she hangs out with a roommate but avoids most social spaces. Like Ian, Erica's campus life is largely contained within classes, work, and a single friendship or two, as well as time alone in her room.

Mirroring much of what we see in sociological literature on first-generation students at selective campuses,[1] the largest portion of the first-generation National Longitudinal Survey of Freshmen (NLSF) sample (41%) fall into Disconnected geographies (compared to 29% of continuing-generation students). Like Ian and Erica, students in Disconnected geographies struggle to make friendships or find a niche, whether through classes, clubs, or social circles. While respondents in Work Hard geographies formed "tiny little communities" (in the words of Jack, a Latino/multiracial student), students in what we call Disconnected geographies felt almost or totally alone. As described in Chapter 1, Disconnected students are at the bottom end of the distribution across all geography indicators with the exception of studying and working for pay; despite this time studying, they have few strong faculty connections.

Like students in the Work Hard geography, students in a Disconnected geography steered clear of the Hilltop party ethos. However, unlike the Work Hard geography students, these respondents did not have others around with whom to form an alternate community. In contrast to the Multisphere students who could move with ease across peer groups and social spaces, Disconnected students seemed to be virtually shut off from campus life and did not appear to feel comfortable anywhere. Because they felt they did not fit in anywhere, these students spent most of their time outside of class holed up alone in their dorm rooms. Many reported being depressed and regretted their choice to come to Hilltop College (HC). Because of this lack of connection, they feel alienated, often doubting their choice to attend the college in which they are enrolled, and also lose out on opportunities for resources that come from connections to peers and faculty members.

Entry Points: Failure to Launch

This lack of connection began early. While a few respondents unsuccessfully tried to make friends through typical means, most Disconnect students were so overwhelmed by their transition to campus that they initially stayed to themselves. This pattern of delayed and stalled efforts to find meaningful connection within the first few months of college is difficult to overcome. While we might assume that students in this geography are the most economically disadvantaged and/or felt the most pressure to work for pay, Table B.1 shows that this is not the case.

One notable difference, however, between this and other geographies is that most Disconnected interview respondents did not participate in any HC pre-college programs. This meant they did not have an institutionalized space through which to connect with others who shared a meaningful identity in common. Like other respondents in this study, they confronted often extreme differences in wealth upon meeting the majority of their classmates. Without access to an institutionally facilitated "safe space" or connections to construct a college identity around, they looked for friendships among the broader student population in first-year orientation events and seminars, classes, and dorms. These were harder to locate and perhaps harder to envision. By the time they were ready to connect with others, social circles had largely already formed, making it that much more difficult to locate a niche.

To get a sense of the importance of this difference, let's compare two respondents' first days. Clark, a White respondent interviewed during his senior year, recalled how he arrived on campus. His parents drove with him from their small town, arriving with all other new students for regular orientation. Clark did not participate in any SB, thematic, or athletic pre-college program. Clark first made friends with his new suitemates, to whom he initially felt close. Within the wider horizon of campus, however, he told us,

> I found that I had many people to smile at while walking to class in the morning, but significantly fewer people to go for a walk into town with or grab a bite to eat. Even with the pressure to find friend groups within the first few days and weeks of first semester, I found myself sticking to my suitemates and my residence hall floor.

Clark therefore met most of his friends through his residence hall, which he pointed out was somewhat arbitrary—there was no common connection or theme to bond around: "I think I met the most friends through like living with them, living in the dorms. But I think that was just out of convenience. Those definitely weren't the best friends I've ever met."

After introductory conversation topics wore out, Clark found that he did not connect easily with peers and that there were few other people who seemed to share his background as "a first-generation college student coming from a very humble background, a very humble area." He reflected back that because he had done his campus visit over a summer,

> I didn't have any first impressions of the student body until I arrived on campus. At first, I thought the few people who seemed standoffish were just outliers. Then I realized that it was more of a systemic personality. As a whole, I think I just came to accept the fact that I wouldn't connect with a significant chunk of the student body, and I became more and more okay with that as my time at HC went on.

Similarly, although Clark and his suitemates got along well enough their first semester to plan on staying suitemates the following year, by the end of that semester their friendship had fallen away. By that point, Clark was feeling uncomfortable on campus overall: "Probably half way into my first semester [my impression changed]. Just like with things that were said in class, and like the classroom dynamic, I felt like people were kind of watching for me to fail."

By contrast, let's look at Gabby's description of arriving on campus. Also White, Gabby's (Multisphere) first impressions were shock and discomfort at the wealth and lack of racial diversity on campus. As she describes, her family arrived on campus in her "mom's car [that] had duct tape on the door" while other students were arriving in "BMWs and Mercedes and like Hummers, everywhere, and I was like wow, these people must have a lot of money, or they have really good car dealers, like I don't know." She also noticed what she called the "Hilltop dress code . . . with which my wardrobe did not and still does not fit into, a lot of button-ups, a lot of very bright colored pants, like the boat shoes, Sperrys." Overall, she recalled that "everybody just kinda like dressed the same, and everybody was driving the same kind of cars, there were a lot of White people. Which I was like, what the fuck is going on?" This entry into campus was not easy or comfortable for her.

Gabby, however, was quickly able to make close friends through the Summer Bridge (SB) program, students who are still good friends today: "So the first and primary way [I made friends] was through SB, and meeting the thirty or so other students who were in the SB program during my year, and a lot of the folks who I met at SB are still some of my closest friends on campus." If she had not had access to SB, Gabby reflected that it would have been difficult to make friends, to connect to new students:

> I think just because of the kind of person I am it wasn't [easy to connect], and what I mean by that is I am, when I know people in a space I am not a shy person, but when I don't know people in a space I'm a very shy person, and so for me it was kind of like I don't know who wants to talk to me and who doesn't, or like I don't know who's approachable and who's not approachable and that kind of thing, so it was definitely hard at first.

Because of this, Gabby felt that for students who are not wealthy, not outgoing, and not White, it would be difficult to make friends and settle in without SB:

> I think that a part of it is just like, some people are better at new interactions than others, I think that's a part of it, I think there's another deeper component to it though. . . . I think another reason, I'll use myself as an example, another reason I think I had a hard time connecting with people is because it was hard to sometimes find like a common identity, and like, and what I mean by that is like coming from like the class background I came from, there were things that people were talking about that I just could not talk about because I didn't have any of those experiences. Like traveling, or like owning a car, like that was not realities in my life you know, so like it was hard to like connecting with people on those first introductory levels that then lead to deeper friendships.

Without shared life experiences, she found it especially challenging to move from initial connections to "deeper friendships."

In Gabby's estimation, then, there are two levels—personal and institutional—that create difficulties. On a personal level, if you are not outgoing, and you are not wealthy, White, and straight, it's going to be tough to form connections and meet people. Being "outgoing" on a campus like HC often meant interest and/or comfort engaging with affluent, White peers in the more mainstream spheres of athletics and Greek Life.[2] On an institutional level, as we saw in earlier chapters, programs like SB helped students, especially those less interested in these spheres and those who are not out-going, navigate into a positive group of friends and from there acclimate to campus. Students in a Disconnected geography were less likely to have these types of institutional bridges to connection or to make satisfactory individual connections.

Two exceptions from our interview sample are Maria (Latina/multiracial) and Shane (Latino/ multiracial). Each participated in the SB program. While Shane mentions having close friends from SB, he does not name them, talk about them, or include them in his narratives during the interview, suggesting that they are not part of his regular campus life. Maria made no close friends at all. She herself pointed out how different this was from a typical SB student's experience:

> Well something surprising is that although I am an SB student, I did not meet my friends in SB. Our SB class was very cliquey compared to others and I just didn't fit anywhere. I was my own person and group [laughs]. . . . I ate alone in [the dining hall] my freshman and sophomore year until some students of color invited me to eat with them sophomore year.

Maria noted that those students, although briefly her friends, had told her they were "intimidated" by her tattoos and style, and the friendships fell apart. Eventually Maria located another friend and became closer with her and a few others, but she spent most of her college career feeling fairly alone. Maria described herself as shy and worried about moving away from home, but this does not necessarily differentiate her from other respondents during their first years.

One key difference, however, is that Maria was not assigned a roommate, which led to a lack of connection. While many other respondents made friends with their roommates and then effectively pooled their social resources, each introducing the other to new people or activities, Maria was on her own: "I didn't have a roommate. I got lucky and had a single. It was pretty lonely though. I think that's what contributed to my loneliness freshman and sophomore year." Maria's story is a series of missed opportunities for connection, whether through precollege programming, orientation, or even just getting to know a roommate—all steps campuses take to try to knit new students into the college experience.

Respondents understood delays in identifying early meaningful connections as a significant barrier to locating a social niche on campus, or making friends at all. Ian (Latino), for example, reflected back on his own delayed start, "I think it was very hard to try to meet people later in the year because I was pretty quiet in the beginning and everybody was starting to form friend groups. And I was just left on my own with sort of a small group of people." Although Ian made one friend during his orientation, he does not describe that friendship as having either lasted or developed into other connections. Moreover, Ian views this early stall in friendship formation as one of the defining features of his college experience. When asked what advice he would give his high school self, Ian said, "Try to make friends early, I think, because it's, because friendships develop quick and, you know, if you don't do it fast, you're just gonna end up bein' the one outlier, I guess." The image he presents here is almost one of musical chairs or a dance, where others have already grouped off and options for connection have been removed, leaving stragglers with peers to whom they might otherwise feel no connection, except that they are all left behind to form friendships. This is not likely to be the basis of a lasting relationship.

Commonalities

Orientation to Academic Life: Work is a Priority, but Not Always Satisfactory

One thing students in Disconnected geographies shared in common with their Multisphere and Work Hard peers was that they tended to speak about academic work as an important aspect of their time on campus, but they did not develop the same types of supportive academic relationships with faculty and peers. Midway through college, survey results presented in Table B.2 show that Disconnected students, like their Work Hard and Multisphere peers, score higher across all indicators of academic effort and engagement compared to their Play Hard peers. While they report similarly high academic effort as their Work Hard and Multisphere peers, Disconnected students are less likely to identify a college mentor, engage with faculty, and study with peers outside of class compared to their Work Hard and Multisphere peers. For example, only 43% of Disconnected students have a mentor on campus compared to 57% of Multisphere and 65% of Work Hard students. Moreover, the classroom was less likely to serve as a context for forming close college friends (26%) compared to their Work Hard (35%) and Multisphere (34%) peers (Table B.4).

Consistent with these survey results, our interview data show that Disconnected students worked hard, worried about grades, and did their best in their classes. Unlike students in the Work Hard geography, this generally did not lead into a combined social–academic pattern, however, because Disconnected students have few friends with whom to go to brown bags or speakers or with whom to stay in and study. This was something Ian hoped to make happen, although it did not appear he was able to do so—he told us that over time, he had become "more willing to have, to form study groups with people that I've had in class" but despite this, he did not mention any instances of this happening.

For several respondents in a Disconnected geography, academic work was nonetheless a rare and therefore important area of college satisfaction. Although Lauren (White) struggled early in her enrollment, by junior year she had found her pace academically. She described these accomplishments as sources of real pride and satisfaction: "Now that like I'm a junior and I've learned a lot more I'm more confident in my academic abilities . . . so like the classroom space has gotten better for me." Indeed, for some students in Disconnected geographies, academic work was the only place they felt successful, and in some cases they ended up spending a great deal of time on academic work because they had nothing else on which to spend their hours.

However, for respondents who were neither performing well academically nor finding their way socially, academic work was one more source of deflation. This meant they needed to find other sources of affirmation and belonging. In contrast to students in the Play Hard geography, respondents in a Disconnected geography spoke about this as a real source of concern and disappointment. Respondents in the Play Hard geographies tended to see academic work as an area where they could perhaps perform better, but confidence that they *could* do better allayed or boosted their feelings about their existing accomplishments. This was not the case for students in a Disconnected geography.

Erica (White) is the strongest example here. She talked about how unsuccessful she felt on campus, noting that college was not at all what she'd hoped it would be. Despite her strong academic record in high school, Erica was not getting the grades she hoped for and worked for. She noted that, "[I] feel like I'm doing a lot but like in terms of doing things I like, I'm not. . . . I don't have that, I mean, I don't have like the energy to be like doing things that like will make me happy." In fact, the only area in which Erica felt she was succeeding was her campus job. In addition to making money, her job allowed her to have a small sense of self-esteem that was otherwise lacking. She told us,

> I feel like, like I'm just good at having jobs. Like I had multiple jobs before I got to Hilltop. That's just like something that I feel like good at, is working and being an employee. Like in terms of like clubs and stuff, I just feel like I'm not good enough, a job is one of the places I feel . . . what's the word? Competent. Yeah.

Clark (White) echoes this language. Although Clark was ultimately positive about his academic experiences and accomplishments, he worried about how his college experiences might stack up against other students who had a more technically oriented training—a neuroscience major, he planned to go into research. Clark also balanced his academic work with several paid jobs on campus. When we asked him about where he felt good on campus, his work in the campus center was one of the places he named. A volunteer there, he spent hours per week in the information booth, "since speaking to prospective students and families was something I was told I was really good at, so that became my 'safe space.'" The importance of this work—and Clark's interest in spending hours of unpaid time away from studies or paid employment—seems to be rooted in the role this position came to play for him as a "safe space" because it was something he was "told he was really good at." By contrast, asked about places he felt uncomfortable, the classroom was the first place he listed, followed by mainstream social scenes like fraternity parties and bars downtown. Even Lauren, who spoke about becoming more comfortable and confident in her academic abilities, nonetheless reflected that she still had "really bad, like, pathological fear" that she would make a mistake out loud in class and that "people [would] think I'm stupid."

Faculty Relationships

Most Disconnected students reported having lukewarm relationships with faculty that were restricted to discussions of coursework and advising. Their descriptions of faculty relationships were not marked by the warmth or enthusiasm we observed among Work Hard and Multisphere students. For example, Shane (Latino/multiracial) explained, "I like some of them pretty much, but there are others that I don't really like. I don't know." Ian (Latino) only talks with faculty when he is struggling in a class. He also explained that he does not "really interact" with his academic advisors. They only meet twice a year before course registration. Erika (White) adds, "I don't talk to my advisor because he's not genuinely interested." This lack of connection with faculty is very similar to what we observed among the Play Hard students.

All but two of the Disconnected students in our qualitative sample lacked an institutional bridge to connect with faculty, but those who did connect seemed to resemble Work Hard and Multisphere students who also had these types of connections. Like most first-generation students, Clark (White) initially felt uncomfortable with approaching faculty, but this all changed after working as a faculty research assistant. He points to these experiences as transformative in terms of the quality of relationships he formed with faculty: "[They are the] most rewarding academic relationships at HC. I learned so much and got incredible advice." In addition, Clark explained that these closer relationships translated into greater comfort within the classroom: "It was the only time I felt comfortable discussing the materials since it took about two years at HC to feel comfortable answering questions and talking during class." As we saw in other campus geographies, SB, faculty research, or other institutional opportunities are central to facilitating the types of deep relationships that help first-generation students feel more comfortable in the classroom and on campus in general and develop important social capital for navigating campus and the post-college world.

Orientation to Extracurricular and Social Activities: Low Engagement

While most students in each of the other geographies found social connections through extracurricular activities, students in Disconnected geographies did not participate in many, or in some cases any, clubs or campus organizations midway through college. Table B.4 show that Disconnected students are about half as likely as Work Hard students to participate in nonathletic extracurricular clubs (cultural, art, religious, or volunteering). Disconnected students are also not very involved in the social and athletic spheres on campus, with hours partying and participation rates in athletics and Greek Letter Organizations (GLOs) less than half of those in Play Hard geographies (Table B.3). As a result of this low participation, Disconnected students did not identify many close friends in activities outside of class (Table B.3). They were, however, just as likely to be dating or have a serious partner as their more socially engaged peers in Multisphere and Play Hard geographies. Qualitative data suggest that these partnerships are central to helping Disconnected students stay afloat, but it is difficult to discern if these romantic relationships are a cause or a consequence of their larger social isolation during college. Finally, Table B.4 shows that Disconnected students (58%) are less likely to work for pay than Work Hard (78%) students, suggesting their lower level of involvement are not entirely due to work demands or conflicts.

The solitary nature of HC Disconnected students' lives became clear when we asked them to tell us about a typical weekday and a typical weekend day. Disconnect respondents simply reported very few forms of engagement on campus, whether through extracurriculars, sports, or any source of contact with peers, through which to form future friendships They described classes, homework, and sometimes paid employment as predominant, and time alone or with a single friend as their social outlet. Consequently, they missed out on both opportunities for friendships and also, as a number of scholars point out, opportunities to show "leadership" or campus involvement on their resumes, gain cultural capital that they could use in interviews or cover letters, and other corollary outcomes. Of the respondents in our interview sample, only Clark and Lauren participated in more than one extracurricular activity. Each other respondent participated in no clubs or only one.

Maria, a multiracial Latina student, exemplified this. Maria's typical day seemed to include no social or extracurricular time whatsoever. She told us,

> I usually wake up around 8 am. Get dressed and do some homework until class or work. I go to class and usually take a nap in between my two classes. I usually have to go to work again in the evening and then I'll come home at dinner, do more homework, shower and go to bed.

This routine accomplishes the basic requirements of college, but not much else. Weekends look fairly similar:

> Well I don't go out. I used to go out freshman and sophomore year. But I usually just stay in on a Friday and do my reading for the week. I work on Saturday and Sunday. So I don't have time to do much. Honestly, I spend most of my time by myself in my room. I see my one friend once in a while when I do decide to step out to an event, which is rare.

Maria's first, immediate response of "I don't go out" speaks both to her social isolation and to the common understanding that most students in fact do go out—that's what weekends include for many or most students, which further highlights the level to which students like Maria are isolated. Throughout her interview, Maria refers to only one friend. She describes having made efforts earlier in her college life to be social, but has given these up and now spends "most of [her] time by [herself]."

Other respondents fitting this geography described the same combination of few friends, few activities, and a sense of loneliness on campus. Let's look at Erica, for example. A White junior, Erica described herself as having only one friend. When we asked her about a typical weekend, she told us,

> This semester, I have one friend, she's my roommate. I spend all my free time with her, if I'm spending time with anybody. Also, it's usually forced though 'cause she lives on the same [room as I do]. [laughter] But no, I like her presence. Yeah, social life—don't really have one. Sometimes I'll go to like events that I see on Facebook, but I don't really talk to other people that are there. I'm really isolated. I don't spend much time with other people aside from my roommate.

Although Erica laughs during this section of the interview as she uses self-deprecating language to joke that her friend is stuck spending time with her because they live together, she cried several times during the interview. Asked what advice she would give herself as a high school senior, she said that she would tell herself to

> just consider the type of person who's probably gonna be going there and ask yourself like how similar are you to these people and how like, easily will it, or like how easy will [you] be to be able to fit in with these people, or like find people to get along with. Yeah. 'Cause I did look at student reviews and people who go here, like on the internet, that say that they really like it here. So I just assumed like, Oh, it's an awesome place. Like people are really happy here. But like the people who are saying that, it's people who like con-sistently works for them, if that makes sense?

As we see in this excerpt, Erica does not feel that she is the problem. Rather, the other students—who seem to really like campus—are simply too dif-ferent from her. She cannot "fit in with these people." Erica read about Hilltop before arriving; she did the kind of research that many high school students do, not only in checking the academic profile but also reading student reviews to understand campus life—Are people happy at this college? Her reading of those reviews showed here that "it's an awesome place," but she had not taken into account the demographic differences between herself and the kinds of students who likely authored those accounts.

Ian, whom we met at the start of the chapter, echoes Erica's and Maria's experiences. Ian's free time is spent on low-key solitary activities—"read[ing], watch[ing] the computer, do[ing] homework, and then just sleep[ing]." Weekends, he says, he spends alone "doin' nothin'." Ian elaborated that he would like to develop new connections, but he has not been able to do so.

> I think I've been more willing to have, to form study groups with people that I've had in class. The one roommate, my current roommate that I have, that I met last year, he withdrew from his classes and he left in the middle of the year, so I'm basically left just walkin' around.

In a Disconnected geography, the loss of one friend or one study buddy is significant. Ian does talk about having a couple of other friends:

> So, my friendship was with the one person from [archery club] and his roommate. . . . And then I also have met another student, a freshman who's from, who's also from [my home state], and that sort of became the, from there we started to talk more. Yeah. Go to dinner. Have conversations with one another. Either we watch movies on laptops or play FIFA [video game].

His involvement with archery was cut short after the campus range closed, and Ian did not join any other clubs. Although Ian does have a few friends, his account of his connections to them are a far cry from descriptions of close friendships shared by respondents in other geographies.

Contrast these narratives to those of the students in the Work Hard geography. Even those who are the most dissatisfied with their college social lives, like Victoria, who describes her weekend as "It just doesn't [exist]" or "I just don't [do anything]," had a group of friends to spend time with, something students in Disconnected geography lack. Again, even when students in the Work Hard geography reported having less social time or fewer social outlets than they wished for, and even when they described spending many hours in a typical day on classes and homework, their narrations always included mentions of close and trusted friendship ties with multiple college peers upon whom they could rely.

Having very few friends, often referring to only one or perhaps no close friends at all, was the hallmark indicator of respondents in a Disconnected geography. While two respondents in this group (Shane, Latino/multiracial, and Lauren, White) have romantic partners, these partners are their only real social contact. A primary outcome of this small friendship circle is that most respondents in a Disconnected geography are lonely. Even those who describe themselves as "loners by choice" (as Maria [Latina/multiracial] does) say that they are lonely on campus. In some cases, respondents tried to make friends and retreated after those efforts were not satisfactory or successful; others were still struggling to find a social niche after two or more years on campus. It's important to note that in most cases respondents in this geographic pattern felt that they *could* be happy, that they *could* make friends, and that the social structure, norms, and demographics of Hilltop were largely what prevented them from having an enjoyable experience. Their isolation is a reaction to or an outcome of the particular classed and raced institutional world of which they are now members.

Making Space on Campus: Few Places of Comfort

The alienation Disconnected students felt on HC's campus was also clear in their descriptions of where they felt comfortable and uncomfortable. While Work Hard geography respondents talk about finding comfort in spaces where they feel like others share their views, background, and/or thinking, Disconnected students talk about spaces where they can be alone, unjudged, and not excluded. Students in a Disconnected group were more likely to describe feeling comfortable only in their own rooms or being alone than respondents in any other group.

Maria is emblematic here. She named her room as the place she feels most comfortable. This, in and of itself, is not unique, a number of respondents feel comfortable in their rooms or living spaces, which are often where they connect with friends. But Maria's longer response contextualizes her answer more fully to paint a picture of alienation on campus and her room as the rare space in which she feels at ease:

> I don't venture out much. So I have had, like, an identity issue for the longest time that I have just come to terms with. I am multiracial and I identify as a student of color, but my skin is White. I do not feel comfortable going to student organization for students of color because I feel like I am stared at and not accepted. So I tend to like spaces where I am alone. I don't have

many friends on campus. My closest friend graduated last year. So I don't go out either.

Maria is clear and specific that she does not feel comfortable around other people, and among other things, her narrative highlights some of the complexities of racialization on Hilltop's campus. A senior, she has adopted the practice of isolating herself to avoid feeling "stared at and not accepted" by students of color and by White students. She has few friends, and after her one closest friend graduated, she struggled to make new connections or re-engage in social life. She added that there is an academic department space where she feels comfortable "because all of my professors are so nice and it's cozy. . . . I take naps in there and everything. So that's a comfortable space for me." Other than this, however, she told us that she "[doesn't] really enter other spaces unless it's for academic reasons." In other words, Maria avoids virtually all of campus because she does not feel comfortable with other students, unless she has to go to class or some other academic requirement.

Maria's lack of comfortable spaces and her desire to be in spaces in which she does not feel judged are shared by other respondents in Disconnected geographies. Ian (Latino), for example, expressed a similar line of reasoning. He listed four comfortable spaces: "The dining hall, here in the library, in my room, and also the Chinese restaurant [in town]." Like Maria, he described the spaces that are comfortable as those in which he does not feel judged or excluded. He mused that in these spaces,

I feel like everybody's left on their own to do, to think however they want. Nobody seems awkward with one another. You just [pause], it's just places where you feel like it's accepted to just act the way that you are. Yeah. I think the dining hall is just, I could, it's places where I could think, also in the library, and also in the restaurant.

As in Maria's narrative, Ian's description tells us a lot about how Disconnected students feel in other spaces on campus—judged, bothered, awkward, not like themselves.

In fact, most respondents in a Disconnected geography listed their rooms as important comfortable spaces on campus. Most indicated there was "no judgment" (Harry's phrasing) in their rooms. When Shane (Latino/multiracial) is asked about places he feels comfortable, he seemed almost unable to answer:

Um, my room, [coughs] um, I don't know . . . [long pause]. Places I feel most comfortable? . . . Like it's basically my room is the closest home I have . . . I don't know like, maybe I just feel weird, and I'm developing greater and greater neuroses as I drive myself crazy but, like [laughs], I don't know it's like I sit in the dining hall, and all the food's awful and like [sighs], I'm sitting either, probably alone. And like I just don't want to be there. I'd rather be in my room.

Shane is the closest to not being Disconnected—we might think of him as being on the periphery of a Disconnected geography. He has a girlfriend and a few close friends that he made through SB and through a social club for board games. In other words, among Disconnected students, his narrative is the most positive! He nonetheless describes his room as the most, and perhaps only, comfortable place for him. While Work Hard students also described campus overall as fairly alienating, they had strong friendship groups and extracurricular activities that provided social and emotional support. This was not the case for Disconnected students, who felt not only alienated on campus but also experienced that alienation alone.

Because Disconnected students had so few places in which they felt comfortable, they were more likely than respondents in most other geographies to describe wishing they had gone to college somewhere else. We asked respondents whether they ever wished they had not enrolled at Hilltop. Many indicated that—at least occasionally—they had wished that they had not chosen this campus. They wished to be closer to or further from home, to be somewhere warmer, to be in a larger city, or to be nearer to where their high school friends were. Students in a Disconnected geography were the most likely to report feeling this way and felt the strongest. Harry (White), laughing, responded "Yeah, like all the last two years." He elaborated in a sort of back and forth narration:

But, I mean, not every single day, almost every single day, but there were times where like I kind of like just thought, and just kind of like disregarded all the negatives and just kind of like thought of, you know, being at a good school and just kind of was like, "Okay. That's okay. That's all there is to it."

Harry has been able, at times, to focus on his academic accomplishments and see those as enough—"all there is to [college]." But other times, often enough that he has to specify "not every single day," he has wished he were somewhere else. Ian talked about comparing his time at HC with friends who attend larger campuses, wondering about life there:

> I visited my friend at [another campus] and I hung out with his friends and saw how well they were doing, and I always thought, you know, "What did I do that left me with a few friends and not really knowing much about the school?" So yeah, I think sometimes, you know, what could have been if I had applied to that school and what I've been doing now.

Maria described campus as "a toxic place" that "slowly kills you on the inside," noting that she had spent a lot of time crying on campus, wishing to be somewhere else. Erica (White) was more equivocal, but no happier. She told us,

> It's rough 'cause like I wasn't happy where I was before this, but I'm not happy here now. So, I mean, I wish I had gone somewhere else entirely from the very beginning, but like I don't know, like if I hadn't gone here, like chosen to go here when I was applying, like I probably would be at community college. Like I don't know.

Erica cried during this section of the interview, suggesting that this is an especially fraught issue. She is truly unhappy at HC despite having envisioned it as a place in which she might experience what other students seem to— fun, friends, academic success.

Mitigation Efforts: Clark, Lauren, and Maria

Because the largest portion of our quantitative sample is located in a Disconnected geography, it is worth exploring these respondents' narratives in more depth to understand how they remained—and in rare cases, began to get out of—their isolated campus lives. In particular, it is important not to simply see these students as loners or shy introverts. Rather, the same sociological interplay of institutional structure and demographic variables of class, gender, and race are at play.

Clark and Lauren, both White, offer illuminative examples of the work some Disconnect students put in to try to make campus work. Both spoke extensively about how they have tried to change in significant ways to fit in, and although both say that they have friends on campus, neither sounds happy.

Asked whether he sees himself as a "typical Hilltop student," Clark answered: "Yes, because I've made myself into the typical Hilltop student." He elaborated,

> I feel like the typical HC student has a reputation of being White and wealthy and intelligent. And, I feel like I need to fit into that mold. So I need to make sure that I'm outgoing in class, need to make sure that I'm dressing in the right ways.

Clark has a clear vision of what it means to be a Hilltop student, and he has worked hard over the years to become that person. He has spent money on new clothes, shifted his behavior, and sometimes hides things about his home life, such as his parents' jobs, to better fit "that mold." Clark feels this intensely, the "pressure" to make himself something new, because he has always believed that wealthier students seem to be looking down on him. As he put it, "there is that pressure that if you don't come from an elite background, that either you're not, that you yourself aren't worth as much, or you're just going to be seen differently from the general Hilltop population."

Lauren also told us directly that she had worked hard to acclimate to campus, including trying to change herself: "Like I feel like I've changed as a person since I've come to Hilltop in an attempt to fit into more of those spaces." Despite this, Lauren had a lower level of social engagement than she would have liked. When we asked about her typical weekend, she told us, "I'd say usually one night I go out a week, but that's about it. Sometimes, if I don't have anything going on, I go home instead. Um, what do I do on weekends? I'm such a loser. I don't know." Lauren had hoped to find friendships when she enrolled in college, and unlike some other respondents in Disconnected geographies, she remained active in seeking out connections.

Although she had a long-term boyfriend on campus, he seemed to be her only steady social connection. She related, "There definitely have been times where, like, I tell my boyfriend, like, if it wasn't for you, I just would've transferred by now because I hate everyone, which isn't, isn't really the case but sometimes, you feel like that." Lauren had not been invited to participate in SB, but she had done a pre-orientation program available for the general student population and had not especially enjoyed it. She also did not make friends in her First Year Experience course, which she found arbitrary and stilted.

Lauren tried actively to make friends by joining various student clubs over the years. She also tried just striking up conversation with classmates. Neither of these approaches worked well. Recounting her efforts during her first year, she recalled, "People [on campus] seemed cold though. I don't know, like I'm the person that sits down in class and I'm like, 'Hey. Hi.' I say hi to everyone and sometimes, people literally don't say anything back and it's like excuse the fuck out of me." Lauren told us that because of how she perceived students on campus, and because of their reactions to her, she had a hard time imagining connecting with them. She described how she felt that they might have nothing in common, nothing to talk about:

> I didn't know what to talk about with these people, you know what I'm saying? Like I go and what, what am I gonna talk about? Like how I made dinner for my brothers for two years? I played soccer but, yeah, I don't know. They're talking about vacation homes and, and, once again, this is just my perception of it 'cause I was nervous but, um, no, I didn't have a lot in common with too many people. I wasn't making friends at all.

Here again, Lauren is working to make friends but making little progress and perceives that the other students on campus are too different from her.

Moreover, what we hear in Lauren's recollection of her adjustment to campus is not just a sense that she and many of her new peers were different, but also that they might not welcome her—that she might not measure up. She noted, "I see people's Bean Boots. I've never seen Bean Boots before and I don't know. I just, I feel like when you're in a situation where you feel inferior, you automatically kind of resent the people around you and that's not fair at all." Despite her caution that this was "not fair at all," it clearly shaped her initial experiences on campus. Clothing and other signals suggested that in status terms, she would feel—or be made to feel—"inferior." Her high school experiences of caring for her two little brothers and the soccer team were not in the same conversational league as their vacation homes. She felt "nervous" around these people, and also felt that "the people just seemed snooty and not my kind of people."

When we spoke during Lauren's sophomore year, she had joined a pick-up sports team and told us that she "[has] so many friends and it's getting better,

I'm realizing now. Not everyone hates me." However, when we checked back in with Lauren a year later, she told us that these friendships had never really materialized: "I just quit [the team] this year because they're very superficial and [have a] competitive social life that I just can't keep up with." To locate new friendships, Lauren joined a sorority, but did not seem especially engaged with it. In fact, she told us that she often thought about leaving. When she initially joined the sorority, she recalled thinking, "Oh my god they want me, someone wants me, I'm gonna have friends!" She also recalled that because she joined midway through the year, there was not much of a welcome process in place for her as a new member:

> I didn't get a lot of education about what the organization was and like everybody else is doing their own spring semester thing whereas I feel like in the fall they're like, new people are here—make it welcome, make them welcome. Well, I didn't get that and then I went abroad so I seriously considered disaffiliating because I had been there for like seven weeks and then I was gone for six months.

The only thing keeping Lauren in her sorority at this point is her involvement on a diversity committee, which has become very important to her. Of the group as a whole, she's begun to feel that "it's so expensive and it's very superficial," and she therefore "still like really grappled with staying or going. . . . it's also like why am I staying in an organization that I only enjoy when I'm trying to change it?" Thus, as a junior, Lauren still spent most of her time with her boyfriend and seemed to have few other positive and meaningful ties on campus.

In many ways, Lauren sounds like a Multisphere student—she is actively involved in multiple types of activities, and she joined pick up sports teams and a sorority and several other clubs in an effort to make friends. And yet neither these nor her short pre-orientation program have led to lasting friendships on campus. The question of timing looms large here: It is simply difficult to make friends as a first-generation student outside the period in which others have formed their connections. Moreover, pre-college programs and other onboarding activities are not a one-size-fits-all.

A final respondent also helps to illuminate the ways that students experienced and responded to being disconnected. Maria, whom we also previously met, started her time at Hilltop as a member of the SB program. Unlike other respondents, she was not able to find an early friend group. She felt that this was because her personal style was more punk than other women of color in her program, and that they had been "intimidated by [her]." She felt excluded from the nascent social circles of women of color and, once the semester began in full, also excluded by the wealthier White students who arrived in the fall. She eventually made some friendships with students who had also attended SB, also women of color. Her perception of a divide between herself and other women of color grew even larger after she befriended an affluent Latina woman in a sorority who didn't "join everyone else in the social justice work" and also started hanging out with White peers: "My old friends were not happy with my actions and felt I was a traitor."

Maria's campus life was also highly constrained by financial worries. Of all of our interview sample respondents, Maria reported working the highest number of hours, and she cited money as limiting her experience in nearly every way, from studying abroad, class projects, club involvement, joining a sorority, and going on spring break—thereby also constraining some of the options she might otherwise have taken to making more friends. Ultimately, over the course of her four years, Maria had no consistent friendships on campus, and her social life and ties varied widely. Like Lauren and Clark, she described conscious choices to change her dress and language in an effort to fit in, but in the end, she is still on an island. She is only comfortable in her academic department and in her room.

Maria's narrative highlights the way that campus context matters not only in terms of socioeconomic status (in the form of blockages to accessing high-status groups and costs of trying, as we saw for Clark and Lauren) but also ways that race is difficult to navigate on a campus with a minority–majority social divide and very few racially minoritized students. The largest groups of women of color were located in Work Hard geographies, which focused on shared ties and shared interests. As a student who did not seem to fit in that crowd and then did not wish to participate in the shared activity of social justice work, Maria was initially and then again later excluded. While Maria eventually formed friendships with wealthier women of color and White students, these ties were not enough to mitigate her feelings of alienation or to create a real sense of belonging. Indeed, Maria seems to have faced a kind of double-jeopardy in which she did not form friendships with either a small and close-knit group of racially similar other women during SB or the wealthier White students she met during her first year and later felt excluded by co-ethnic peers when she did not adhere to a Work Hard geography focus on social justice engagement.

Variation

Although this geography is the most common among first generation students, Table B.5 shows that 45% of White women and 44% White men are Disconnected compared to only 38% of women of color and 26% of men of color. In light of literature about racism and stereotypes about Black and Latino men,[3] it is especially interesting that men of color are least likely to be in Disconnected geographies. We suspect that this may reflect both the role of the institution in selecting students who meet particular expectations and men of color who are able to attain admission into highly selective predominantly White institutions—and who choose to attend—having become adept at managing negative stereotypes across many years of schooling.[4] These respondents have figured out how to manage niches across multiple spaces on campus. These race and gender differences may also stem from differences in entry points and fit in available campus contexts: Students of color are invited to participate in academic programs, such as SB, and identity-based extracurricular clubs. Women are more likely to be socialized toward these forms of reciprocal support and also more affirmed for academically focused geographies. Men, by contrast, are more likely to be affirmed in social settings and may meet resistance in presenting academically focused selves.[5] Moreover, they are more likely to meet friends through other formal institutional and informal social entry points around sports.[6]

White first-generation men and women at Hilltop have fewer venues that attract them *and* are targeted to their backgrounds and needs. For some, this lack of fit is counterbalanced by being able to visually blend in, but clearly not for all. As sociologist Jenny M. Stuber writes, being White "provid[es] a sense of invisibility and similarity that allows these students to 'blend in.'" However, she continues, the stereotypical association of Whiteness with "higher levels of socioeconomic status" also means that White students are assumed to be continuing-generation. Thus, Stuber notes, Whiteness may "render invisible White students who come from economically disadvantaged backgrounds [and] . . . hinder the possibility that they may identify others with whom they might share experiences and from whom they might draw strength or a sense of validation."[7] Moreover, a superficial appearance of belonging does not necessarily quell doubts or feelings of alienation that make connecting with new peers difficult and/or unappealing.

Because the number of interview respondents in a Disconnected geography is quite small,[8] variation is difficult to assess using our qualitative data.

However, there is some indication that a difference exists along racialized lines between those who proclaim that they are "social loners by choice" and those who wish to make friends. Maria and Shane, both multiracial students, each use language that implies that they have opted out of social life on campus, choosing to limit their social connections. This may indicate that they have determined that this campus cannot offer them a satisfying social life or meaningful friendships. The students who describe strong, continuing desires to make friends are White. Lauren, Erica, Clark, and Harry all were clear about their expressed wish to have stronger social connections on campus, perhaps indicating that they understood the problem as lying more with them than with the campus as a whole. (Ian, a Latino respondent, does not fit this pattern, and also expressed a greater desire to have more friends.) In a small interview sample, it is difficult to be able to discern whether this is a pattern or simply incidental similarities. However, these potential variations suggest intersectional dynamics that should be further elaborated through future research.

Conclusion

Disconnected students are the other side of the Multisphere coin. Just as the Multisphere students seem to be able to access the best of the Play Hard and Work Hard worlds or approaches, Disconnected students are trapped between them. They do not feel at home on campus, and most often report feeling most at ease alone in their own rooms. While academics are important, they report classrooms as very stressful. Their friendships are few in number, sometimes only one or two, and rather than the "us against the world" feeling shared by the Work Hard students, Disconnected students' friendships seem not to buffer their overall discomfort. Even significant others do not seem to ease this feeling. Because they are not able to gain success or satisfaction in any of the three spheres we focus on—academic work, extracurricular activities, or social life—it is difficult for them to construct a meaningful or fulfilling identity as a college student.

One important commonality among Disconnected respondents was a delay in forming friendships: these students could not form early connections, and described how difficult it is to make friends after the initial rush of being new together. This issue of timing also highlights the role played by the institution. As we show in other chapters, institutional programming often provides important connections—although as we see in this chapter, such ties are not a guaranteed outcome. However, what seems clear from Disconnected students' accounts is that early connections, whether through programming or not, are crucial.

There is, of course, variation, both across respondents and along each respondent's own personal trajectory. Some became closer to peers, made more friends, and become more at home on campus over the years of enrollment. Clark, especially, talks about the hard work and struggle he put in and the payoffs he received. He talks about finally, after years, becoming more comfortable on campus and finding his stride academically, and mentions a few friends. Lauren, too, in her senior year, sounds more at home, having found meaningful employment and doing better in her classes than in earlier years and still with her boyfriend. However, in contrast to students in other geographies, even these more settled respondents stand out for their continued sense of alienation, and indeed some in Disconnected geographies report having *fewer* friends and social ties in the latter years of college because their few initial friends have graduated or left campus.

Like other students, respondents in Disconnected geographies came to college with high hopes and, perhaps, high expectations. The presentation that campuses like Hilltop make, and that is shown in American movies, TV, and other media, is of college as a time when students find themselves, make lifelong friends, take intellectually stimulating courses, perhaps participate in keggers and all-nighters, and generally have the best four years of their lives. Students in Disconnected geographies experienced none of these elements. At a fundamental level, these students have not been able to take advantage of the opportunities selective colleges like those in the NLSF and like Hilltop pride themselves in offering. These visions of involvement, fulfillment, and friendship are not mere marketing, but important to students' college outcomes—a great deal of research shows that students' friendships on campus and overall level of engagement in campus life are important not only to their happiness, but also in connecting them to activities and opportunities and even staying enrolled from year to year. For the students whose narratives we focus on in this chapter, however, college is an isolated pursuit characterized by limited engagement or connection. In Chapter 7, we examine the ways that this lack of connection moves Disconnected respondents—the largest portion of our national survey sample—toward post-college outcomes.

Notes

1. See, for example, Aries and Seider, 2005; Aries, 2008 Ostove and Long, 2007; Stuber, 2011a; Armstrong and Hamilton, 2013.
2. In other work, we show that Disconnected and Work Hard students were somewhat less likely than those in Play Hard and Multisphere geographies to participate in high school athletics and have friends involved in the party scene, suggesting they may be less primed to engage in these areas of college life.
3. For example, Wilkins, 2014; see also Feagin, Vera, and Imani, 1994; Willie, 2003; Torres and Charles, 2004; Torres, 2009.
4. For an example of the potential role of admissions officers' screening students around racially linked characteristics, see Thornhill (2019), Jaquette and Salazar (2018) and Han, Jaquette, and Salazar (2019). See also Massey, Mooney, Torres, and Charles (2007). See also Megan Holland (2012) on similar dynamics in high school.
5. Wilkins, 2014.
6. Eitzen, 2009.
7. Stuber, 2011b: 132.
8. HC's longstanding SB program targeting first-generation students is one reason why we may have had fewer students fitting the Disconnected profile in our qualitative sample. They also may have simply been more difficult to locate and/or recruit.

7

Connecting to Post-College Life and Locating Success

Introduction

In the preceding chapters, we examined the ways that students in different geographies varied in their orientations toward academic and social life and their connections to similar and cross-class peers. In this chapter, we take up the question of what these variations may ultimately bring students in terms of their post-college mobility. Because our interviewees had not yet entered their post-college lives, we cannot analyze their career outcomes. However, we can examine the ways selective campuses set students up for success and how this may be different across the geographies in which students are situated.

Selective colleges like Hilltop offer several potential resources beyond human capital and job skills that are emphasized by sociologists and by campuses alike. One is social capital, or connections to alumnae who can offer advice, internships, connections, and even jobs after graduation. Students may also conceptualize their peers as connections—friends now who can provide opportunities later. Networking is so prevalent on campuses such as Hilltop College (HC) that it almost seems natural, as if everyone learned how to do it in primary school along with arithmetic. However, research suggests that, in fact, the social knowledge of networking, the blending of work and social, is "cultivated" through socialization practices that teach youth to be comfortable asking for help, interacting with and questioning adults, and negotiating to get their needs met.[1]

A second set of resources is high-status cultural capital, such as clothing, food, music tastes, or even linguistic shifts. As sociologist Lauren Rivera shows, white-collar employers routinely and perhaps subconsciously draw on class-based micro-interactional signals and bases of knowledge favoring affluent candidates to make both initial and final choices that lead to hiring or not hiring a candidate.[2] For example, employers looked for potential

Geographies of Campus Inequality. Janel E. Benson and Elizabeth M. Lee, Oxford University Press (2020). © Oxford University Press. DOI: 10.1093/oso/9780190848156.001.0001.

employees who made them "feel comfortable," enjoyed "hanging out with," and who could "make tough times kind of fun."[3] Unlike academic and formal job search strategy skills, these presentations of self and taste preferences that employers referred to as "fit" are more difficult to learn because they require lots of practice within particular classed and racialized contexts to be performed with ease.[4]

In this chapter, we examine the ways that accumulating these two types of resources are shaped by geography. We show that opportunities to network and practice new cultural capital are not automatic, or built through a few conversations, but rather gained through ongoing informal interactions within campus geographies. Developing these skills is challenging for first-generation students overall, but especially for those from multiply-marginalized groups who need to transverse more than just class differences. We also examine respondents' understandings of these opportunities—how students make sense of them, and the ways respondents saw themselves changing since enrolling at HC. These questions are important not only for thinking about how institutions support first-generation students' access to post-college mobility, but also—given what we now know about how students are distributed across different geographies in terms of race, ethnicity, and gender—whether their access to mobility or to particular types of mobility are similarly stratified.

Commonalities

Most respondents across all four campus geographies shared the understanding that, because of their families' financial and occupational circumstances, they would not be able to find jobs through connections at home. This made college especially valuable. It also set them apart from their peers in terms of the resources on which they believed many of their affluent classmates could draw. Many respondents told us that they had "nothing to fall back on" (Aleyda, Work Hard, Latina) if things didn't work out in their college job search. Victoria (Work Hard, African American), for example, reflected that others might have the luxury of being able to not worry about grades because of their family connections:

> Like some people . . . can get Cs and they're still gonna get a job because
> whoever they know will slide them through, and I know there are some

people who can pass their resume around and get a job too, and I know that the pressure I put on myself, maybe it's invisible, maybe I'm making it all up but it's really real for me and that is a big motivator, so I know I need to have good grades to get a good job and propel myself to the next level, like it's not a joke. That's my life.

Similarly, Grant (Multisphere, White) linked a higher family income to "just more security in terms of just you have a fall back in terms of money, . . . access to outside help, external sources for academic achievement, things like that." Some respondents also felt that wealthier peers did not need to work as hard. Kaelin (Work Hard, Latina/multiracial) and Jay (Play Hard, Latino) both talked about "mommy and daddy" financially supporting wealthy college students, wording that highlights the immaturity with still relying on adults.

Race and ethnicity provide some additional nuance here. Several respondents of color spoke about being additionally aware of hurdles to obtaining jobs because of racism. Carlos (Work Hard, Latino), for example, spoke about this potential problem: "I mean, like, even in the job search right now. I mean people are gonna see my name 'Carlos' and they're not gonna see me. . . . So that in and of itself is already disadvantaging." Andrew (Work Hard), a Black student, similarly reflected,

> I feel like I have to do better than other people. For example, my first year, I heard if you have a Black-sounding name your resume gets thrown out 50% more. Like, I don't have a father who works at a hedge fund [where] I can get a job after [graduating].

Thus, for students of color, the stakes of not having family or home community connections to career on-ramps was potentially a source of even greater stress.

This pressure was exacerbated by the ways respondents understood their education as being intimately tied into their families' futures. They wanted to succeed as role models for younger siblings and extended family members, to make parents proud, and, in many cases, to be able to support their families financially. This was the case for Rico (Play Hard, African American), who told us, "My family is lower class so I feel like I have to succeed to help my family out. It's not just all about me." Many described parents or other family members pushing them to do better or get particular kinds of jobs, and most described intense internal pressure. Tommie (Play Hard, White), for instance, told us about how his uncles and extended family members joke about how when he is a doctor, he'll be able to help support them all—a joke that he knows might be rooted in some very real expectations about his economic success.

This feeling was very common across race/ethnicity and genders. Like Tommie, Manesha (Work Hard, African American) told us,

> I know that my dad's really proud of me and I know that my other siblings haven't been as successful. So, sometimes I do feel like there's, like, this pressure for me to do well just so they have something to show for it. Um, so, I'm, like, the star, the golden child and my family, my, um, extended family joke around that I'm the star of the family but, you know, it does put a little bit of pressure on you 'cause it's, like, you can't disappoint them.

As we see in Tommie's and Manesha's words, the value of their accomplishments might be both financial and symbolic.

Moreover, respondents often perceived that their families made great investments and sacrifices, so that they could attend college—something their parents had not been able to do themselves. This heightened respondents' understanding of the importance of their college outcomes to family members: It was not a simple matter of getting a job, but rather the fruition (or not) of a decades-long series of expectations, plans, and sacrifice. As Brianna (Work Hard, African American) put it, "my mother invested so much for me to, like, even, like, be here. My ancestors invested so much for me to even be in this space that wasn't created for me, so yeah there's a lot of pressure." Respondents therefore felt a great deal of stress about turning their college achievements into concrete post-college gains. Whether they planned to financially "take [the] family to the next level" (Jordan, African American, male) or simply make their parents proud, there was enormous pressure to succeed.

Geographies: Varied Strategies and Beliefs

Play Hard

The Network-Only Pathway
First-generation Play Hard respondents in the qualitative sample were confident that they would be successful after college and that the college

would provide them with the tools they needed. In Play Hard respondents' narratives, those tools fit with primary approaches prescribed by the campus, namely, networking and drawing on institutional prestige. Jay (Latino), when asked whether Hilltop College has set him up for success, answered emphatically: "Yes!" He describes the reasons for his confidence: "Because of all the Alumni and the people you meet here. . . the network is unbelievable. HC people look after HC people when it comes to after graduation and I feel like that alone is setting me up for success more than another university will." Mike (African American) also echoes the importance of connections: "Alumni know how tough it is to go through a place as rigorous, so they're very helpful giving jobs after you graduate." In contrast to other groups, these respondents did not plan to rely on academic achievements to obtain that success—in fact, two mentioned that academics are not as important as who you know. Institutional support, such as the career center, also did not rank highly as a means of gaining success. We have therefore called their approach the "network-only pathway" to post-college outcomes.

Play Hard respondents spoke the most and the most positively about the concept of networking. More than any other group, they have internalized and appreciate the institutionally sanctioned approach of making connections to current peers and to alumnae as a means of securing access to jobs later in life. They are most likely to have learned how to network: what it means, how it works, what to expect—in other words, they not only understand the *concept* of networking, but also have learned and practiced the concrete strategies of how to make it happen.

One reason that respondents in a Play Hard group are most likely to speak about networks is that they are often already part of organizations on campus—fraternities, sororities, and athletic teams—that stress the importance of membership and connection, not only to current peers but as part of a larger family that includes alumnae. These connections allowed frequent interactions with wealthier peers, who might themselves have family, and friends' parents who could offer job opportunities or other resources and, importantly, offered a model for how networking operates. Many described close friends gaining internships and post-college opportunities through family networks. In addition, several of their athletic teams and Greek Letter Organizations (GLOs) offered alumni mentoring programs specifically geared toward identifying jobs and internships. Play Hard respondents who are not themselves part of such a group may internalize this understanding from friends who are members.

As described in Chapter 3, students in Play Hard geographies are least focused on academics, and for some, this is part of a larger belief system they
have developed about getting ahead. Not only are connections key, but also
some respondents told us specifically that they are less worried about their
academic work because they have learned that grades are not ultimately the
only or even most important outcome of college.[5] Nick (White), for example,
explained:

> I feel like I'm an average student grade wise. Nothing special, nothing fancy.
> I don't put in the most effort. Well, I did at first, but since then I have man-
> aged to level off, I don't put in as much effort and I just get decent grades.
> I think I'm doing fine.

Asked about his stress level around academics, Nick elaborated:

> Full disclosure, I don't really care about academics since I've come here.
> Like I'm doing fine and that's good enough for me. I have made a lot of good
> connections, met a lot of good people. I feel like it's about who you know
> at this point more than what you know. That's one of the biggest things I've
> learned here.

Similarly, John (Latino) told us that while he felt like he could be doing better
academically, "but then I realize, who cares about grades. The jobs I apply to
no one's asking me for my GPA, at this point I don't really care about grades.
I don't really read anymore, now I'm just trying to get out." Others, like Rico
(African American), told us they did enough academic work to facilitate
other, larger priorities—that is, being able to play the sport about which they
were passionate and that they hoped would bring them professional opportunities, whether as a player or in another capacity, after graduation.

This conceptualization of the role of academic work in mobility was
rarely expressed in our interview sample and only by respondents in Play
Hard geographies. Interestingly, this echoes what other sociologists show
are key differences between middle or upper socioeconomic status students
and lower socioeconomic status students: those with greater socioeconomic
advantages perceive social activities and connections as valuable resources
for post-college life and—crucially—are able to use them effectively even
in the face of lower grades. Lower-socioeconomic status students perceive
hard work, indicated high academic achievement and other human capital

related activities such as work experience, as more valuable.[6] We argue that first-generation students learn this networking-only approach from their wealthier peers within their geography who are themselves planning to draw on connections rather than grades.

Building these connections and learning this type of mobility approach depended on being able to "chill" together, in the words of many respondents. This mirrors the toolkit that Play Hard respondents are learning for later life networking—not only connections to peers and the shared jokes, habits, and memories that create ongoing bonds,[7] but also the understanding that social spaces and workspaces may be interrelated. As sociologist Annette Lareau points out, white-collar workplaces often bleed over into social life, with client dinners, happy hours, weekend golf, and the informal chatting that results in learning the ropes and perhaps forming bonds that link participants to new opportunities.[8]

This social connection is more complicated than it sounds and more difficult to achieve, because it involves subtle performances of status culture, which may explain in part why so few first-generation students in the NLSF sample (17%) are located in these geographies. While many "chill" activities involved simply sitting around and goofing off in a dorm room, locker room, or athletic field, some relied on being able to buy a round for the group out at a bar, to contribute to a pizza run, pay dues to a GLO, or buy the right clothes for different social occasions. Moreover, respondents seeking membership in these venues must be able to conform to the norms of behavior that are set by much wealthier peers and that include complex interactional performances that are classed and also often racialized and/or gendered, posing additional challenges for women and students of color. For example, performances of upper-class femininity are focused much more on appearance, clothing, and accessories than upper-class masculinity,[9] making it more difficult for lower-income women to access and find comfort in Play Hard spaces. For students of color, spending time in predominantly White, wealthy spaces may mean having to ignore, downplay, or otherwise cope with racial micro-aggressions and perhaps viewing friendships with White peers as temporary, strategic, or instrumental.

Change Over Time
These context-based identity expectations influence not only whether one builds ties but also the types of middle-class cultural practices one gains from these spaces. Overall, men, regardless of racialized position or ethnicity,

described a much easier time navigating upper-class masculine spaces, reported less class-based pressure to change, and found the changes they made to be more positive and less burdensome than women did. They reported developing maturity, ambition, and communication skills, with nearly all respondents noting improved vocabularies. Todd (White), for example, told us, "From high school to college, I definitely became a hard worker especially in school and [my team]. I also became more mature, I would say, in just being able to talk to people and holding conversations." Like Todd, many respondents noted increased confidence in holding conversations, a skill that is critical for networking. While a few men described changes to their physical appearance and wardrobe, they saw these changes, like their changes in speech, as a reflection of becoming more mature rather than someone else. As Jeff (Black) explained, "I guess I have matured a lot here, grown to be my own person—more independent. I guess my fashion style has reflected that." Like Jeff, men may be able to view these changes as positive rather than threatening because their connections to more affluent peers were built around engaging in more class-neutral hegemonic masculine rituals, such as playing sports and/or working out, drinking, and picking up women.[10]

While women in Play Hard geographies also described being more mature, nearly all described facing pressures to make wide-ranging and costly changes in their appearances to fit into their new peer groups. They spoke about needing "new wardrobes" (in the words of Kristen, White) to fit in and the pressure that came with trying to meet mainstream social expectations associated with the party scene and/or Greek Life.[11] Their location within a Play Hard geography thus brought both financial and also social pressure. Kristen, previously quoted, spoke in fairly positive terms about this. Asked how she had changed, she told us,

> I'm more preppy now and I don't wear t-shirts and jeans to class anymore, [laughter] so I've conformed a little bit, which is I don't know if that's a good thing or not but I have . . . I . . . basically got a whole new wardrobe at Thanksgiving freshman year. I just completely changed everything, and it's continued to change. I never—I would not have been able to see myself [like this] in high school.

While Kristen at least can laugh (if ruefully) about these changes, most female respondents in a Play Hard geography, especially women of color, spoke in more fraught terms. Maggie (Black) was the strongest example. Like

Kristen, Maggie had spent a lot of money her first year to better fit in. Unlike Kristen, she spoke with regret and even self-recrimination about those choices, but also told us that she continues to try to meet these standards:

> My freshman year, I had a really bad shopping habit. . . . I think it par-
> tially comes from, like, being overwhelmed and being like, "Oh my God,
> I need, like, better clothes or, like, I need to look cuter." And so, I spent a
> lot of money on, like, online shopping and then, now I definitely, like, plan
> out my paychecks. Well now, I just finished paying my last payment plan
> part of my sorority so, like, partially, it's, like, paying for that because mom
> and dad, if I even tried to explain to them what a sorority is, they're gonna
> be like, "Bitch, what? Like we're not paying for you to, like, hang out with
> people. Like that's stupid." So, I think that's usually the first thing that I'm
> trying to get out the way and then, groceries now that I'm not on a meal
> plan. Less on clothes now 'cause I just have realized how dumb I am. Ugh,
> I regret a lot of my purchases.

While Maggie describes being better at budgeting, the costs she chooses to cover are substantial. We also see the way that Maggie is very negative about herself, referring to "how dumb" she is and regretting her choices. Importantly, Maggie relates this directly to being part of Greek Life and to being a woman of color on a small, predominantly White campus:

> The pressures here definitely feel like, I've noticed my self-perception of
> myself, like, definitely changed. . . . I think this also comes with the whole
> identity of, like, being a part of Greek life and, like, going to social events
> where I definitely feel uncomfortable and, those things, like, aren't great,
> and I think the same thing goes for the romantic relationships and like
> being one of, like, what, 25 women of color on campus.

These "pressures" to fit in lead not only to Maggie's lowered self-esteem and "self-perception," they also result in a profound dislike of campus. Despite being part of a fun-oriented geography, Maggie does not seem to be enjoying the social aspect. Rather, she describes herself as "drained and . . . very tired" because of the pressures of being on campus and in this particular geography. She narrated a ritual of sorts that she has developed that seems to speak to this evocatively: "I don't know what happens to me but when I sit in the passenger [seat], you can ask everyone who's ever been in a car with me when I go home for break. I literally roll down the window and I yell, like, "Goodbye! Fuck everyone!" Because of these feelings of exhaustion, of feeling pressure to fit in with expensive norms and practices, a number of female respondents in Play Hard geographies ultimately opted to leave or reduced involvement in their sororities after several years and described their confidence and growth as coming from those difficult experiences.

Work Hard

Achievement-Focused Pathway

Rather than spending their time in leisure activities developing networks, students and their peers in Work Hard geographies were intensely focused on excelling in classes and gaining leadership roles in campus clubs. For them, building a strong transcript and resume of activities was the way to gain a foothold into the white-collar world. In essence, these respondents applied the same achievement-oriented model they used in high school. However, many felt that the stakes were higher and the pressure more intense because of the understanding that while high school achievements were about gaining access to college, college achievements are about the rest of one's life, about setting oneself up for success. The structure of Work Hard geographies reinforced this intensity and pressure: Respondents were largely friends with, and spent time around, peers who share those beliefs, creating a fishbowl effect.[12]

Work Hard students, not surprisingly, were most likely to talk about their academic skills and strong grades as what will get them a job. When asked whether HC set her up for success, Manesha (African American) describes what she has learned and points to "professors in like [my major] department." Carlos (Latino) spoke about valuing the "critical thinking, time management, and a whole list of skills and knowledge already come with the rigorous education at Hilltop." Work Hard students locate their post-college chances in the academic training they have received and prospectively attribute their successes to their academic work. This is, of course, what young adults are taught to look for in a college, and particularly in a liberal arts college or any selective campus: its academic rigor and its level of academic selectivity. The entry into such a space is largely academic in nature, and for these respondents, the exit out seems to be as well.

Part of the reason Work Hard students relied on their own achievement is because they expressed the most doubt about whether campus prestige and resources, such as the Career Development Center, would be able to (or would) help them secure employment. For example, Angela (Latina) reflected on whether the college has positioned her for success,

> Mmm, I think yeah? I'm gonna give a tentative yes because, like, the classes I take are really great and like, my, the classes I choose to take in Gender Studies and Education. They're really great and they really, like, help me with social justice activism and stuff but, like, there's not a lot of resources, like, in the Career Development Center for my interests. Like if you're not in the sciences or if you're not an econ major, it's really hard to really find anything.

Thus, rather than relying on networks or the institutionalized cultural capital of their alma mater's name recognition, respondents in a Work Hard geography, like Angela, rely on the same tools that had gotten them into college and the same tools that had supported them through their college lives, namely, achievement.

In particular, Work Hard students had doubts about networking and its link to post-college success. They understood the concept, but many did not see this as a meaningful option for themselves. First, forming connections to wealthier peers would cost money—whether spent on joining organizations, sharing social time together, or making sure to have the right clothes or other goods to relate. Several respondents in a Work Hard geography highlighted that this was prohibitive. Jack (Latino/multiracial), for example, told us that

> having a fake ID costs a shit-ton of money and going to, you know, bars to talk with upperclassmen frat guys and buy them drinks, that costs a lot of money. Buying the right clothes, that costs a lot of money. It's all this big show, and if you don't have money, you can't show yourself off as well.

Second, some respondents in a Work Hard geography also described feeling uncomfortable with the interactions they anticipated having as part of the social venues where networking with affluent peers takes place, whether at mainstream parties or Greek events. Brianna (African American) explained that while she sees the networking benefits, she saw joining a GLO as both unattainable and undesirable:

I feel like these organizations are very like exclusive so like you're very limited to um the people you interact with and your friends to a certain extent.
Also . . . I don't think it would be worth it in terms of like the dues you have
to pay, the monetary aspect of it. . . and also like. . . the pledging process. For
me, I don't think I could do it.

Similarly, Kaelin (Latina) spoke about the reasons that she is not likely to join
a sorority, despite knowing that they would provide social connections and
even having teammates in a sorority who recommend it. She told us, "Like
I definitely feel like that's not something that I would ever want to do 'cause
I always associate that with, um, more upper class. . . people." For Kaelin,
a place or activity that is "more upper-class" is not for her. Finally, in some
cases respondents were morally uncomfortable with the idea of networking,
and with the idea of developing connections for later use. For example, Jack,
whom we met previously, told us that although he wished he had done a
better job of making friends beyond the dorms, "networking feels like you
are taking" and makes him feel ill at ease.[13]

Respondents in a Work Hard geography, the second largest group in the
NLSF sample, were aware of the networking logic—aware that friendships
with a broad range of peers could offer connections for post-college use—
but, in the end, they gained little practice learning how to do it. Their
concerns about both the financial and the social costs highlight the ways that
a network pathway requires participants to develop essentially a new habitus, a new way of thinking about and interacting with the world, that is at
odds with their core values and identity. In the end, many lament losing out
of this opportunity. For example, Andrew (Black), a business major, told
us that like other students in his major, he wants a career in finance, but he
feels limited because he doesn't "have a family history of that. Or the whole
idea of networking and schmoozing it up with people. And the fact that
I don't party. You want to talk to alums, the first thing they ask is about the
[downtown bar]."

From one perspective, then, Work Hard respondents are not taking advantage of one primary potential benefit of a selective college—networking with
alumnae or through forming wide-ranging friendships that included more
wealthy and/or White students or joining campus organizations that promote social ties to large groups (such as GLOs or athletic teams). However,
social ties to co-ethnic peers are especially important for women of color.
They are associated with with increased "academic self-worth"[14] and overall

satisfaction,[15] and students more broadly benefit from close relationships with peers who provide close emotional support, especially around shared experiences or backgrounds.[16] In short, these ties are crucial for students and should not be underestimated.

Change Over Time

Although both Play Hard and Work Hard students are situated on a largely White, affluent campus, outside of the classroom setting, Work Hard students have less sustained interaction with this particular demographic. They therefore face different pressures to change or conform. Manesha (African American) illustrates this aptly: When asked whether she ever felt excluded on campus, she paused to think but responded, "Not really. I don't feel like I run in the circles to feel excluded because of my social class." She went on to explain how many of her closest peers share her background and that among those peers—with whom she spends much of her time and who are the people she cares about on campus—she feels included.

Therefore, while Work Hard respondents similarly felt they had developed confidence and grown both personally and intellectually during college, they reported less pressure to change their appearance, and the changes they did make were much smaller. As with Play Hard respondents, these appearance-related pressures were felt more acutely by women than men, and women were more likely to specify that they could not afford to do so, reflecting a sense of limitation if not distress. Kaelin (Latina), for example, told us that she "still dresses like a middle school kid:"

I still dress the same. I still dress like a middle school kid, you know. Like those skinny jeans and all of that, you know, like, . . . I don't wear leggings. I don't have the body type for leggings. Um, I don't wear, like, rain boots. You know, I don't have any, like, high-fashioned anything, you know. I shop at thrift stores. I have, like, no name-brand clothing or anything like a lot of students do here.

Similarly, Rebecca (White) told us that "this is what I would wear in high school pretty much. The same style of clothing. . . . I guess there's no way I would attain the level of dress that is like the Hilltop dress." For both Rebecca and Kaelin, college did not bring big shifts in style to try to fit in or assimilate, because the costs were simply too high. The description of dressing like one did in high school seems to imply a lack of some expected development, a devaluation of style by associating it with one's younger years.

A second pattern among female respondents in a Work Hard geography was to note that they had not changed much but to concede they had made shifts in style—as Brittney (African American) put it, "just a little bit"—to try to fit in. Angela (Latina), for example, told us that she did not want to spend a lot of money, but "I've noticed, like, I've bought more sweaters. I've bought more, like, leggings, which is actually an investment for me 'cause regular pants don't fit me." Her phrasing of "I've noticed" suggests that she is reflecting back on something that happened slowly over time, rather than the more deliberate and early efforts of women in a Play Hard geography. Similarly Briana (African American) told us that she has become "more preppy" and that "sometimes I catch myself putting on certain things and I'm just like 'No, Briana, look again.'"

Finally, several women reported that they made less effort on campus because their social lives are so low key—there's no one to bother dressing up for, particularly because the dating pool feels inaccessible. Samirah (African American) mused in response to our question about how her style had changed,

> Style? I became basic. Like I used to dress up in high school but I . . . maybe it's because I'm stressed and also cause everybody else is wearing sweatpants and leggings so I feel like I can get away with it too now. Um yeah, like I've definitely like toned down. I used to wear make up a lot. I don't wear makeup anymore. Like I never wore glasses. [Now] I'm wearing glasses. I have my contacts and I still haven't opened them.

Perhaps most indicatively, Samirah told us that at home she makes more effort even for family: "I'll comb my hair for my mom. I'm not going to comb my hair for nobody here if I don't feel like it." For many women of color, campus romance and hook-up markets were discouraging enough to minimize their efforts, while countervailing pressures to fit in with wealthier White peers also meant sometimes spending more money on different, preppier shoes, leggings, bags, or other items. These latter efforts were more widespread among Play Hard women, but engaged in selectively by Work Hard women, suggesting the strength of the normative peer style: Even women highly critical of campus culture found themselves feeling at least some pressure to conform.

Multisphere

Networking and Achievement

Like Play Hard students, Multisphere respondents learned how to use the network mobility framework. However, they also believed that academics were highly important, and their descriptions of what they gained from attending HC included discussion of both. For example, when asked how HC set her up for success, Leslie (White, female) points to both the social and academic benefits of her education:

> I think the social aspects of HC helped me gain more confidence. I think also, even though my job didn't end up being through HC network connections, I think just talking to people in a variety of careers. I also think trying different things and learning about different things. I think in general I've had to work hard here.

Leslie's college engagement ran the gamut, including joining a sorority, working in the dean's office, and serving as a research assistant in a professor's lab. Each was important, but perhaps most emblematic of her geography, Leslie describes the advantages of trying out a range of experiences during college.

Because Multisphere students were tapped into the mainstream social centers of campus, they also gained intimate knowledge and practice with how upper-class social networks operate. These respondents are gaining knowledge about what we might call the rules of the game in white-collar work settings, to which many of them aspire after graduation. Jordan (African American, male) is perhaps the strongest example. Jordan, a member of a GLO, sees a large portion of his college education as being outside of academic work—although that has been important and is something he values strongly. When he talks about what he has learned in college, part of what he describes is about learning how the social world works, how this opened up his eyes: "I see a lot of people who are being plugged into positions, very very highly paid positions. This is how things works, this is how people got to where they are now."

One notable aspect of Jordan's thinking here is the way that he understands that this kind of exclusive access—obtained through membership in a small circle of primarily wealthy peers—is not "fair" (as we saw in Chapter 5). Indeed, Jordan stressed that he had had to "wake up" to the realities of his peers' advantages in their academic preparation and what this meant for him: He reflected that he would tell his high school self to figure out the way things work. . . . People's test scores are so high on the SAT because they [took] study drugs in the junior year of high school. They lied to get extra time, and because of that, things are stacked against you in a way you can ever imagine. Because of that, you don't have to time slack.

Jordan has developed a strong sense of a different kind of hidden curriculum: Although it is not "fair," he understands that people from advantaged backgrounds have access to invisible resources. As a graduate from Hilltop, he will now also have access to some insider advantages, and he plans to draw on those after college. Like Jordan, Multisphere respondents had overall positive expectations about post-college life and the role that networking would play, and many had begun conceptualizing college activities as venues for developing connections.

Change Over Time
What is unique about Multisphere students is that they do not have their eggs all in one basket—that is, their connections were not located exclusively in one peer culture. Unlike Work Hard and Play hard students, these respondents had friends who valued both academics and mainstream social life. Moreover, these students were involved in the broadest array of extracurricular activities, from sports to the arts, exposing them to peers with a range of interests and priorities. Thus, they did not feel the same types of pressure to tightly conform to one particular group. As described in Chapter 5, however, very few first generation students are located in a Multisphere geography.

Multisphere students, much like those in other geographies, saw themselves as more mature, but when they spoke about changes to their personal style, it was more a matter of fact or part of a broader perceived process of maturation, rather than a source of self-questioning or something in which they wished they could participate. Anna (White), for example, told us that she had changed "materialistically, definitely." She elaborated to say, "Hilltop has a sense of nicer dress and presentation than where I grew up, so that's definitely influenced how I dress." Roy (Latino) also spoke about dressing differently: He told us,

In terms of how I dress, I think I got a couple more formal pieces of clothing. I think it's because my uncle, he used to dress like that too. I feel like I can do it here. In the city you have to be more urban and shit, but it's different here.

As part of this shift from "urban" dressing to "more formal," he sold his sneaker collection and reflected, "I guess I just removed certain things, I didn't really add on." For Jordan (African American, male), this shift in style is part of a greater feeling of comfort, safety, and even creativity on campus as compared to home. While at home he felt constrained to fit in with an "urban" style, and he also felt less safe in his home neighborhood. He told us that at home he stayed in most of the time, reading books and not going out. By contrast, on campus he goes to music performances and dancing because he feels "sheltered." He can develop these new interests alongside his shifting personal style.

Multisphere students also were more likely to use language about expanded horizons, specifically—seeing more of the world, being more open to the world—than other respondents when describing their change. For example, Emma (White) told us, "This is probably gonna sound like super clichéd but I feel like my world views changed a little bit." She spoke about noticing these differences when going home: "It felt like I was like, like everybody had changed and then I realized like, 'Oh, wait. No. It was me.'" Emma had grown up in a small homogenous town. Going to Hilltop had not only taken her outside that town, but allowed her to meet people different from herself, go on study abroad, and generally shift her thinking:

> Like a lot of people where I live, kind of like don't leave that general area, so coming back and talking about like, "Oh, like I was in like France for spring break and, like, doing this, and like, traveling here, and like, seeing, like experiencing all of these different kinds of things." Like, "Oh yeah, I've eaten food here or like done this kind of activity here."

Thus, for Emma and others in a Multisphere geography, the changes they saw in themselves were positive, rather than threatening, and directly linked to growth they experienced through attending HC.

Disconnected

Self-Reliance
As we saw in Chapter 6, respondents in Disconnected geographies—the largest proportion of first generation students on selective campuses—have only a few, often unstable connections to friends and peers on campus. Some

respondents in this geography also struggled with their coursework, unable to find their stride either academically or socially. Both avenues for mobility, then, seem uncertain. And, as opposed to those in some other geographies, they often do not have models of what a successful strategy might look like through friends who have already graduated and obtained jobs.

Given this impasse, respondents in Disconnected geographies were the most likely to report that they planned to rely on themselves, and perhaps only themselves, as the means of post-college success. For example, Maria (Latina/multiracial) told us, "I think that this institution has given me the skills for future success in my career, however I don't think it has set me up with connections or anything that they brag about to help with this success, which is OK because I'll do it myself." Maria locates post-college success in her own efforts: what *she* will need to do—as she has always done—to look out for herself. While a few Disconnected respondents reported that they believed that the institutional resources of the campus—the Career Development Center and other formal types of support—were helpful, only one respondent in this geography expected that the alumnae or social networks promised by the college would support their opportunities after college, and only one described relying on their academic learning.

Respondents in this geography also expressed some doubts about what they would get from Hilltop as an institution. Clark, for example, told us:

> I can't lie and say that I don't sometimes doubt the benefits of a liberal arts education because I mean like right now, a student who went to a tech school, or who went to a more industrial based school knows probably more technical information than I do. They probably can tell me more things about science than I know. But it takes me having faith in the sense that I, in the long run, will be a quicker learner and I will able to advance more quickly than my friends who have gone to more industry-based schools. So that kind of gives me a little bit of uncertainty with how well HC has prepared me. But then I look at the success of Hilltop alumni and I look at all these amazing opportunities and networking possibilities and things that I have already accomplished. And then I always wonder how I could ever think I should have gone somewhere else.

As we see here, Clark seems to go back and forth between wanting concrete skills and having faith in what he is promised. Like many other respondents, and especially those in neither GLOs or athletic teams, he has only abstract examples of the ways Hilltop's elite cultural and social capital can help him get access to later opportunities. Earlier in the interview, Clark credited his own sense of "drive" as key to his future success. This back and forth between highlighting networks versus hard work illustrates the internal contradictions many respondents feel in not being able to rely on networks themselves but being surrounded by a discourse that highlights the value of those networks.

Disconnected respondents were aware of the possible network benefits and wistful about the ways such opportunities were opaque and/or inaccessible to them. One primary example here is Greek Life. Although only one Disconnected student successfully joined a GLO, most spoke about the benefits of both current emotional-community connections and long-term networking connections. For example, Maria (Latina/multiracial) recounted that she "[had] considered joining, but I know I wouldn't be able to balance all of my jobs and schoolwork with their activities. I also know that I wouldn't be able to afford the dues and stuff you have to pay. But I would have loved to join because of the connections and I feel like I would have a good job by now." Strikingly, Maria—who has little belief that Hilltop has provided her with the tools for success and that she will largely need to make connections on her own—feels that had she been able to join a sorority, those connections would have helped her "have a good job by now." Unlike respondents in Work Hard geographies, who spoke about why they did not want to join, respondents in a Disconnected geography regretted ways that GLOs were inaccessible to them because of their socioeconomic background.

The two Disconnected students who attempted to rush and join a GLO in search of these benefits were left deeply disappointed. Lauren joined a sorority because "I wasn't making very good friends and I was like well maybe I can try this . . . in the hopes of making more friends and connections on campus um and because my sorority seems to be like the nice people house." Lauren had already joined a pick-up sports team, but found that the friendships on her team were superficial, and although she was initially excited about her sorority, overtime, she was becoming dissatisfied with those relationships as well as the cost. Similarly, Clark viewed rushing as something he felt he needed to do to fit in on campus and identify job opportunities. He was not accepted, however, and the process left him disenchanted: "The interactions seemed completely fake, but I was there because I felt socially obligated to go along with it. For some, Greek life serves the purpose they hoped it would, but for me, it wouldn't." Overall, Disconnected students desired social connections and the benefits that accrue from them, but could not find a successful avenue into real friendships that could later transform into a post-college network.

Change Over Time

As we saw in Chapter 6, Disconnected described their intentional and continued efforts to fit in and gain social mobility during and after college. However, they did not reap the kinds of social rewards they were seeking. As in other geographies, gender played an especially important role as respondents sought to fit better into what they understood to be appropriate presentations of middle-class femininity.

Maria (Latina/multiracial), for example, recounted,

> I came in freshman year and I had a nose piercing, used to wear my favorite brand of sneakers, Jordans, and dressed with my own style how I used to dress back at home. But I noticed how I stuck out. I stopped dying my hair all these cool colors and went natural. I don't really wear sneakers unless they are Nike Roshes. I wear Sperry's now which a new thing. I don't have any piercings anymore. So I tried to fit in more hoping I would look less intimidating and would make friends. I also stopped cursing so much. I tend not to use slang that much anymore. Hilltop has definitely changed me, but the changes were conscious. I knew that I was making them in order to fit in.

Despite this, Maria was still unable to make lasting friendships until late in her college career.

While respondents in every geography talked about code switching or making shifts between home and school, respondents in a Disconnected geography were most likely to talk about people at home thinking they had changed too much, getting "above" themselves in class terms or in some cases, becoming "too White." These accusations made personal and intellectual change much more fraught and ambivalent, leaving respondents not as clear about whether their growth was positive or negative. Respondents in this geography were also deeply concerned about appearing "snobby" to friends and family at home or seeming to have changed too much. Here we can look to Maria's experience. She told us that when she goes home,

> I have to, like, take it down a notch and stop acting all "scholarly". They look at me weird when I bring up a topic and discussion that they would

rather not talk about. Um, I used slang more. I don't really police my behavior as much. I do this because I get the "oh you think you're better because you went to college" from people or "you think you know everything." And I don't like making people feel belittled in any type of way.

Respondents in other geographies did sometimes mention this worry, or at least the possibility. They did not describe it as an active threat, however. Bernard, for example, who was in a Play Hard geography, told us about how his family teases him: "Like my family will throw around jokes like, oh you don't fuck with us no more." However, he quickly adds, they are only joking and are happy for him to be at a good college. Their teasing is not a reprimand or an underhanded critique of the ways he has changed. For students in Disconnected geographies, the shift from school to home was perhaps more fraught because the changes they made, whether intentional or unintentional, seemed to be less welcome and even cause for derision at home.

These accusations might also feel especially threatening because for some Disconnected respondents (although not all), home remained a much more comfortable place than campus. Losing a feeling of belonging at home would therefore have been very threatening. Erica (White) spoke at length about how much better she feels at home. She told us,

> I'd say I'm happier at home 'cause I don't have classes to worry about, and I can focus on like things that I like doing outside of . . . cooking and like exercising and like, I don't know, I'm, like, more conscious of other people. Like I take care of my family members a lot. I go grocery shopping and all that, so I'm like, I don't know, very like motherly, my responsibilities are much different. So yeah, I just feel like more like in my zone when I'm home.

As we saw in Chapter 6, campus is not her "zone" because it does not provide meaningful opportunities for Erica to feel competent and connected. While students in other geographies found some way to identify shared interested around which to build a community, Disconnected students remained on a proverbial island with only the dominant campus culture against which to compare themselves. Work Hard students also felt alienated from the larger student body, but they were able to carve out spaces to be with others who shared at least part of their backgrounds, reducing some of these pressures to conform and therefore making campus somewhat more manageable.

Conclusion

This chapter shows that while first-generation respondents may be exposed to middle-class cultural knowledge and peers on selective campuses, the process of gaining new social ties and cultural practices is not automatic or without cost. First-generation students share a number of perceptions and experiences in common and may come to campus with particular plans and aspirations in place, but the approaches they see to attaining that success are also patterned by geography and suggest stratified pathways—and potentially stratified outcomes. Campus geographies provide gateways to particular types of social and institutional ties that offer different types of resources. This includes strategies for obtaining post-college success and cultural repertoires that signal employability and talent to white-collar employers.

Play Hard respondents expect to succeed by using network resources, and learn to socialize and relax with middle and upper socioeconomic status peers—the coin of the realm. By contrast, Work Hard students learn to double down on their studying, aware that the social or situational venues required for a network approach are untenable to them. They emphasize the academic route to success, the path that has supported them into and through college. These respondents also expressed the most doubt about whether the campus could or would support their success, and this may stem from a discordance between how they want to achieve and the dominant institutional message about what success looks like and how one is supposed to obtain it. Multisphere respondents acquired networking cultural practices but also emphasized the importance of the learning that happened inside and outside the classroom. Respondents in Disconnected geographies were at a loss socially and, often, academically. They were more likely than respondents in other geographies to talk about needing to rely on themselves for their future outcomes. Although some also expressed a desire to connect with the campus in ways prescribed by the network approach, they gained little or no experience doing so. Importantly, two-thirds of the first-generation NLSF sample are located in campus geographies without strong connections to cross-class peers and social worlds.

The variations we tracked over the previous four chapters matter not only during college, but also as respondents begin to think about how to capitalize on their college experiences in their adult lives. Understanding these differences should shape college approaches to supporting first-generation students, who may have not only a range of tools at their disposal depending on their college experiences but also a range of beliefs and attitudes about whether and how to use those tools and about where success will come from. This schism is important because this tells us that while first-generation students understand the concept and mechanics, they may still choose not to participate or have uneven opportunities to practice these skills. Colleges should not count on students accessing informal learning and need to step up the formal options.

Notes

1. Lareau, 2003.
2. Rivera, 2016.
3. Rivera, 2016, p. 1007.
4. Khan, 2010.
5. Armstrong and Hamilton (2013) develop a similar analytical focus on the role of partying in college experiences, considering who is able and unable to participate in this dominant social activity. They describe the "party pathway" through college and into post-college life, noting that for women from socioeconomically advantaged families, a college enrollment focused on social activities may be neutral or even helpful because they can secure job connections through family or a wide network of peers developed through those social activities. However, for women without socioeconomic advantages, participating in a party pathway may be alienating or simply prohibitive in college and likely will not pay off after college because they cannot draw on parents' social networking or financial support.
6. Armstrong and Hamilton, 2013; Stuber, 2009, Martin, 2012.
7. Milner, 2004.
8. Lareau, 2003; see also Rivera (2016) on the value of social knowledge in obtaining jobs.
9. Stuber, Klugman, and Daniel, 2011; 438.
10. Stuber, Klugman, and Daniel, 2011; Chase, 2008; Kimmel, 2008.
11. As described in Chapter 3, first-generation Play Hard students are slightly more economically advantaged than those in other geographies, but importantly, all first-generation students, regardless of geography, come from significantly less-resourced households than their continuing-generation counterparts.
12. Aleman (2000) and Baker (2015) similarly find that friendships among college women of color often support and reinforce academic strengths.
13. Similarly, Walker (1995) finds that working-class friendships are based on high expectations of interdependence and reciprocity, while middle-class respondents'

friendships were based on shared leisure. Expectations of taking without clearly being able to give back therefore might therefore violate established expectations about what it means to be a friend.

14. Aleman, 2000: 145.
15. Baker, 2015.
16. See, for example, McCabe's "tight knitters" (2018).

8

Conclusion

Our analyses offer a number of important takeaways. The most fundamental is simply that first-generation students have a wide range of experiences at college. Upon enrollment, students are not entering a cohesive college space, but rather entering into smaller campus geographies characterized by distinct peer cultures as well as academic, extracurricular, and social engagement.

Our second key takeaway is that while students' individual preferences and experiences come into play as they make friends and decide how to spend their time, their options are conditioned to a large degree not only by the context of a predominantly White and wealthy campus, in which being first-generation and/or a student of color places one into a minority status, but also by the college's administrative and social structures. These institutional structures codify students not only into categories of first-generation or continuing-generation, but also in racialized and gendered terms that link students to particular programmatic opportunities such as Summer Bridge.

Finally, we show how respondents gain informal social knowledge—accrue particular tools, resources, and inclinations—through their campus geographies. These may be more or less helpful both in college and as they prepare for post-college life. They also have both relative advantages and challenges that stem from these locations and their intersectional racialized, gendered statuses. Let us briefly elaborate on each of these findings.

First-Generation Students Are Not a Cohesive Group

We began the book by describing the first-generation student population that attends selective colleges and universities in the United States and how they are collectively different from their continuing-generation peers, who are the majority demographic of these campuses. While both groups excel in academics and extracurricular activities during high school, first-generation students were situated in largely unengaged school climates surrounded by a handful of other academically oriented peers. Because these students often

Geographies of Campus Inequality. Janel E. Benson and Elizabeth M. Lee, Oxford University Press (2020). © Oxford University Press. DOI: 10.1093/oso/9780190848156.001.0001.

don't have parents who could help them with the college process, let alone launching into a career with advice and/or networks, first-generation students often needed to be self-starters and to rely on fewer resources in high school than continuing-generation students. By contrast, they see most of their college peers as having that support through family connections, and they perceive this to be an important difference.

Despite these collective similarities, the most important takeaway of this book is that there are significant and meaningful differences among first-generation students along intersectional lines. First-generation college students have uneven experiences both inside and outside of the classroom that, in turn, shape how they approach post-college opportunities. Campus geographies, where and with whom students spend their time, are a central mechanism in this stratification process. These peer contexts, created and re-inforced in part by institutional structures, powerfully shape the ways first-generation college students from different race and gender positions invest in and experience college life, from academic engagements and study habits to extracurricular and social life. It is in these smaller contexts where students also develop cultural models for upward mobility. Moreover, students find varied levels of comfort and belonging within campus geographies that support and/or challenge them as students.

Within scholarly and popular literature, and in campus programming and discourse, however, first-generation students are generally treated as a cohesive whole, in terms of their outcomes, needs, and, by implication, their identities. Such treatments are far too broad. Rather, this book speaks to a much more complicated process whereby students' intersectional identities and preferences work along with institutional structures to sort first-generation students into one of several small contexts that then lead to different types of connections with faculty, peers, extracurricular activities, and social engagements.

Consistent with previous research[1], this book shows that large numbers of first-generation students have trouble finding strong sources of connection on selective campuses, but this is not the entire story. We also find first-generation students in Play Hard and Multisphere geographies are deeply engaged with more affluent peers in Greek Life and other party-oriented social scences. Their relative comfort levels on campus and broad friendship circles contrast with many findings that show first-generation students as isolated and dissatisfied.[2] While one take on these students' experiences might simply be that they are exceptions—they certainly represent a smaller percentage of first-generation students—we see their experiences as significant because they highlight the potential range of ways that first-generation students can be more fully included on selective campuses.

Moreover, given their struggles on campus one might assume that Disconnected students are the most economically disadvantaged among first-generation students. We find, however, that this is not the case. There are only marginal socioeconomic differences among first-generation differences. Indeed, the largest socioeconomic differences are between first- and continuing-generation students. One might also expect that Disconnected students spend the most hours working for pay, a key explanation for student isolation. We find that Work Hard students, however, devote the most time to work. As we will discuss in the next section, Disconnected students have access to fewer institutional bridges to inclusion than other first-generation students.

Our interview and survey samples also highlight racialized and gendered patterns in both the geographies that respondents occupied and their abilities to fit comfortably within them. Some of these racialized and gender patterns cut across geography. For example, men and women of color shared concerns about being positioned as a representative of their putative community or called out by a faculty member—or, by contrast, about being ignored by a faculty member. White respondents felt discomfort for class-related reasons, but were more often able to blend in or pass, despite a sense of difference or even alienation. Overall, women more readily identified connections through academic and nonathletic extracurricular activities whereas sports, gaming, and leisure were more common gateways for men; men who did not wish to connect with same-gender peers through traditionally masculine scripts struggled to find male friends. Women of color felt excluded from the dating and sexual markets on campus, while White men, women, and men of color did not. Women often felt unsafe in fraternity houses—even those who regularly attended Greek events—and women of color worried about themselves and male friends of color being mistreated because of their racialized identities.

While these commonalities are important, one aim of this book is to avoid essentializing around race and gender. Just as we do not treat being first-generation as determinative, we do not consider race or gender to be the "reason" that students move through college with such different experiences. Moreover, we are not making an argument that first-generation students *should* have more friendships with wealthier students or that students of color who have primarily same-race friendships are segregating themselves from White students. To the contrary, our respondents were in almost constant contact with White and wealthier students in classrooms and shared campus spaces, through the very ethos of the college, and, in some cases, through their social choices. Rather, we emphasize the role that the campus plays in shaping and contextualizing students' varied experiences and choices. In other words, the issue at hand is not students' reactions to campus or choices in managing their time at Hilltop. Rather, it is that the campus needs to be less uncomfortable for first-generation students whether they are students of color or White students. Moreover, the campus needs to carefully think about its role in categorizing and sorting students and the resources made available to students depending on those decisions. This brings us to the second fundamental takeaway, which is the role of the institution.

Importance of Structure and Role of the Institution

Colleges provide the infrastructure underlying these campus geographies and their peer cultures, shaping students' pathways into and through campus. Students arrive on campus not only with their own particular backgrounds and goals but also through variously structured programs that unevenly serve first-generation students. Students of color are more likely to arrive through Summer Bridge programs than White students, and male students are more likely to arrive through recruited athletic programs than female students. These entry points, in turn, lead to different types resources and connections: Students who are recruited to athletic teams often arrive with a lengthy preseason, getting to know older students and forming cross-demographic ties. Students participating in Summer Bridge similarly arrive weeks before the semester begins for a pre-orientation that emphasizes academic work and are positioned in contact with peers who share a similar background.

We find this especially notable in contrasting the two most prevalent geographies among first-generation students, Work Hard and Disconnected. While students in both geographies are either unable to or uninterested in engaging in the mainstream social scene, nearly all Work Hard students participated in a lengthy Summer Bridge program that connected them to faculty members and demographically similar peers. We argue that without these early connections to close friendships and to the advising and academic resources that allowed them to become closer to institutional insiders—that is, those who knew how to get support when needed—Work Hard students would have been similarly disconnected. Indeed, we suspect that one reason the qualitative sample had so few Disconnected students is because of HC's longstanding, robust SB program. However, that some Disconnected students were not well-served by their own orientation experiences also shows that institutional programs and other guided entry points can increase but not guarantee inclusive pathways to connections.

Structure can help us understand students experiences, but is not the whole story: Student social dynamics around race, status, and power remain in play. Among those who did not enter college through institutionalized entry points, White women seemed best able to still access the Play Hard geography that required (and offered) the greatest levels of cross-class inter-action. We also see the power and value in the close, protective communities created by Work Hard students that offered an alternative to the mainstream White and wealthy party scene. For those located in this geography, their ties offered an oasis but not a strong means of developing networks with cross-class peers. By contrast, for women of color who participated in the Play Hard geography, their friendship ties did not shield them from the emotional and financial stresses of trying to "keep up with the Joneses." Moreover, they felt the least comfortable and satisfied in this geography, suggesting they may not reap the same benefits from participating as men and White women. This again highlights the contextual importance of race and gender.

Finally, of course, we see that students also exercise their own agency: Disconnected students keep seeking connections despite early disappointments; women, and to a lesser extent, men of color, in the Play Hard geography stick with it despite misgivings or leave their Greek Letter Organizations because they become untenable. However, we need to be able to think about students making choices not only based on their individual preferences or background but also based on the available social world, the dominant social structure, and the ways in which they have been invited into campus with particular opportunities and resources.

Hidden Curricula and Social Learning

Finally, we show that these geographies place students in contact with others who embody and reinforce a particular orientation toward campus life.

Geographies are the spaces in which students learn the hidden curricula for potentially traversing class boundaries through white-collar jobs and social life after college. As we show in Chapter 7, simply broadcasting the importance of networking is not enough. First-generation students must learn how to perform the subtle interactions involved in this middle-class cultural form of communication through ongoing practice. Importantly, this practice often happens in more informal leisure settings, such as hanging out over drinks or playing ping pong, where norms of behavior are often set by their more affluent (and White) peers. In this way, a student's ability to locate and navigate these more casual interactions that typically take place in Play Hard or Multisphere geographies shape whether students learn the process of networking, with potentially long-term implications. Notably, only about one-third of first-generation students had the opportunity to practice these skills. Campuses need to make this process more formally available for those students who do not have opportunities to engage in it within their peer circles.

In addition to networking, campus geographies also offer different pathways and orientations toward faculty mentoring relationships. While these relationships can be an important source of academic, social, and professional support both during and after college,[3] first-generation students often miss out on these opportunities. Sociologist Anthony Abraham Jack shows in his recent book that while first-generation students, especially those who attend public schools, are socialized to believe that faculty and other authority figures "should be treated with deference and left unburdened by their questions and needs," their more affluent peers, who have more experience and comfort interacting with teachers and adults, often feel "entitled" to faculty time and resources.[4]

Although this pattern initially applied to most first-generation students in our study, those with access to institutionally supported links to faculty through Summer Bridge, faculty research, and other sustained engagements developed strong relationships and learned why they are important. As Anthony Abraham Jack argues, the "My door is always open"[5] policy is simply not enough to cultivate faculty–student relationships, and institutions and faculty need to do more to provide opportunities for sustained and meaningful faculty contact, especially outside of class and in the first year.[6]

What Happens Next?

Respondents used different types of approaches to plan for their post-college lives and, more specifically, about how to locate jobs. Students in the Play

Hard geography learned to use a networking strategy, reflecting the predominant advice provided by Hilltop and adhering to the idea that this was one key benefit of attending this highly selective college. Respondents in the Work Hard geography, although they were aware of the push to network, relied on their academic achievements to support their post-college goals. Multisphere students drew on both academics and networking, and Disconnected students, the largest group in the sample, expected to rely on neither approach, but rather on themselves.

Recent sociological work suggests that first-generation students may not benefit as much as they hoped from any one of these strategies. On the one hand, it is not clear that Play Hard students will be able to draw effectively on the tool kits they have amassed.[7] These students might be overly optimistic about the job search process and how far their new networks will take them after graduation. Research by sociologists Elizabeth Armstrong and Laura Hamilton reveal that a network approach often works best when students have parents who can financially support them as they find their feet in new locales and supplement students' campus network connections with their own.[8] Less advantaged students—like the respondents in this book—cannot rely on these supports.[9] Indeed, other work shows that first-generation graduates of similar selective colleges report being disappointed in the actual experience of using their college's resources after college.[10] Although selective campuses actively market their networks as a key advantage of attendance, this book shows that students have uneven access to these networks and the resources required to fully take advantage of them.

On the other hand, there are no guarantees that grades will provide the benefits that Work Hard students anticipate. Audit research suggests that this investment approach will not yield the strongest post-college return for women and may be particularly detrimental for women of color. Sociologist Natasha Quadlin shows that women who achieve at a "moderate" academic level, rather than the highest achieving women, have the strongest labor market outcomes because they are perceived by employers as having the best social skills and are rated highest on likeability.[11] The highest achieving women are often overlooked because employers have concerns about their social skills, "likeability," and "personality." These concerns are rarely expressed about male candidates regardless of their academic performance. We might also think about ways that "likeability" is assessed and how class-coded forms of likeability or sociability may be learned. For respondents in the Work Hard and Disconnected geographies, these will be difficult to attain: Shared leisure time may be not only expensive but also rely on classed (and gendered, racialized) interactional forms learned more easily or fully through Play Hard or Multisphere geographies. Moreover, there is strong evidence that white-collar hiring processes continue to be substantially shaped by socioeconomic factors like cultural capital markers.[12] This suggests that women, especially (and men to a lesser extent) in the Work Hard geography may actually reap negative outcomes from their hard work, and men in this geography will not gain from their academic outcomes.

Men—especially White men—are more likely than women to be embedded within campus geographies that value and reward networking. Often, but not always, this investment strategy comes with a cost to academic performance. While some may be concerned about the post-college labor market costs of this strategy, audit study results suggest that men's college achievement is not linked to employer perception of their capacities.[13] While our respondents should certainly be proud of themselves for their achievements in and outside of the classroom, and while they have obtained a credential that continues to be among the strongest economic dividing lines, they may not be as well equipped to gain career success in highly paid white-collar jobs as they desire.

Implications for Selective Campuses

What can campuses do to mitigate the stratified experiences and outcomes discussed here? First, administrators must examine the role that campuses play in creating different types of locations through which students make friends and seek support and the ways they may not be accessible or comfortable for all students. Our work highlights that college campuses must consider the ways in which first-generation students may be differently marginalized by campus structures and cultures. Here we have focused especially on early institutional pathways into campus in the forms of orientation programming.[14] However, campuses might also consider other institutional strategies for creating early on-ramps to meaningful connections through housing, learning communities, dining, support for student clubs and organizations, and even scheduling. As we learned from the success of Summer Bridge, institutions must also invest in infrastructure and resources to provide ongoing and sustained support beyond the first year. Of course, as other scholars have also highlighted, tackling these larger issues might also include questions about admissions' practices as well as the role of athletics and

Greek Life[15] on campus and to what degree colleges support or even permit these kinds of organizations. As institutions construct additional opportunities for connection and belonging, they should carefully consider their matrices of selection and their goals, as well as the categories and underlying assumptions being used.[16]

A more fundamental concern that underlies each of these is that selective and highly selective campuses, in particular, must improve their recruitment of low-income first-generation students and students of color. These campuses lag far behind others in educating the students who are the focus of this book, and they have not improved significantly over recent decades. According to a recent Pew Research Center Report, the percentage of undergraduates from lower-income backgrounds increased from 12% to 20% between 1996 and 2016, but only increased from 10% to 13% at the most selective institutions.[17] Campuses must improve outreach to lower-income schools and community-based organizations that work with low-income students, and invest in programs, such as the College Advising Corp and Questbridge, that connect underrepresented students with selective colleges and what they have to offer.

Chapter 2 showed how first-generation students had less college knowledge and were less able to go on campus visits; they also had fewer opportunities to seek advice from other students and adults who graduated college. Campuses need to pick up this slack through increasing recruitment opportunities, campus visits, and programming that supports the diverse needs of first generation students. These recruitment efforts need to be paired with expanding the diversity of campus staff and carefully considered institutional supports that do not end the first semester—access is not enough on its own. As one piece of this ongoing effort, campuses should recognize faculty mentorship and support for first-generation students as a meaningful form of campus service. This mentorship should not be limited to faculty members who are themselves first-generation, female, and/or faculty of color.

Second, administrators must take seriously the idea that first-generation is an intersectional category, more or less meaningful for individual students, and intertwined with other identities such as race, gender, and income. Although colleges and universities are increasingly recognizing social class and first-generation status as important aspects of students' lives, efforts stemming from that recognition need to develop more nuanced discussions of intersectionality. While we have focused on some of the ways that race and gender come into play, other dimensions may be as important or even more important, such distinctions among other marginalized racial and ethnic groups, immigration background, sexuality, or ability/disability. In short, simply having first-generation programming and support on campus is not sufficient. We argue that siloed efforts recognizing one aspect of marginalization, such class or race, will be largely incomplete without also considering how systems of power underlying campus structures are classed, raced, and gendered in ways that unevenly impact the experiences of students from multiply-marginalized communities. First-generation support systems and programming that have monolithic presentations and/or do not engage with the other issues shaping students' lives will miss substantial ways in which their needs vary.

Importantly, the ways that marginalized students experience campus is shaped not simply by the larger campus culture but also by how their identities are represented (or not) and understood (or not) within the smaller spaces that make up their everyday lives. In this way, campuses need to think about the campus culture that exists not simply on campus as a whole but also in the smaller spaces where students spend time. Our work shows that students feel most comfortable in spaces where they are understood and can be themselves.

Third, colleges must think especially strategically about not only student support services but also those intended to help usher students into post-college life. As we see in Chapter 7, respondents held fairly different ideas about how they would be able to become successful after college. While all understood that networks should theoretically provide connections to potential jobs, not all were engaged in developing their networks, and some had doubts about whether networks or the institution would support them at all. Even when students learn about the idea of networking, being from a low-income first-generation background may shift how that mechanism works. Students may be unsure about how to actually navigate the process of networking or simply feel uncomfortable with it. Moreover, although all were familiar with the Career Development Center, many felt that their services were not geared toward them or their interests. In fact, very few named the support services found there as beneficial. More commonly, first-generation students relied on themselves and focused their efforts on building their resumes through activities and achievement. While selective campuses have expanded and even boast about career-related services as a key benefit, campus administrators need to develop more specific efforts and programming that supports first-generation students, including tailored advising along with the earlier stages of internship support, mentoring programs, and so forth. Although not all first-generation students aspire to work in the white-collar world, colleges should equip them to make an informed choice; moreover, students' ability to prepare for that post-college option should not be constrained by class, gender, or race.

Final Thoughts

We are completing this book at a time when selective campuses both proclaim their diversity in terms of race and socioeconomic background and yet also remain homogenous in racialized and socioeconomic terms. Although college attendance for first-generation students have ticked up over time, it still is far below continuing-generation students. This remains a meaningful division: While there are public worries about the costs of college and whether a college degree is really necessary to gaining a job that pays a living wage, data continue to show that a four-year degree is significant and that adults with four-year college degrees have substantial economic advantages over those with high school diplomas only. Moreover, increases in first-generation college attendance are most pronounced in one- and two-year degree programs and in nonselective four-year campuses. While these programs are also valuable, selective and highly selective four-year campuses have higher rates of post-college job placement and graduate school admission. Questions about where students attend are therefore also significant.

However, we should also think about other contemporary contexts. Campuses remain places in which students experience threats and violence— both symbolic and physical— predicated on their gender and/or racialized social positions and class positions. Again, while race and gender matter everywhere, they are always contextualized: Women and people of color (and first-generation students) are othered on these campuses because of the ways campuses are and have been populated. We see news stories of African American students being reported by White peers or personnel to the police for napping in their own dorm's shared spaces or for simply sitting around in a campus building, and Latinx and Native American students face similar levels of discrimination. Affirmative action policies continue to be attacked through the court system. The #MeToo movement has brought to more public light the kinds of sexual harassment faced primarily by women, and campus sexual violence is an ongoing threat. Students of recent immigrant background or whose parents or grandparents may have been immigrants face threats of their own or family member arrests as the Deferred Action for Childhood Arrivals program is under long-term threat and as political system acts against communities of color through Immigration and Customs Enforcement and police.

As of May 2020, campuses are struggling with how best to serve students during the global pandemic. We are just beginning to understand how campus closures and shifts to online learning impact first-generation students and their families. First-generation students' lives have been especially disrupted, losing access to dependable internet, places to study, campus jobs, and on-campus support services. Many also face housing and food insecurity and an increased need to support family members.[18] While many selective campuses with strong endowments remain committed to providing student aid, how will they meet the unique needs of lower-income and first-generation students if students do not return to a physical campus in the fall? Moreover, summer bridge programs that target first-generation students have been moved online or canceled, and many campuses are planning virtual orientation events. How will campuses provide first-generating students with high-touch mentoring and opportunities for belonging in this new virtual world, especially as they face devastating budget cuts and uncertainty around student enrollment?

Taken together, these social dynamics create additional sources of stress for first-generation students. Although we have listed them separately, they are always experienced and caused intersectionally, reflecting social positions of race, class, and gender. When students need to manage these day-to-day tensions and threats, they are less able to focus on their studies, their friends, and their overall well-being.

Our findings highlight the ways that first-generation students at predominantly White selective institutions use different approaches to try to make the most of it. They are confronted by challenges both shared and geography-specific. We expose deeply rooted organizational practices that shape students' engagement on campus, and the ways that engagement in social, extracurricular, and academic spaces is profoundly influenced by class, race, and gender. It is important to begin developing policies that takes this variation—and many other forms—into account. We hope that our work helps make this possible.

Notes

1. Armstrong and Hamilton, 2013; Martin, 2012.
2. Stuber, 2009, 2011a; Jack, 2019; Landers, 2018.
3. Chambliss and Takacs 2014; Jack, 2019.
4. Jack, 2019: 82.
5. Jack, 2019: 80.
6. For a similar point, see Lee (2016) and Chambliss and Takacs (2014).
7. Armstrong and Hamilton, 2013.
8. Armstrong and Hamilton, 2013.
9. Whether students from lower-income backgrounds reap the same economic returns to a selective college degree as their more affluent counterparts is currently debated. While large-scale quantitative studies (i.e. Manzoni and Streib, 2019) generally find smaller class differences than qualitative work, a recent study by Pfeffer (2018) suggests that scholars may underestimate class differences by not considering the increasing role of wealth in intergenerational disparities. Although lower-income students from selective college may initially have somewhat similar earnings as their more affluent peers, they do not benefit from economic transfers that pay for initial start-up costs, such as housing, and reduce the need for college and other forms of debt.
10. Lee, 2016.
11. Quadlin, 2018.
12. For example, see Rivera, 2016.
13. Quadlin, 2018.
14. Chambliss and Takacs (2014) also find that pre-orientation and Summer Bridge programs, "high-contact" extracurricular activities, and dorms arrangements can be gateways to strong connection.
15. Hamilton and Cheng (2018) find that selective colleges with a greater Greek Letter Organizations presence have a wider class gap in graduation rates, suggesting that the organizational practices impact students' abilities to succeed. See also Armstrong and Hamilton, 2013; Stuber, 2011a.
16. For an example, see Charles et al.'s (2009, Chapter 8) discussion on constructing effective affirmative action policies.
17. Pew Research Center, May 2019, "A Rising Share of Undergraduates are From Poor Families, Especially at Less Selective Colleges." See also Chetty et al. (2017) for a similar discussion of slow growth in the percentage of lower income students at the most selective colleges despite efforts to increase enrollment and financial aid.
18. Casey, Nicholas, 2020.

Methodological Description

As described in Chapter 1, we employ a multimethod approach that pairs interviews with 64 first-generation students at one selective northeastern university with survey data from the National Longitudinal Study of Freshmen (NLSF). By employing these two rich data sources, we illustrate how first-generation student experiences within campus geographies play out on interrelated macro- and micro-levels. We provide a broad over-view of these geographies and their shared characteristics using survey data, and then we draw upon qualitative interview data to contextualize how these geographies fit within the larger campus social worlds, including status hierarchies and campus practices and how students themselves make sense of their own position within these divergent communi-ties. In this appendix, we more fully describe the data collection and analysis techniques.

Survey Sample

The survey analyses in this book use data from Waves 1, 2, and 3 of the NLSF, a proba-bility sample of approximately 4,000 students who entered 28 selective U.S colleges and uni-versities in the fall of 1999. Wave 1 was conducted during the fall of 1999 when students ($n = 3,924$) were in their first semester of college, Wave 2 was conducted in the spring of 2000 at the end of the first year of college, and Wave 3 was conducted in the spring of 2001 at the end of the second year.[1] As noted in Chapter 1, the NLSF oversampled students from racial/ethnic minority groups, allowing us to examine within-group differences among first-generation students.[2] We conceptualize first-generation college student in this book as those students who grew up in households where neither residential parent or caregiver graduated from a four-year college. We choose to focus on African American and Latinx students rather than other marginalized racial and ethnic groups because they share sim-ilar disadvantaged educational outcomes compared to White students,[3] and they make up a significantly larger proportion of first-generation college students.[4] Race/ethnicity is operationalized as a dichotomous variable, coded 0 for White and 1 for African American or Latinx. The sample includes a considerably small weighted percentage of African American and Latinx students, as shown in Table A.1, and recoding race in this way also provides more power to identify race-gender patterns, a key focus of this book. In Chapter 2, we restrict the sample to include White, African American, and Latinx students from both first-generation ($n = 718$) and continuing generation backgrounds ($n = 1,832$) to provide a comparison be-tween these two groups. In Chapters 3, 4, 5 and 6, however, we look at differences among first-generation students and restrict the sample to only these students.

Survey Measures and Analysis

In Chapter 2, we use a range of measures from Wave 1 to capture students' high school and family experiences, and we briefly describe them here. In addition to first-generation

Table A.1 Demographic Composition of Survey Sample (*N* = 2,550)

	% Entire Sample	% First-Generation	% Continuing-Generation
Black women	5	10	4
Latina women	5	11	4
White women	44	43	45
Black men	3	5	2
Latino men	5	9	4
White men	38	22	41
Total	100	100	100%

college status, we include several measures of family socioeconomic and household context. To capture family economic context, we include dichotomous variables for whether the respondent's family ever received public assistance and whether the household income falls below $35,000.[5] We also include dichotomous measures for whether the respondent applied for financial aid, received loans, and works for pay to finance college.

Family context measures include middle-class cultural capital and strictness of discipline. Middle-class cultural capital is measured using an additive index (α = 0.76) of the following indicators at aged 13 and 18, where 1 equals "often or very often," or otherwise zero. Aged 13 indicators include homework help; participation in parent–teacher conference; taken student to art museum, science museum, library, plays or concerts, or sporting events; domestic travel, international travel; or sent to educational camp during the summer. Aged 18 indicators include check if homework complete, met personally with teachers, helped with homework, taken student to plays or concerts or sporting events, domestic travel, or international travel. Strictness of discipline is measured using an additive index (α = 0.86) of the following indicators at aged 13 and 18 that are coded from zero ("never or strongly disagree") to 4 ("always or strongly agree"): punished for bad grades, punished for disobedience, limited time with friends, forbade respondent things when displeased, made life miserable when got poor grades.

We also include a number of measures of academic and extracurricular engagement in high school. High school academic indicators include grade point average, number of advanced placement courses taken, number hours studying per week, course difficulty (scaled 1–10, with 10 being "very difficult"), and plans to graduate and attend graduate school. Extracurricular indicators include dichotomous measures of activity participation in athletics, arts (drama, band, or dance), student government, volunteer work, media use (watching TV, listening to music, or playing video games) and working for pay, which are coded 1 if respondent participated "often" or "very often," and zero otherwise.

We capture high school environment by type of high school, students' evaluation of school quality, and students' exposure to disorder and violence. We measure high school type in two categories: public or private high school (private and religious). School quality includes dichotomous measures of student reports of the following dimensions as "excellent": school buildings, classrooms, audiovisual equipment, libraries, computers, teacher interest, teacher preparedness, strictness of discipline, fairness of discipline, overall school quality, public reputation of school, and school spirit.

We measure violence and disorder found within respondents' neighborhood and school contexts using the Seelin–Wolfgang weights[6] developed for the National Survey of Crime Severity (see Massey et al., 2003). Neighborhood disorder weighted index ($\alpha = 0.91$) captures students' exposure to homelessness, prostitution, drug paraphernalia, use of illegal drugs, public drunkenness, and graffiti at aged 6, 13, and 18. Neighborhood violence weighted index ($\alpha = 0.90$) includes students' exposure to gangs, selling of illicit drugs, physical violence, gunshots, stabbings, and muggings at aged 6, 13, and 18. School disorder weighted index ($\alpha = 0.90$) captures students' exposure to truancy, verbal abuse of teachers by peers, vandalism, theft, and use of alcohol, tobacco, and illegal drugs at aged 6, 13, and 18. School violence weighted index ($\alpha = 0.84$) includes measures of students' exposure to fighting, violence directed toward teachers, peers carrying concealed weapons (knives, guns), gang activity, and the presence of security guards and metal detectors at aged 6, 13, and 18.

High school peer group values were measured as dichotomous variables coded 1 if respondent reports that their "close friends think it is very important to" regularly attend classes, study hard, get good grades, finish high school, participate in religious activities, conduct community or volunteer work, play sports, hold a steady job, have a steady romantic partner, or be willing to party or get wild. We also include dichotomous measures of peer behavior, coded 1 if respondent reports that their "closest friends have": used illegal drugs or alcohol or had sex.

We measure college selection using questions that ask students to rate the importance of the following criteria from zero (not important at all) to 10 (very important): cost, financial aid, scholarships, sports program, academic support, recruitment efforts by school, course availability, athletic reputation, social prestige social life, theme dorms, distance to home, religious environment, campus safety, job placement record, graduate school placement, admissions' standards, comfort and size of own ethnic group, size of school, parents' connections to school, parents' opinions of school, and friendship with students or alumni.

At the end of Chapter 1, we generate four campus geographies using indicators measured in Wave 2 at the end of the first year of college. Although we can learn a lot about college student engagement by examining discrete indicators such as the number of friends or groups joined, hours dedicated to activities and studying, and how often students attend faculty office hours, campus geographies provides a more holistic perspective on campus engagement that identifies larger patterns of concurrent academic, social, and extracurricular pursuits. We include time use measures (hours per week) of studying, extracurriculars, partying, athletics, sleeping, employment, and volunteer work. Indicators of peer group values are based on questions that ask students to rate the importance from zero (no importance) to 10 (utmost importance) their "friends and close acquaintances at college" place on the following behaviors: be willing to party, get wild, work full-time, study hard, get good grades, and go on to graduate school. We make an additive index of peer academic values using the last three indicators ($\alpha = 0.79$). Faculty engagement is an additive index of five questions that ask students on a scale from zero (never) to 10 (always), the degree to which they ask professors questions in class, raise their hand during lecture when they don't understand something, approach professors after class to ask a question, meet with professors in their offices to ask about material they don't understand, and meet with professors to talk about other matters ($\alpha = 0.77$). Peer academic engagement is an additive index of three questions that ask students on a scale from zero (never) to 10 (always) the degree to which they engage with peers (α= 0.75). These indicators include studying with other students, organizing a study group, and seeking help from a classmate or friend.

The campus geography framework emerged inductively from the qualitative interviews where we saw that students' lives were organized around larger constellations of engagement lived out alongside peers with particular types of orientations toward campus life. To capture these larger patterns, we examine how indicators of academic, extracurricular, and social engagement and peer culture characteristics, as previously described, clustered together to form homogeneous subgroups using a statistical technique called latent class analysis. Through this process, we were able to sort students into groups that share similar configurations across these academic and social dimensions. Before fitting our latent class analysis model, we recoded all of our model variables into dichotomous indicators that equal 1 if the respondent scored above the sample mean, and zero otherwise.[7]

We constructed models with two, three, four, and five class solutions, assessing absolute model fit with the likelihood-ratio statistic and the number of classes that fit the data with Bayesian information criterion.[8] We found that the Bayesian information criterion was smallest for the four-category solution. Next, we used the posterior probability of belonging to each latent class to create four dummy variables for each geography type by assigning respondents to the class for which the probability is the largest. We then named each of the resulting clusters, Work Hard, Play Hard, Multisphere, and Disconnected, based on their unique characteristics (shown in Figure 1.1).

In Chapters 3 through 6, we examine how different campus geographies lead to various types of orientations toward campus life midway through college. Here we draw on Wave 3 measures of academic engagement, extracurricular activities, social life, and friendship collected at the end of the sophomore year. We include indicators of academic effort, rated from zero (no effort) to 10 (maximum effort) based on hours studying each week and whether respondents have college mentors. Measures of faculty and peer academic engagement are asked in multiple waves. We measure them in the same way we did in Chapter 2, but with Wave 3 questions. We also include a distracted studying space index based on questions that ask students how often their studying was distracted, ranked on a scale from zero (never) to 10 (everyday), by conversations, someone playing a stereo, someone watching television, friends partying, or friends talking them into going out.

Extracurricular engagement includes dichotomous indicators of participation in the following activities: cultural groups, art groups, religious groups, volunteer work, working for pay, varsity athletics, and intramural athletics. We also include measures for hours per week spent in athletics (both intramural and varsity), working for pay, volunteering, extracurricular activities, and sleeping. Social life indicators include involvement in a Greek Letter Organization and dating on campus. We also include hours per week spent socializing with friends, consuming media, and partying. Finally, we include measures for how students met their closest friends. These are dichotomous variables are coded 1 if respondents reported meeting at least one of their four best friends in the dorms, classrooms, Greek Letter Organizations, Clubs, or athletics, and zero otherwise.

Qualitative Sample and Analysis

Between 2014 and 2016, we aimed to interview an equal number of first-generation students from each targeted race/gender category: African American women, Latinas, White women, African American men, Latinos, and White men. We used purposive and snowball sampling techniques to recruit members of sample target groups because we were unable to access a list of all first-generation students enrolled at Hilltop College (HC). In the first 18 months of data collection, we interviewed 52 first-generation sample members through snowball sampling techniques, with respondents helping us locate additional sample members. In the final three months of data collection, HC's Institutional Research Office sent out an email to all enrolled first-generation students inviting them to opt into the interview part of this study. This strategy yielded 12 additional respondents, 10 of whom were White, suggesting that we may have not been able to locate our African American and Latinx sample members had we relied solely on this type of opt-in approach.

The final sample of 64 first-generation students includes an approximately equal number from each target group, with White females somewhat overrepresented and Latinas somewhat underrepresented. As Table A.2 shows, the sample is composed of 11 African American women, 7 Latina women, 14 White women, 11 African American men, 10 Latino men, and 11 White men. Consistent with the survey sample, students in the qualitative sample did not live with a parent who had earned a four-year degree. A few respondents, however, reported having a parent enrolled in four-year programs during their high school years. Most respondents' parents were gainfully employed in blue- or pink-collared jobs. Mothers and female caregivers tended to work in service-oriented jobs, including grocery clerks, home healthcare aids, waitresses, retail workers, house cleaners, custodians, and administrative assistants. Fathers and male caregivers worked as cab and truck drivers, contractors (electrical, lawn care, construction), mechanics, security officers, and government workers. Table A.3 describes the pseudonym, gender, race/ethnicity, school type, entry point, and campus geography for all qualitative respondents.

A team of trained HC student research assistants conducted the interviews over a two-year period. We believed that first-generation respondents on campuses such as HC would be more open about discussing their experiences with others who shared their background. To this end, our research team was composed of students from each race/gender group in the sample, and all but one identified as a first-generation

Table A.2 Demographic Composition of the First-Generation Students in the Qualitative Sample

	n	%
Black women	11	17
Latina women[a]	7	11
White women	14	22
Black men	11	17
Latino men[b]	10	16
White men	11	17
Total	64	100

[a]Includes the two female multiracial Latinx respondents.
[a]Includes the two male multiracial Latinx respondents.

Table A.3 Characteristics of the Qualitative Sample

Pseudonym	Gender	Race/Ethnicity	High School Type	Entry Point	Campus Geography
Brianna	Female	Black	Public	Summer Bridge	Work Hard
Brittney	Female	Black	Public	Summer Bridge	Work Hard
Samirah	Female	Black	Public	Summer Bridge	Work Hard
Victoria	Female	Black	Private	None	Work Hard
Zendaya	Female	Black	Public	Summer Bridge	Work Hard
Manesha	Female	Black	Public	Summer Bridge	Work Hard
Angela	Female	Latina	Public	Summer Bridge	Work Hard
Sarah	Female	Latina	Charter	Summer Bridge	Work Hard
Aleyda	Female	Latina	Public	Summer Bridge	Work Hard
Katie	Female	White	Public	Summer Bridge and Athletics	Work Hard
Rebecca	Female	White	Public	None	Work Hard
Jen	Female	White	Public	Summer Bridge	Work Hard
Kaelin	Female	White/Latina	Public	Summer Bridge	Work Hard
Ed	Male	Black	Public	Summer Bridge	Work Hard
Andrew	Male	Black	Public	Pre-Orientation	Work Hard
Carlos	Male	Latino	Public	None	Work Hard
Smokey	Male	Latino	Private	Summer Bridge	Work Hard
Jack	Male	Latino/White	Private	Summer Bridge and Athletics	Work Hard
Akeira	Female	Black	Public	Summer Bridge	Multisphere
Gabby	Female	White	Public	Summer Bridge	Multisphere
Emma	Female	White	Public	Pre-Orientation	Multisphere
Leslie	Female	White	Public	Pre-Orientation	Multisphere
Anna	Female	White	Public	None	Multisphere
Jordan	Male	Black	Public	Summer Bridge	Multisphere
Roy	Male	Latino	Private	Summer Bridge	Multisphere
Phillip	Male	Latino	Public	Pre-Orientation	Multisphere
Grant	Male	White	Public	None	Multisphere
Kyle	Male	White	Public	Summer Bridge	Multisphere
Erica	Female	White	Public	None	Disconnected
Lauren	Female	White	Public	Pre-Orientation	Disconnected
Maria	Female	White/Latina	Public	Summer Bridge	Disconnected
Ian	Male	Latino	Public	None	Disconnected
Clark	Male	White	Public	None	Disconnected

Pseudonym	Gender	Race/Ethnicity	High School Type	Entry Point	Campus Geography
Harry	Male	White	Public	None	Disconnected
Shane	Male	White/Latino	Charter	Summer Bridge	Disconnected
Jason	Male	Black	Public	Summer Bridge	Play Hard
Rico	Male	Black	Private	Athletics	Play Hard
Rick	Male	Black	Private	Summer Bridge	Play Hard
Kobe	Male	Black	Private	Athletics	Play Hard
Bernard	Male	Black	Private	Summer Bridge and Athletics	Play Hard
Jeff	Male	Black	Private	Summer Bridge and Athletics	Play Hard
Mike	Male	Black	Private	Athletics	Play Hard
Lebron	Male	Black	Private	Athletics	Play Hard
Charles	Male	Latino	Public	Pre-Orientation	Play Hard
Jay	Male	Latino	Public	Athletics	Play Hard
John	Male	Latino	Private	Summer Bridge	Play Hard
Brian	Male	White	Public	None	Play Hard
Nick	Male	White	Public	Summer Bridge	Play Hard
Oliver	Male	White	Public	None	Play Hard
Richard	Male	White	Private	None	Play Hard
Dan	Male	White	Private	Athletics	Play Hard
Todd	Male	White	Public	Athletics	Play Hard
Tommie	Male	White	Public	Athletics	Play Hard
Maggie	Female	Black	Private	Summer Bridge	Play Hard
Peaches	Female	Black	Public	Summer Bridge and Athletics	Play Hard
Selita	Female	Black	Private	Summer Bridge	Play Hard
Nadya	Female	Black	Private	None	Play Hard
Gretchen	Female	Latina	Public	Athletics	Play Hard
Beth	Female	Latina	Public	Summer Bridge and Athletics	Play Hard
Brooke	Female	White	Private	None	Play Hard
Julie	Female	White	Public	None	Play Hard
Katherine	Female	White	Public	Athletics	Play Hard
Kristen	Female	White	Public	None	Play Hard
Pam	Female	White	Public	Pre-Orientation	Play Hard

student. This allowed us to match interviewer and respondent generational status and race/gender for 85% of the interviews. The recorded interviews followed a semi-structured interview schedule, were conducted in a setting of the respondent's choosing, and lasted an average of 90 minutes each. Student research assistants helped develop and pilot the interview protocol,[9] providing critical insider knowledge about student culture and campus life. To protect participants' confidentiality, we asked them to select a pseudonym. We also changed any potentially identifying information, such as the names of respondents' hometowns, dorms, activities, and friends. We aimed to maintain the integrity of each respondent's narrative while also disguising any identifying information.

The transcribed interviews were analyzed in multiple stages. We first read through the interview transcripts multiple times and wrote analytic summaries to capture individual narratives. From there, we developed our initial set of analytic codes and began coding the transcripts using QSR International's NVivo 11 qualitative data analysis software. To insure consistency and intercoder reliability, we began this process by having the authors and research team members code several of the same interviews and comparing the results. Moreover, we met frequently with the research team to discuss the coding process and the development of new codes emerging from the data. We are incredibly grateful to our research team for their efforts, careful insights, and on-the-ground knowledge of HC student culture.

Notes

1. The NLSF is one of the most comprehensive existing longitudinal survey on highly selective campuses. The NSLF sample were collected when there were few if any programs that focused specifically on first-generation students; there are more now. Despite this time lag between the survey data and interview data collection, these geographies are locatable in each data source, suggesting both that the survey data are still highly relevant and that the interview data are not reflective only of HC patterns.
2. We weight survey analyses to adjust for this sampling design. See Massey et al. (2003) for full description of NLSF design.
3. Rothwell, 2015; Massey et al., 2003.
4. A recent U.S. Department of Education report indicates that the racial composition of first-generation college students is 49% White, 14% Black, 27% Latinx, 5% Asian, and 5% other (Redford and Hoyer, 2017).
5. This income cut-off closely approximates two-times the Federal Poverty Line in 1999 for a family of four ($33,400). The National Center for Children in Poverty argues that families need at least two times the Federal Poverty Line to cover basic expenses. Moreover, Jack (2014) also identifies low-income families in the NLSF in this way.
6. Wolfgang, Figlio, Tracy, and Singer, 1985.
7. Quadlin and Rudel (2015) use a similar approach, but they included only time use variables in their model, leaving out critical aspects of peer culture. They generated

three, rather than four clusters, and labels these groups serious students, inactive students, and socially engaged students. Our results include a fourth type of category that we call Multisphere, which captures a pattern of student engagement that includes a strong orientation toward both academics and social life.

8. Schwarz, 1978.
9. The interview schedule was adapted from Lee's (2016) study of first-generation students.

Appendix Tables B.1–B.5

Table B.1 Family Background Indicators by Geography Type Among First-Generation College Students

	Among First Generation Students (%)							
	Continuing-Generation (%)	First-Generation (%)	*P* value	Work Hard	Disconnected	Multisphere	Play Hard	*P* value
Family income <35K	5	29	p <. 001	28	28	32	25	
Family received public assistance	4	14	p <. 001	22	12	14	9	<0.10
Applied for financial aid	63	94	p <. 001	99	97	96	89	<0.01
Received loans to pay for college	32	62	p <. 001	59	69	67	45	<0.01
Works for pay to finance college	22	47	p <. 001	50	46	50	43	

Table B.2 Academic Engagement Midway Through College by Geography Type Among First-Generation College Students

	Work Hard	Disconnected	Multisphere	Play Hard	P value
	Mean/%	Mean/%	Mean/%	Mean/%	
Academic effort, mean	7.08[d]	7.08[d]	7.69[d]	6.06[abc]	
Study hours per week, mean	28.62[bd]	23.60[ad]	26.91[d]	19.42[abc]	
Distracting study environment, mean	2.85[bcd]	3.56[a]	4.07[a]	3.41[a]	
Faculty engagement, mean	4.01[bd]	3.37[ad]	3.84[d]	2.26[abc]	
College mentor, %	65	43	57	36	<0.01
Peer academic engagement, mean	3.64[bcd]	3.37[cd]	4.86[abd]	2.52[abc]	

Note: Means significantly different ($p < 0.05$) from Work Hard, Disconnected, Multisphere, and Play Hard.

[a] Work Hard.

[b] Disconnected.

[c] Multisphere.

[d] Play Hard.

Table B.3 Social Engagement and Friendships Midway Through College by Geography Type Among First-Generation College Students

	Work Hard	Disconnected	Multisphere	Play Hard	*P* value
Percentage involved in					
Greek Life organization	13	9	25	37	<0.001
Campus dating or partnership	73	88	93	90	<0.01
Varsity athletics	5	2	12	7	<0.05
Intramural sports	22	26	41	41	<0.05
Mean hours spent each week:					
Media	20.06^d	23.01^d	22.41^d	28.55^{abc}	
Socializing with friends	6.92	7.15	6.42	7.71	
Partying	5.23^{bc}	5.48^{bc}	9.67^{ab}	11.24^{ab}	
Athletics (varsity and intramural)	3.15^{cd}	2.61^{cd}	7.81^{ab}	5.12^{ab}	
Percentage met close friend through					
Dorm	61	55	59	49	
Classes	35	27	34	15	<0.05
Greek Letter organizations	5	2	3	29	<0.05
Clubs	31	16	23	7	<0.05
Athletics	5	2	10	8	<0.05

Note: Means significantly different ($p < 0.05$) from Work Hard, Disconnected, Multisphere, and Play Hard.

[a] Work Hard.

[b] Disconnected.

[c] Multisphere.

[d] Play Hard.

Table B.4 Extracurricular Engagement Midway Through College by Geography Type Among First-Generation College Students

	Work Hard	Disconnected	Multisphere	Play Hard	P value
Percentage involved in					
Cultural group	48	23	20	13	<0.001
Art group	31	17	14	8	<0.05
Religious group	32	17	11	11	<0.05
Volunteer work	49	21	35	21	<0.05
Working for pay	78	58	44	55	<0.05
Mean hours spent each week					
Working for pay	13.12^{bc}	8.21^a	6.71^a	8.84^a	
Volunteering	3.51^{bcd}	0.83^a	1.79^a	0.84^a	
Extracurricular activities	10.81^{bcd}	4.36^a	5.86^{ad}	3.68^{ac}	
Sleeping	45.01^{bd}	47.96^{ac}	45.53^{bd}	50.38^{ac}	

Note: Means significantly different ($p < 0.05$) from Work Hard, Disconnected, Multisphere, and Play Hard.

[a] Work Hard.

[b] Disconnected.

[c] Multisphere.

[d] Play Hard.

Table B.5 Geography Types by Race and Gender Among First-Generation College Students

	White Women (%)	Women of Color (%)	White Men (%)	Men of Color(%)	Total Sample(%)	P Value
Work Hard	25	36	9	33	25	<0.01
Disconnected	45	38	44	26	41	<0.01
Multisphere	16	16	20	22	17	<0.01
Party Hard	13	10	27	19	17	<0.01

References

Alemán, Martínez. 2000. "Race Talks: Undergraduate Women of Color and Female Friendships." *The Review of Higher Education* 23(2):133–52.

Allison, Rachel, and Barbara J. Risman. 2014. "'It Goes Hand in Hand With the Parties': Race, Class, and Residence in College Student Negotiations of Hooking Up." *Sociological Perspectives* 57(1):102–23.

American College Health Association. 2016. *American College Health*. Hanover, MD: American College Health Association.

Aries, Elizabeth. 2008. *Race and Class Matters at an Elite College*. Philadelphia: Temple University Press.

Aries, Elizabeth, and Maynard Seider. 2005. "The Interactive Relationship Between Class Identity and the College Experience: The Case of Lower-Income Students." *Qualitative Sociology* 28:419–43.

Armstrong, Elizabeth A., Paula England, and Alison C. K. Fogarty. 2012. "Accounting for Women's Orgasm and Sexual Enjoyment in College Hookups and Relationships." *American Sociological Review* 77(3):435–62.

Armstrong, Elizabeth A., and Laura T. Hamilton. 2013. *Paying for the Party: How College Maintains Inequality*. Cambridge, MA: Harvard University Press.

Aronson, Pamela. 2008. "Breaking Barriers or Locked Out? Class-Based Perceptions and Experiences of Postsecondary Education." *New Directions for Child and Adolescent Development* 119:41–54.

Attinasi, Louis C., Jr. 1989. "Getting In: Mexican Americans' Perceptions of University Attendance and Implications for Freshman Year Persistence." *Journal of Higher Education* 60:247–77.

Baker, Christina. 2015. "Gender Differences in the Experiences of African American College Students: The Effects of Co-Ethnic Support and Campus Diversity." *Women, Gender, and Families of Color* 3(1):36–57.

Bergerson, Amy Aldous. 2007. "Exploring the Impact of Social Class on Adjustment to College: Anna's Story." *International Journal of Qualitative Studies in Education* 20(1):99–119.

Bettie, Julie. 2003. *Women Without Class: Girls, Race, and Identity*. Berkeley: University of California Press.

Bourdieu, Pierre, and Jean-Claude Passeron. 1990. *Reproduction in Education, Society and Culture*. London: SAGE.

Bowen, William G., Martin A. Kurzweil, and Eugene Tobin. 2005. *Equity and Excellence in American Higher Education*. Charlottesville: University of Virginia Press.

Byrd, W. Carson, Rachelle J. Brunn-Bevel, and Sarah M. Ovink (eds.). 2019. *Intersectionality and Higher Education: Identity and Inequality on College Campuses*. New Brunswick, NJ: Rutgers University Press.

Calarco, Jessica M. 2014. "Coached for the Classroom: Parents' Cultural Transmission and Children's Reproduction of Educational Inequalities." *American Sociological Review* 79(5):1015–37.

Carnevale, Anthony P., and Stephen J. Rose. 2004. "Socioeconomic Status, Race/ Ethnicity, and Selective College Admissions." Pp. 101–56 in *America's Untapped Resource: Low-Income Students in Higher Education*, edited by Richard D. Kahlenberg. New York: Century Foundation.

Casey, Nicholas. 2020. "College Made Them Feel Equal. The Virus Exposed How Unequal Their Lives Are." *New York Times, April 6*. Retrieved May 1, 2020 (https://www.nytimes. com/2020/04/04/us/politics/coronavirus-zoom-college-classes.html).

Chambliss, Daniel F., and Christopher G. Takacs. 2014. *How College Works*. Cambridge. MA: Harvard University Press.

Charles, Camille Z., Mary J. Fischer, Margarita A. Mooney, and Douglas S. Massey. 2009. *Taming the River: Negotiating the Academic, Financial, and Social Currents in Selective Colleges and Universities*. Princeton, NJ: Princeton University Press.

Chase, Sarah A. 2008. *Perfectly Prep: Gender Extremes at a New England Prep School*. New York: Oxford University Press.

Chetty, R., J. N. Friedman, E. Saez, N. Turner, and D. Yagan. 2017. *Mobility Report Cards: The Role of Colleges in Intergenerational Mobility* (No. w23618). National Bureau of Economic Research.

Collins, Patricia Hill. 1991. *Black Feminist Thought: Knowledge, Consciousness, and the Politics of Empowerment*. New York: Routledge.

Cookson, Peter, and Caroline Hodges Persell. 1985. *Preparing for Power: America's Elite Boarding Schools*. New York: Basic Books.

Crenshaw, Kimberlé. 1991. "Mapping the Margins: Identity Politics, Intersectionality, and Violence Against Women." *Stanford Law Review* 43(6):1241–99.

Crosnoe, Robert. 2000. "Friendships in Childhood and Adolescence: The Life Course and New Directions." *Social Psychology Quarterly* 63:377–91.

Crosnoe, Robert., Shannon Cavanagh, and Glen H. Elder Jr. 2003. "Adolescent Friendships as Academic Resources: The Intersection of Friendship, Race, and School Disadvantage." *Sociological Perspectives* 46(3):331–52.

Eisen, Daniel. 2015. "Constructing 'Hawaiian,' Post-Racial Narratives, and Social Boundaries at a Predominantly White University." Pp. 46–63 in *College Students' Experiences of Power and Marginality: Sharing Spaces and Negotiating Differences*, edited by Elizabeth M. Lee and Chaise LaDousa. New York: Routledge.

Eitzen, D. Stanley. 2009. *Fair and Foul: Beyond the Myths and Paradoxes of Sport*. Lanham, MD: Rowman & Littlefield Publishers.

Erickson, Lance D., Steve McDonald, and Glen H. Elder Jr. 2009. "Informal Mentors and Education: Complementary or Compensatory Resources?" *Sociology of Education* 82:344–67.

Espenshade, Thomas J., and Alexandra W. Radford. 2009. *No Longer Separate, Not Yet Equal: Race and Class in Elite College Admission and Campus Life*. Princeton, NJ: Princeton University Press.

Feagin, Joe R., Hernan Vera, and Nikitah Imani. 1996. *The Agony of Education: Black Students at White Colleges and Universities*. New York: Routledge.

Fischer, Mary. 2007. "Settling Into Campus Life: Differences by Race/Ethnicity in College Involvement and Outcomes." *Journal of Higher Education* 78(2):125–61.

Furstenberg, Frank, Jr., Thomas D. Cook, Jacquelynne Eccles, Glen H. Elder Jr., and Arnold Sameroff. 1999. *Managing to Make It: Urban Families and Adolescent Success*. Chicago: University of Chicago Press.

Giancola, Jennifer, and Richard D. Kahlenberg. 2016. "True Merit: Ensuring Our Brightest Students Have Access to Our Best Colleges and Universities." Jack Kent Cooke Foundation. http://www.jkcf.org/assets/1/7/JKCF_True_Merit_Report.pdf

Goldrick Rab, Sara. 2006. "Following Their Every Move: An Investigation of Social-Class Differences in College Pathways." *Sociology of Education* 79(1):67–79.

Grazian, David. 2008. *On the Make: The Hustle of Urban Nightlife.* Chicago: University of Chicago Press.

Guiffrida, Douglas A. 2003. "African American Student Organizations as Agents of Social Integration." *Journal of College Student Development* 44(3):304–19.

Guiffrida, Douglas A. 2006. "Toward a Cultural Advancement of Tinto's Theory." *Review of Higher Education* 29(4):451–72.

Hamilton, Laura T. 2016. *Parenting to a Degree: How Family Matters for College Women's Success.* Chicago: University of Chicago Press.

Hamilton, Laura T., and Simon Cheng. 2018. "Going Greek: The Organization of Campus Life and Class-Based Graduation Gaps." *Social Forces* 96(3):977–1008.

Hamilton, Laura T., Josipa Roksa, and Kelly Nielsen. 2018. "Providing a 'Leg Up': Parental Involvement and Opportunity Hoarding in College." *Sociology of Education* 91(2):111–31.

Han, Crystal, Ozan Jaquette, and Karina Salazar. 2019. "Recruiting the Out-of-State University: Off-Campus Recruiting by Public Research Universities." The Joyce Foundation. https://emraresearch.org/sites/default/files/2019-03/joyce_report.pdf

Holland, Dorothy C., and Margaret A. Eisenhart. 1990. *Educated in Romance: Women, Achievement, and College Culture.* Chicago: University of Chicago Press.

Holland, Megan M. 2012. "Only Here for the Day: The Social Integration of Minority Students at a Majority White High School." *Sociology of Education* 85(2):101–20.

Hoxby, Caroline M., and Christopher Avery. 2012. *The Missing "One-Offs": The Hidden Supply of High-Achieving, Low-income Students* (Working paper no. 18586). National Bureau of Economic Research.

Hurst, Allison L. 2010. *The Burden of Academic Success: Loyalists, Renegades, and Double Agents.* Lanham, MD: Lexington Books.

Hurtado, Sylvia, and Deborah Faye Carter. 1997. "Effects of College Transition and Perceptions of the Campus Racial Climate on Latino College Students' Sense of Belonging." *Sociology of Education* 70:324–45.

Hurtado, Sylvia, Jeffrey F. Milem, Alma R. Clayton-Pedersen, and Walter R. Allen. 1998. "Enhancing Campus Climates for Race/Ethnic Diversity: Educational Policy and Practice." *Review of Higher Education* 21:279–302.

Jack, Anthony Abraham. 2014. "Culture Shock Revisited: The Social and Cultural Contingencies to Class Marginality." *Sociological Forum* 29:453–75.

Jack, Anthony Abraham. 2019. *The Privileged Poor: How Elite Colleges Are Failing Disadvantaged Students.* Boston: Harvard University Press.

Jackson, Brandon A. 2018. "Beyond the Cool Pose: Black Men and Emotion Management Strategies." *Sociology Compass* 12(4):1–14.

Jaquette, Ozan and Karina Salazar. 2018. "Colleges Recruit at Richer, Whiter High Schools." *New York Times,* April 13. https://www.nytimes.com/interactive/2018/04/13/opinion/college-recruitment-rich-white.Html

Johnson, Dawn R., Matthew Soldner, Jeannie Brown Leonard, et al. 2007. "Examining Sense of Belonging Among First-Year Undergraduates From Different Racial/Ethnic Groups." *Journal of College Student Development* 48(5):525–42.

Kendall, Diana Elizabeth. 2011. *Framing Class: Media Representations of Wealth and Poverty in America*. Lanham, MD: Rowman & Littlefield.

Khan, Shamus. 2011. *Privilege: The Making of an Adolescent Elite at St. Paul's School*. Princeton, NJ: Princeton University Press.

Kimmel, Michael. 2008. *Guyland: The Perilous World Where Boys Become Men*. New York: HarperCollins.

Kobrin, Jennifer L., and Rochelle S. Michel. 2006. *The SAT as a Predictor of Different Levels of College Performance* (Research report no. 2006-3). College Board. https://files.eric.ed.gov/fulltext/ED563073.pdf

Landers, Kerry. 2018. *Postsecondary Education for First-Generation and Low-Income Students in the Ivy League*. Cham, Switzerland: Palgrave MacMillan.

Langhout, Regina D., Peter Drake, and Francine Rosselli. 2009. "Classism in the University Setting: Examining Student Antecedents and Outcomes." *Journal of Diversity in Higher Education* 2(3):166–81.

Lareau, Annette. 2003. *Unequal Childhoods: Class, Race, and Family Life*. Berkeley: University of California Press.

Lee, Elizabeth M. 2016. *Class and Campus Life: Managing and Experiencing Inequality at an Elite College*. Ithaca, NY: Cornell University Press.

Lerma, Veronica, Laura T. Hamilton, and Kelly Nielsen. 2020. "Racialized Equity Labor, University Appropriation and Student Resistance." *Social Problems* 67:286–303.

Manzoni, Anna, and Jessi Streib. 2019. "The Equalizing Power of a College Degree for First-Generation College Students: Disparities Across Institutions, Majors, and Achievement Levels." *Research in Higher Education* 60:1–29.

Martin, Nathan D. 2012. "The Privilege of Ease: Social Class and Campus Life at Highly Selective, Private Universities." *Research in Higher Education* 53(4):426–52.

Massey, Douglas S., Camille Z. Charles, Garvey F. Lundy, and Mary J. Fischer. 2003. *The Source of the River: The Social Origins of Freshmen at America's Selective Colleges and Universities*. Princeton, NJ: Princeton University Press.

McCabe, Janice. 2009. "Racial and Gender Microaggressions on a Predominantly-White Campus: Experiences of Black, Latina/o and White Undergraduates." *Race, Gender & Class* 16:133–51.

McCabe, Janice. 2016. *Connecting in College: How Friendship Networks Matter for Academic and Social Success*. Chicago: University of Chicago Press.

McDonough, Patricia. 1997. *Choosing Colleges: How Social Class and Schools Structure Opportunity*. Albany: State University of New York Press.

Milner Jr., Murray. 2004. *Freaks, Geeks, and Cool Kids: American Teenagers, Schools, and the Culture of Consumption*. London: Routledge.

Moffatt, Michael. 1989. *Coming of Age in New Jersey: College and American Culture*. New Brunswick, NJ: Rutgers, The State University of New Jersey Press.

Mullen, Ann. 2010. *Degrees of Inequality: Culture, Class, and Gender in American Higher Education*. Baltimore: Johns Hopkins University Press.

Museus, Samuel D., and Dina C. Maramba. 2011. "The Impact of Culture on Filipino American Students' Sense of Belonging." *Review of Higher Education* 34(2):231–58.

Museus, Samuel D., and Stephen John Quaye. 2009. "Toward an Intercultural Perspective of Racial and Ethnic MINORITY College Student Persistence." *Review of Higher Education* 33(1):67–94.

Nenga, Sandi Kawecka, Guillermo A. Alvarado, and Claire S. Blyth. 2015. "'I Kind of Found My People:' Latino/a College Students' Search for Social Integration on

Campus." Pp. 37–53 in *College Students' Experiences of Power and Marginality*, edited by Elizabeth M. Lee and Chaise LaDousa. New York: Routledge.

Ostrove, Joan, and Susan Long. 2007. "Social Class and Belonging: Implications for College Adjustment." *Review of Higher Education* 30(4):363–89.

Pager, Devah, and Hana Shepherd. 2008. "The Sociology of Discrimination: Racial Discrimination in Employment, Housing, Credit, and Consumer Markets." *Annual Review of Sociology* 34:181–209.

Pew Research Center. 2019. "A Rising Share of Undergraduates Are from Poor Families, Especially at Less Selective Colleges." May 2019. https://www.pewsocialtrends.org/2019/05/22/a-rising-share-of-undergraduates-are-from-poor-families-especially-at-less-selective-colleges/

Pfeffer, Fabian T. 2018. "Growing Wealth Gaps in Education." *Demography* 55(3):1033–68.

Quadlin, Natasha. 2018. "The Mark of a Woman's Record: Gender and Academic Performance in Hiring." *American Sociological Review* 83(2):331–60.

Quadlin, Natasha, and Daniel Rudel. 2015. "Responsibility or Liability? Student Loan Debt and Time Use in College." *Social Forces* 94(2):589–614.

Ray, Rashawn, and Bryant Best. 2015. "Diversity Does Not Mean Equality: De Facto Rules that Maintain Status Inequality Among Black and White Fraternity Men." Pp. 83–101 in *College Students' Experiences of Power and Marginality: Sharing Spaces and Negotiating Differences*, edited by Elizabeth M. Lee and Chaise LaDousa. New York: Routledge.

Ray, Rashawn, and Jason A. Rosow. 2012. "The Two Different Worlds of Black and White Fraternity Men: Visibility and Accountability as Mechanisms of Privilege." *Journal of Contemporary Ethnography* 41(1):66–94.

Reardon, Sean F., and Ann Owens. 2014. "60 Years After Brown: Trends and Consequences of School Segregation." *Annual Review of Sociology* 40:199–218.

Redford, Jeremy, and Kathleen M. Hoyer. 2017. *First-Generation and Continuing-Generation College Students: A Comparison of High School and Postsecondary Experiences* (Stats in Brief, NCES 2018-009). Washington, DC: National Center for Education Statistics.

Rendón, Laura I., Romero E. Jalomo, and Amaury Nora. 2000. Theoretical Considerations in the Study of Minority Student Retention in Higher Education. Pp. 127–56 in J. Braxton (Ed.), *Reworking the Student Departure Puzzle*. Nashville, TN: Vanderbilt University Press.

Reskin, Barbara. 2012. "The Race Discrimination System." *Annual Review of Sociology* 38:17–35.

Rivera, Lauren. 2016. *Pedigree: How Elite Students Get Elite Jobs*. Princeton, NJ: Princeton University Press.

Rothwell, Jonathan. 2015. *The Stubborn Race and Class Gaps in College Quality*. Washington, DC: Brookings Institution.

Saenz, Victor B., Sylvia Hurtado, Doug Barrera, et al. 2007. *First in My Family: A Profile of First-Generation College Students at Four-Year Institutions Since 1971*. Los Angeles: Higher Education Research Institute.

Schwarz, Gideon E. 1978. "Estimating the Dimension of a Model." *Annals of Statistics* 6(2):461–464.

Smith, Daryl G. 2015. *Diversity's Promise for Higher Education: Making It Work*. Baltimore: Johns Hopkins University Press.

St. John, Edward P., Shouping Hu, and Amy S. Fisher. 2011. *Breaking Through the Access Barrier: How Academic Capital Formation Can Improve Policy in Higher Education.* New York: Routledge.

Stevens, Mitchell L., Elizabeth A. Armstrong, and Richard Arum. 2008. "Sieve, Incubator, Temple, Hub: Empirical and Theoretical Advances in the Sociology of Higher Education." *Annual Review of Sociology* 34:127–51.

Stuber, Jenny M. 2015. "Pushed Out or Pulled In? How Organizational Factors Shape the Extracurricular Experiences of First-Generation Students." Pp. 118–35 in *College Students' Experiences of Power and Marginality: Sharing Spaces and Negotiating Differences,* edited by Elizabeth M. Lee and Chaise LaDousa. New York: Routledge.

Stuber, Jenny M. 2011a. *Inside the College Gates: How Class and Culture Matter in Higher Education.* Lanham, MD: Lexington Books.

Stuber, Jenny M. 2011b. "Integrated, Marginal, and Resilient: Race, Class, and the Diverse Experiences of White First-Generation College Students." *International Journal of Qualitative Studies in Education* 24(1):117–36.

Stuber, Jenny M. 2009. "Class, Culture, and Participation in the Collegiate Extra-Curriculum." *Sociological Forum* 24(4):877–900.

Stuber, Jenny M., Joshua Klugman, and Caitlin Daniel. 2011. "Gender, Social Class, and Exclusion: Collegiate Peer Cultures and Social Reproduction." *Sociological Perspectives* 54(3):431–51.

Swidler, Ann. 1986. "Culture in Action: Symbols and Strategies." *American Sociological Review* 51(2):273–86.

Thornhill, Ted. 2019. "We Want Black Students, Just Not You: How White Admissions Counselors Screen Black Prospective Students." *Sociology of Race and Ethnicity* 5(4):456–470.

Tinto, Vincent. 1987. *Leaving college: Rethinking the causes and cures of student attrition.* Chicago: University of Chicago Press.

Tinto V. 2010. "From Theory to Action: Exploring the Institutional Conditions for Student Retention." Pp. 51-89 in *Higher Education: Handbook of Theory and Research* (Vol. 25), edited J. Smart. Dordrecht, The Netherland: Springer.

Tierney, William G. 1999. "Models of Minority College-Going and Retention: Cultural Integrity Versus Cultural Suicide." *Journal of Negro Education* 68(1):80–91.

Torres, Kimberly. 2009. "'Culture Shock': Black Students Account for Their Distinctiveness at an Elite College." *Ethnic and Racial Studies* 32(5):883–905.

Torres, Kimberly C., and Camille Z. Charles. 2004. "Metastereotypes and the Black–White Divide: A Qualitative View of Race on an Elite College Campus." *Du Bois Review* 1(1):115–49.

Wachen, John, Joshua Pretlow, and Karrie G. Dixon. 2018. "Building College Readiness: Exploring the Effectiveness of the UNC Academic Summer Bridge Program." *Journal of College Student Retention: Research, Theory & Practice* 20(1):116–38.

Walpole, MaryBeth. 2003. "Socioeconomic Status and College: How SES Affects College Experiences and Outcomes." *Review of Higher Education* 27(1):45–73.

Wilkins, Amy C. 2014. "Race, Age, and Identity Transformations in the Transition from High School to College for Black and First-Generation White Men." *Sociology of Education* 87(3):171–87.

Willie, Sarah Susannah. 2003. *Acting Black: College, Identity, and the Performance of Race.* London: Routledge/Taylor Francis.

Wingfield, Adia Harvey. 2007. "The Modern Mammy and the Angry Black Man: African American Professionals' Experiences with Gendered Racism in the Workplace." *Race, Gender & Class* 14(1):196–212.

Winkle-Wagner, Rachelle. 2010. *The Unchosen Me: Race, Gender, and Identity among Black Women in College*. Baltimore: Johns Hopkins University Press.

Wolfgang Marvin E., Robert M. Figlio, Paul E. Tracy, et al. 1985. *The National Survey of Crime Severity*. Washington, DC: U.S. Government Printing Office.

Index

Page numbers followed by *f* indicate figures; page numbers followed by *t* indicate tables. *For the benefit of digital users, indexed terms that span two pages (e.g., 52–53) may, on occasion, appear on only one of those pages.*